SON OF HEAVEN

T0381568

LI SHIH-MIN, EMPEROR T'ANG T'AI TSUNG

Reproduced from a rubbing of the ancient stone at Li Ch'üan, Shensi, West China.

SON OF HEAVEN

*A Biography of Li Shih-Min, founder of
the T'ang Dynasty*

BY

C. P. FITZGERALD

CAMBRIDGE
AT THE UNIVERSITY PRESS
1933

CAMBRIDGE
UNIVERSITY PRESS

University Printing House, Cambridge CB2 8BS, United Kingdom

Cambridge University Press is part of the University of Cambridge.

It furthers the University's mission by disseminating knowledge in the pursuit of
education, learning and research at the highest international levels of excellence.

www.cambridge.org
Information on this title: www.cambridge.org/9781107495081

© Cambridge University Press 1933

First published 1933
First paperback edition 2015

A catalogue record for this publication is available from the British Library

ISBN 978-1-107-49508-1 Paperback

CONTENTS

PLATES

NOTE.—Plates I, II and III are reproduced from drawings of three of the six bas-reliefs which formerly decorated the approach to Li Shih-Min's tomb at Chao Ling, in Shensi. These reliefs were executed during the lifetime of Shih-Min from drawings made by the artist Yen Li-Pen. A short inscription and a poem composed by the emperor himself were engraved on each monument. Translations of these will be found under the plates.

MAPS

PERSONS OF IMPORTANCE IN THIS HISTORY

BILGÄ KHAN. Turk. Rival to Qadir Khan.

CHAI SHAO. General. Brother-in-law of Li Shih-Min.

CHANG CHIEH-YÜ. Concubine of Li Yüan.

CHANG-SUN, THE LADY. Empress. Consort of Li Shih-Min.

CHANG-SUN WU-CHI. Minister. Brother-in-law of Li Shih-Min.

CH'ÊN SHU-TA. Minister. Scion of Ch'ên dynasty.

CH'ÊNG HSIN. Boy minstrel. Favourite of Crown Prince Ch'êng-Ch'ien.

CH'IN SHU-PAO. General.

CH'ÜAN KAI-SU-WÊN. Regicide and dictator of Korea.

CHUR KHAN. Ruler of the Turks. Brother of Qadir Khan.

CH'U SUI-LIANG. Minister.

CH'Ü-T'U T'UNG. Sui general. Submitted to T'ang dynasty.

FANG HSÜAN-LING. Minister and friend of Li Shih-Min.

FU-YUN KHAN. Tartar. Ruler of the T'u-yü-hun.

HÔ-KAN CH'ÊNG-CHI. Assassin. Served Prince Li Ch'êng-Ch'ien.

HOU CHÜN-CHI. General.

HSIAO HSIEN. Pretender of Liang dynasty.

HSIAO, THE LADY. Empress. Consort of Yang Ti.

HSIAO YÜ. Minister. Brother of the Empress Hsiao.

HSÜEH CHÜ. Pretender in Kansu.

HSÜEH JÊN-KUO. Son and successor of Hsüeh Chü.

I CH'ÊNG, PRINCESS. Sui princess. Wife of four Khans.

KAO K'AI-TAO. Pretender. Called Prince of Yen.

KAO SHIH-LIEN. Minister. Uncle of Empress Chang-Sun.

LI CH'ÊNG-CH'IEN. Son of Shih-Min. Crown Prince.

LI CHIEN-CH'ÊNG. Elder brother of Shih-Min. Crown Prince.

Li Chih.	Son of Shih-Min. Afterwards Crown Prince.
Li Ching.	General. Conqueror of the South.
Li Hsiao-Kung.	Prince Chao. General. Cousin of Shih-Min.
Li Mi.	Pretender. Submits to T'ang dynasty but rebels.
Li Shên-T'ung.	Prince Huai An. Uncle of Shih-Min. General.
Li Shih-Chi.	Formerly Hsü Shih-Chi. General.
Li Ta-Liang.	General.
Li T'ai.	Prince Wei. Son of Shih-Min by a concubine.
Li Tao-Hsüan.	Prince Huai Yang. Cousin of Shih-Min. General.
Li Tao-Tsung.	Prince Jên Ch'êng. Cousin of Shih-Min. General.
Li, The Lady.	Sister of Shih-Min. Wife of Chai Shao.
Li Tzŭ-T'ung.	Pretender in south-east China.
Li Yu.	Prince Chi. Son of Shih-Min by a concubine.
Li Yüan.	Father of Shih-Min. Emperor T'ang Kao Tsu.
Li Yüan-Ch'ang.	Prince Han. Half-brother of Shih-Min.
Li Yüan-Chi.	Prince Chi. Younger brother of Shih-Min.
Liang Shih-Tu.	Pretender in north Shensi.
Liu Hei-T'a.	Rebel in north-east China.
Liu Wên-Ching.	General. Early T'ang supporter.
Liu Wu-Chou.	Pretender, in north Shansi. Ally of the Turks.
Lo I.	General. Governor of Yu Chou (Peking).
Lo Shih-Hsin.	Young general.
Ma Chou.	Minister and censor.
P'ei Chi.	Eunuch in charge of Fên Yang Palace.
Qachashar.	Turk. Brother of Tutar Khan.
Qadir Khan.	Ruler of the Eastern Turks.
Sibir Khan.	Elder brother of Qadir Khan. Ruler of the Turks.
Sung Chin-Kang.	General of Liu Wu-Chou.
Tou Chien-Tê.	Pretender. Called Emperor of Hsia.

Tu Fu-Wei.	Rebel against Sui. Submits to T'ang dynasty.
Tu Ju-Hui.	Friend and minister of Li Shih-Min.
Tutar Khan.	Turk. Nephew of Qadir Khan.
Wang Hsüan-Ts'ê.	Ambassador to Indian kingdoms.
Wang Shih-Ch'ung.	Pretender. Called Emperor of Chêng.
Wei Chêng.	Minister.
Yang Chien.	Emperor Sui Wên Ti, founder of Sui dynasty.
Yang Hsüan-Kan.	Rebel against Sui Yang Ti.
Yang Ti.	Emperor Sui Yang Ti.
Yang T'ung.	Sui Prince Yüeh. Grandson of Yang Ti.
Yang Yu.	Sui Prince Tai. Grandson of Yang Ti.
Yin Hung-Chih.	Maternal uncle of Li Yu Prince Chi.
Yü-Ch'ih Ching-Tê.	General of Liu Wu-Chou, later captain of Shih-Min's guard.
Yü-Wên Hua-Chi.	Regicide. Son of Yü-Wên Shu. Pretender.
Yü-Wên Shih-Chi.	Son of Yü-Wên Shu. T'ang general.
Yü-Wên Shu.	Sui general. Scion of Northern Chou Tartar dynasty.

and

Li Shih-Min.	Second son of Li Yüan Duke of T'ang. Founder of the T'ang dynasty, Emperor T'ang T'ai Tsung. Born, A.D. 600. Ob. A.D. 649.

GENEALOGICAL TABLE
OF THE T'ANG IMPERIAL FAMILY

Li Kuang, general in the Han dynasty

Li Kao, Prince of Liang A.D. 400.

Li Yin ——— Li Shun, last prince of Liang

Li Hsi, grandson of Li Shun

Li Hu, grandson of Li Hsi

The Lady Duku (Tartar) = Li Ping, duke of T'ang

(1) The Lady Tou = *Li Yüan* = concubine

Emperor T'ang Kao Tsu ——— Li Yüan-Ch'ang Prince Han

Li Chien-Ch'êng (Crown Prince) | LI SHIH-MIN Prince Ch'in | Li Yüan-Chi Prince Chi | Lady Li = Chai Shao

(1) Empress Chang-Sun = LI SHIH-MIN = concubines

Emperor T'ang T'ai Tsung ——— Li T'ai Prince Wei | Li Yu Prince Chi

Li Ch'êng-Ch'ien (Crown Prince) | *Li Chih* Prince Chin and Emperor T'ang Kao Tsung

COLLATERALS

Li Shên-T'ung Prince Huai An, cousin of *Li Yüan*
Li Hsiao-Kung Prince Chao
Li Tao-Tsung Prince Jên Ch'êng, cousin of LI SHIH-MIN
Li Tao-Hsüan Prince Huai Yang, cousin of LI SHIH-MIN

NOTE

NOMENCLATURE

In this book, which deals with a subject unfamiliar to most western readers, I have endeavoured to simplify the difficulties of Chinese nomenclature. As far as is consistent with lucidity I have omitted the names of minor characters. The reader who succeeds in memorising the names of persons which still remain may be comforted with the knowledge that they all relate to people of importance, prominent in the history of the time.

Place-names have also been reduced to a minimum. With one or two exceptions the modern name has been employed, seventh-century city names being used only when the city no longer exists, or where, as is commonly the case in Shansi, Shensi, and Honan, the old name is still in use. Turkish and Central Asiatic names have been rendered in their native form, not as given in the Chinese texts. The Wade system of romanisation for Chinese words has been adhered to throughout, except in the case of some recognised variations, such as the names of the provinces.

It should be realised that in Chinese the surname precedes the personal name. Thus in "Li Shih-Min", Li is the surname, Shih-Min the personal name. Personal names may be single or double. "Li Yüan" is an example of a single personal name. In the seventh century double surnames, now rare, were still common. In such names as Chang-Sun Wu-Chi or Yü-Wên Shu, the first two words, linked by a hyphen, are the double surname, the second pair or single word, the personal name.

In place-names I have omitted the hyphen sometimes placed between the words composing the name, in order to avoid any risk of place-names being mistaken for personal names.

A full list of all prominent persons mentioned in this biography will be found on p. vii.

BIBLIOGRAPHY

The principal source used is the *Mirror of History* or *Tzŭ chih t'ung chien*, by Ssŭ-Ma Kuang (A.D. 1019–86) of the Sung dynasty, with the commentary of Hu San-Shêng of the Yüan dynasty. Quotations and direct translations unless otherwise indicated are from this work.

Other Chinese texts consulted include *Chiu t'ang shu*; *T'ung chien chi lan*; *T'ang tai tsung shu*; *Ch'ang an chih*; *T'ang liang ching ch'êng fang k'ao*; and the great encyclopedia compiled by order of the Emperor K'ang Hsi, the *Ch'in ting ku chin t'u shu chi ch'êng*.

European books include *Histoire Générale de la Chine*, by P. de Mailla (Paris, 1778), a Jesuit translation of the *T'ung chien kang mu*; *A Thousand Years of the Tartars*, by Parker (London: Kegan Paul, Trench, Trübner & Co., 1928); *The Formation of the Chinese People*, by Li Chi (Cambridge, Harvard University Press, 1928); *Recherches sur les superstitions en Chine*, by P. Henri Doré (Shanghai Mission Catholique, 1916); *Buried Treasures of Chinese Turkestan*, by A. von Le Coq (London: George Allen & Unwin, 1928).

The Maps are prepared from the *Atlas of China*: London, China Inland Mission, and from a Japanese *Historical Atlas of China*.

Old place-names and sites have been identified by indications in the Chinese texts and by two ancient Sung dynasty maps of China engraved on a stone tablet in the Pei Lin at Ch'ang An. For the topography of battlefields and sieges I have visited the ground at Ch'iao Shu Ku, Huo Chou (in Shansi), and Ch'ang An, Lo Yang and Ssŭ Shui.

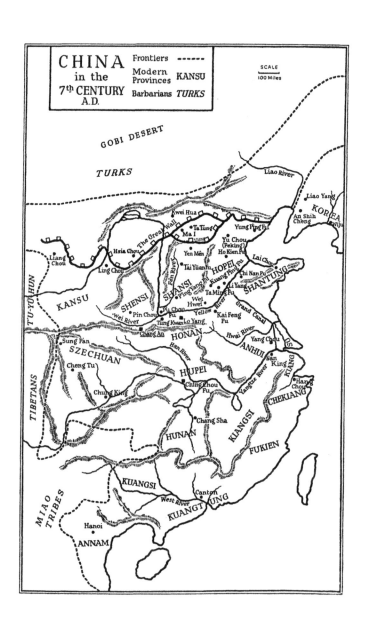

CHINA
in the
7th CENTURY
A.D.

Frontiers -----
Modern
Provinces KANSU
Barbarians *TURKS*

SCALE
100 Miles

GOBI DESERT

TURKS

Liao River

Liao Yang

KOREA

An Shih
Cheng

Hwei Hua
Ta Tung
Ma I
Yung Ping Fu
Yen Mén
Yu Chou
(Peking)
Ho Kien Fu
Lai Chou
Hsia Chou
The Great Wall
Tai Yüan Fu
Chi Nan Fu
Ling Chou
HOPEI
Kuang Ping Fu
Li Yang
SHANTUNG
Liang
Chou
Fên River
SHANSI
Ping Yang Fu
Ta Ming Fu
TU-YÜ-HUN
KANSU
SHENSI
Wei
Hwei
Pin Chou
Pi Chou
Fu
Yellow
Kai Feng
Fu
Grand Canal
Wei River
Tung Kwan
Lo Yang
Chang An
HONAN
Hwai River
Yang Chou
Sung Pan
Han River
ANHUI
Nan King
KIANGSU
TIBETANS
SZECHUAN
Cheng Tu
HUPEI
Chung King
Ching Chou
Fu
Yangtze River
Hang
Chou
CHEKIANG
Chang Sha
KIANGSI
FUKIEN
HUNAN
MIAO
TRIBES
KUANGSI
West River
Canton
KUANGTUNG
Hanoi
ANNAM

PROLOGUE

CHINA IN THE SEVENTH CENTURY A.D.

The significance of the life and achievements of Li Shih-Min, who reigned from A.D. 626–49 as the emperor T'ai Tsung of the T'ang dynasty, cannot be appreciated without some knowledge of the age which immediately preceded his birth. It is necessary to paint, as a background to his life, a picture of sixth-century China, its social organisation and the political trends which dominated the times.

At the dawn of the seventh century China was neither so large nor so populous a country as the modern republic. For more than two thousand years the Chinese people had steadily expanded from their early home in the Yellow river valley, colonising new territories, absorbing or exterminating the aboriginal inhabitants. This expansion had by the seventh century carried the Chinese race and rule south of the Yangtze valley, but had not yet made a permanent conquest of what are now the south-western provinces of the Chinese republic. The northern frontier of the empire was defined by the Great Wall, beyond which lay the country of the nomad Tartars, the secular enemies of the Chinese cultivators. To the south the boundary was less clearly marked. Canton and the coast-line had been brought under Chinese rule some centuries earlier, but this strip was still a colonial territory largely inhabited by non-Chinese races.[1]

The south-western provinces, Yunnan and Kueichou, with parts of Szechuan, Kuangsi and Hunan, were not then part of the Chinese empire, though strong dynasties had from time to time established garrisons at various points. Even on

[1] Shans. The south coast was anciently called Yüeh, and the people of Yüeh were non-Chinese. There are still non-Chinese tribes in Fukien, close to the coast, and in the island of Hainan.

the southern bank of the Yangtze, in Hunan and Kiangsi, Chinese colonisation was as yet sparse, and aboriginal tribes were still found in the mountains.[1]

The Yangtze valley was thus the real southern limit of seventh-century China. Farther south there was a colonial region standing ethnographically in the same relation to the true Chinese territory as Indo-China and Malaya stand to the modern republic. The important difference was that South China in the seventh century had already been subjected to Chinese rule, whereas the modern Chinese settlements in southern Asia are outside the frontiers of the Chinese state. The centre of gravity in the seventh-century empire was still the great plain lying between the Yellow and Yangtze rivers and the plateaux of the north-west. The powerful Han dynasty (206 B.C.–A.D. 220) had indeed ruled over a far wider area, including Mongolia, Central Asia, Korea, southern Manchuria and even Annam, but these far-flung dominions were in no sense part of "China". They were foreign conquests held by the power of the sword. By the end of the sixth century these extraneous territories had all been lost.

The great Han dynasty was succeeded, after a period of division, by the quarrelsome Tsin dynasty (A.D. 265–419) under which the defence of the northern frontiers was neglected. In A.D. 311 invading Tartars captured the Tsin emperor in his capital at Lo Yang and conquered the northern part of China. The Tsin dynasty managed to retain the south, where in A.D. 318 the dynasty was re-established with its capital at Nanking. The northern provinces were left in the hands of several competing Tartar princes who were only prevented from conquering the whole empire by their violent intestine dissensions.

This disaster led to three hundred years of partition. The unity of the empire was lost, the work of the Han dynasty

---

[1] *Tzŭ chih t'ung chien*, by Ssŭ-Ma Kuang. Reprinted by the Commercial Press, Shanghai, Book 183. In which mention is made of ManTzŭ aborigines in the mountain country of south Kiangsu province.

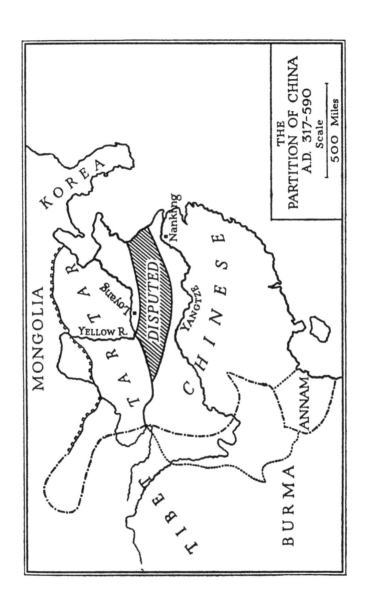

THE
PARTITION OF CHINA
A.D. 317–590
Scale
500 Miles

MONGOLIA

KOREA

TARTAR

Loyang
Yellow R.

DISPUTED

Nanking

Yangtze

CHINESE

TIBET

BURMA

ANNAM

utterly destroyed. The northern provinces from the Great Wall to the southern edge of the great plain were divided up between a number of short-lived Tartar dynasties, only one of which, the Wei (A.D. 390–500), succeeded in uniting the whole north under one ruler. The southern empire remained in Chinese hands, the Tsin being succeeded by four other dynasties, none of which occupied the throne for more than a lifetime.

During this period of partition the situation in China closely resembled the condition of Europe in the Dark Ages. Just as the Roman empire, partly overrun by barbarians, only maintained its authority in the eastern provinces, so the old Han empire of all China lost the north to the barbarian Tartars, but managed to retain its hold on the southern provinces. Nanking, like Constantinople, was the centre of the polite arts, the last refuge of refined civilisation; and the southern Chinese empire, like Byzantium, was preserved more by the incoherence of its enemies than by its own military prowess. The sequel proved different. Europe remained permanently divided, losing not only political unity but also the language and culture of the classical past. The Chinese absorbed the Tartars, reconstructed the old unified empire, revived the ancient culture and carried it to a perfection never previously attained.

In this splendid achievement, which changed the history of the eastern world, Li Shih-Min played a major part, for the Chinese recovery was consolidated under the dynasty which he founded. The reasons why the Chinese succeeded where the eastern Roman empire failed are worthy of examination. There were two important differences between the plight of Europe and that of China in the fifth and sixth centuries. The Roman empire was assailed not only by the Teutonic barbarians of the north, but also by the Persians, and later by the Arabs, from the south. The Chinese had only to contend with the Tartars of the north, for no formidable power ever developed among the aborigines of South China.

Secondly the Graeco-Roman population had for some centuries steadily diminished and had never been an ethnographic unity; but the Chinese, a people bound together by a common language and literature, were infinitely more numerous than their enemies. Consequently the Tartar conquerors were rapidly absorbed by the native stock, which yet remained essentially Chinese. In Europe the descendants of Roman citizens and barbarian invaders blended to form new Latin peoples, but in China the Tartars were too few to breed a new mixed race. Political ascendancy was therefore easily recovered by the Chinese majority.

There is no authority for positive statements about the size of the population of China at the close of the sixth century. An estimate has been made, which, while in conformity with such evidence as exists, does not conflict with commonsense or historical probability.[1] According to this computation the population of the northern provinces which had been under Tartar dynasties was in the year A.D. 618 102,300,000, that of the southern, less populous, region which had remained under Chinese rule was 27,150,000. The population of the whole empire being 129,450,000.

The re-assertion of Chinese supremacy was unquestionably mainly due to the fact that, in spite of three centuries of Tartar rule, the overwhelming majority of the population was still of Chinese race. Though the Tartars were always formidable enemies, there is no reason to believe that their hordes compared in point of numbers with the Chinese inhabitants of the empire. Such historical references as can be found all point the other way. The Chinese historians prided themselves on their punctilious accuracy in matters of fact and date, but they cared little for statistics. The histories tell of Tartar invasions, wars and conquests, but there is no record of how many Tartars survived the war

[1] The detailed arguments and data upon which this estimate is based will be found in the appendix. This estimate was first published in *The China Journal*, Shanghai, in the numbers January and February 1932, and is reprinted by the courtesy of the editor of that journal.

and settled in China, nor of how many Chinese remained in the conquered territory.

The researches of modern historians dealing with the very similar and almost contemporary invasions of the Roman empire by the Teutonic barbarians have tended to discount the traditional belief in vast overwhelming hosts which swept across Europe exterminating the inhabitants. It has been shown that such huge hordes could not have come from the uncultivated forests of northern Europe nor obtained provisions and transport for long marches across the length and breadth of the continent. Their success, it is now believed, was due, not so much to their numbers, as to their superior fighting spirit and the listless resistance of the degenerate subjects of Rome.

The Tartar incursions in North China were unquestionably of the same character. It is against reason to suppose that the semi-desert Mongolian steppe could ever have supported a population equal to that of the North China plain, one of the most highly cultivated areas on the earth's surface. The Tartar tribes, then, as now, were nomads, compelled to range over enormous distances to find pasture for their flocks. Hardiness, horsemanship, and the dissensions among their adversaries were the chief advantages of the Tartar raiders, who made up for their small numbers by superior mobility. Just as the barbarians first gained a foothold in the Roman empire as mercenaries in the service of the emperor, so the Tartars were invited into China to assist in the fratricidal quarrels between the princes of the Tsin dynasty.

When they decided to assume the mastery themselves, they encountered only a feeble resistance. The Chinese population, weary of the misgovernment of the Tsin princes, accepted a Tartar ruler with indifference, if not with relief. The later invasion in A.D. 390 was even easier. These Toba tribes who afterwards founded the most enduring Tartar dynasty, the Wei, first entered China at the expense of the earlier Tartar dynasty, which the Tobas conquered. It was not until A.D. 450

that the new invaders tried conclusions with the Chinese empire in the south. Their conquest of the northern provinces was not opposed by the Chinese, who felt no interest in the fate of their established rulers. When new Tartars attacked the old settlers, the real natives stood by content, no doubt pleased at the spectacle.

The Toba invasion was in fact a change for the better. The new conquerors were of Tungusic stock, a more intelligent and adaptable race than the earlier Tartar invaders who were Huns (Hiung Nu). The Toba Wei dynasty gave North China peace after a century of ceaseless wars. The Tungusic newcomers speedily adopted the Chinese civilisation and freely intermarried with the natives of the soil. A hundred years after the foundation of this Wei dynasty the Tartar emperor himself issued a decree prohibiting the use of the Tartar language, costume and customs, marking the change by abandoning his name of Toba in favour of the Chinese surname Yüan, which had the same meaning. The Tartars were now so identified with the Chinese that they built new lengths of the Great Wall to defend themselves, in the Chinese manner, against the untamed nomads of the Mongolian steppe.

History confirms the theory that the Tartar invaders formed only a very small minority of the North China population. In A.D. 500, when the Wei emperor issued his sinifying decree, the province of Honan, immediately south of the Yellow river, had a Tartar population of only 14,700. Yet it was in this province that the Wei emperor held his court at Lo Yang. The first Tartar invasion in A.D. 304 is said to have had a fighting force 50,000 strong. If the whole of this horde counting women and children was five times as numerous, it would still have been only a small fraction of the population of one Chinese province.[1]

[1] Evidence that the Chinese did not regard the Tartars as exceedingly numerous can be quoted from other periods. In Han times a Chinese renegade is recorded as remarking to a chief of the Huns, "Your whole horde does not equal the population of two Chinese prefectures". Again, in A.D. 750, a

If there was no likelihood that the Tartar conquest would result in the permanent mutation of the Chinese race and its culture, language and civilisation, as happened to the Roman population of the western empire, yet there seemed to be a great danger that it would make an end of Chinese unity, effecting a lasting partition into two or more empires. It was the very limitation of the Tartar strength that made for the permanency of the schism. In the dry plains and plateaux of the north the Tartar horsemen found a country admirably suited to their methods of warfare, the traditional Scythian cavalry tactics, which are described by the Chinese historians in almost the very words which Herodotus uses about the Scythian enemies of King Darius. But when the Tartars raided beyond the confines of the central plain into the valley of the Yangtze, they came into a country in every way unsuited to cavalry. The swampy rice-fields, abrupt, wooded hills, and narrow, wet valleys of the southern provinces were unfamiliar and dangerous ground for the northern horsemen.

The Tartar invasions of the Yangtze valley were in every case failures. Three times, in A.D. 379, 450 and 467, they raided to the very banks of the river, but each time they were defeated and driven from the country. It was not until A.D. 540, when the Tartars, almost entirely absorbed, were freely using Chinese armies, that they profited by the dissensions of the south to make themselves overlords, through a Chinese tributary, of the western half of the Yangtze valley. By that time the pure Tartar blood was rare in the north: the descendants of the free horsemen of the conquest had become elegant and cultivated courtiers, indistinguishable from their Chinese colleagues.

The southern Chinese, though they made several attempts, were equally unsuccessful in their efforts to recover the

counsellor of the Turkish khan remarked in the course of discussion with his master, "The population of the Turks is small, not one hundredth part of China's".

northern provinces. Their troops were mainly infantry, the horse being a rare beast in the south of China, where grazing land is seldom found. The southerners, however, excel as sailors and watermen. Conducting amphibious operations along the navigable rivers, they three times penetrated as far north as the Yellow river (A.D. 380, 417, 450), temporarily reconquering the whole central plain and part of the western plateau. Unfortunately these conquests proved as transient as the Tartar dominion in the Yangtze valley. China seemed doomed to be permanently divided, but without the stability of a lasting clearly defined frontier.

No geographical feature marks the boundary between North and South China. In the west, mountain ranges, by no means impassable, provide an adequate frontier, but in the east the great, dry, millet-growing plain south of the Yellow river shades off imperceptibly into the flat, rice-growing valley of the Huai river, which communicates by channels and lakes with the Yangtze. There is no frontier, only a gradual, indeterminate change in the character of the country. Consequently the history of all partitions of China is ceaseless border warfare punctuated by short intervals of uneasy truce. Peace in China has ever depended on unity.

This border warfare in the fifth and sixth centuries was characterised by endless sieges, for the southern Chinese were skilful and obstinate in the defence of fortified places, while the horse-riding Tartars were unused to siege work. The southern empire, owing its preservation more to its frontier fortresses and its climate than to the valour of the army in the field, seemed likely to endure indefinitely, but entertained no real hope of reconquering the north. Reunion, when at last it came, was the work of the northern Chinese. By the middle of the sixth century the pure Tartar stock had practically disappeared, but in the process of absorption the northern Chinese had acquired something of the virile energy of the nomads, while retaining their Chinese character, language and culture, to which the Tartars could make no useful contribution.[1] It was from this fortified race in the north, Chinese in all essentials, but rendered more dynamic by the addition of some Tartar blood, that the artificers of reunion were drawn, their work being facilitated by the close relationship existing between the aristocracy of both empires.

Although the Chinese feudal system properly so called had been finally overthrown by the foundation of the centralised Han dynasty eight hundred years earlier, Chinese society at the close of the sixth century was still essentially aristocratic. With the collapse of the united empire under the Tsin dynasty, many great families established in the south became locally very powerful. Governorships were passed on from father to son; influential clans dominated whole provinces, claiming an hereditary right to positions of authority.

This was the principal weakness of the southern empire, which was forever spending its strength in suppressing rebellious governors instead of fighting the Tartars. In the north political power was at first confined to the Tartar ruling clans, the Chinese aristocracy having fled south when Lo Yang fell. But as the Tartar stock became absorbed a new Chinese aristocracy rose to power, these families often having some admixture of Tartar blood.

Throughout the whole period of partition there was much intermarriage between the ruling classes of both empires. Princes and governors of the southern state frequently fled to the north when some political complication at Nanking made life in the south unsafe; while the many and sanguinary revolutions in the Tartar kingdoms sent another exodus of refugees across the southern frontier. The short duration and violent perturbations of the dynasties ruling both empires tended to depress the imperial authority and prestige. Few families occupied the throne for more than forty or fifty

[1] It is possible that the Tobas brought with them from a west Asiatic source the art for which their Wei dynasty is famous—sculpture in stone. Against this view there is the earlier evidence of Han sculpture at Hsiao T'ang Shan in Shantung, and the contemporary Liang stone lions at Nanking. But Greek influence is present in the Wei Buddhistic figures.

years. A powerful minister or successful general was always regarded as a potential future emperor. This absence of established loyalties emphasised the selfish clan spirit with which the aristocracy of both empires was imbued.

Yang Chien, founder of the Sui dynasty, who first re-united the empire under one sovereign, was a member of the northern Chinese aristocracy, and father-in-law of the last emperor of the Tartar Northern Chou dynasty. Himself a Chinese, Yang's principal wife was of Tartar blood (the Duku family) and his daughter was the consort of the Tartar emperor. In A.D. 580 Yang dethroned his sovereign and made himself emperor. The significant change, which brought back a Chinese family to the imperial throne, was performed without any opposition from the descendants of the Tartars, who now felt themselves to be Chinese. Ten years after this revolution, the new Sui emperor despatched several armies which rapidly conquered the effete southern empire, then ruled by an artistic but indolent emperor, who could not even be bothered to open the despatches in which his generals informed him of the progress and approach of the enemy.

After 267 years of partition China was once more united under a dynasty of native stock, but this dynasty was itself of short duration. Yang Chien, the founder, was a man of slight education who made no attempt to conciliate the official class. Indeed he retrenched the educational establishments which had existed under his Tartar predecessors. His rule, though harsh and unsympathetic, might have established a lasting dynasty had not his successor, the celebrated mad-man Yang Ti, by his extravagant conduct and improvident expenditure, plunged the empire into an anarchy more intolerable than the Tartar conquest.

The foundation and consolidation of the dynasty which put an end to this anarchy, the T'ang, was the life's work of Li Shih-Min, known to history under his imperial posthumous title of T'ai Tsung of the T'ang dynasty. Although reckoned as the second emperor of the new dynasty, Li Shih-Min was the original instigator of his father's rebellion against the Emperor Yang Ti of the Sui dynasty, and the final victory of the T'ang army was due to his leadership and genius.

The first part of this book traces the course of the desperate warfare between the T'ang leader and his many rivals for the throne. The second part of the book deals with the reign of Li Shih-Min after he had succeeded his father as emperor. In these chapters the success of the emperor as an administrator is contrasted with his failure to control the evil propensities of his own sons. The man who could achieve and consolidate the reunification of the empire and extend its limits far beyond the confines of China proper, could not reform the character of his heir, or train a successor worthy to maintain the authority of the imperial throne.

Finally an attempt is made to assess the historical importance of Li Shih-Min's achievements. By restoring peace, unity, and ordered government to the vast territories inhabited by the Chinese race, Li Shih-Min saved the civilisation of eastern Asia from collapse and ruin. His work made possible the glorious culture of the middle T'ang period, one of the great creative epochs in the history of the world.

This is his title to fame; and now that the ancient Chinese culture is becoming known to the west, it is one which merits a wider recognition.

CHAPTER I

THE DOWNFALL OF THE SUI DYNASTY

It was a troubled world, where loyalties were uncertain and the future menacing and obscure, into which Li Shih-Min was born at Ch'ang An in western China, in the year A.D. 600.[1] He was a younger son of an old and distinguished aristocratic family descending from Li Kuang, a celebrated general of the Han dynasty.

The Li family subsequently settled near Liang Chou in the province of Kansu, the extreme north-west corner of China. There the family became very powerful. In the year A.D. 400, during the confusion that followed the fall of Lo Yang to the Tartars, the head of the family, Li Kao, made himself sovereign prince of the district, calling his state West Liang (Hsi Liang). Li Kao and his two sons reigned over Liang for some twenty years, until the principality was conquered by a Tartar dynast. The Li clan survived this catastrophe, subsequently moving east to Ch'ang An, then the capital of the western division of the Wei dynasty. Several members of the clan served the emperors of Wei and Northern Chou with honour. Li Ping, the sixth descendant of the last prince of Liang, was awarded the honorary title of duke of T'ang for his services. Li Ping married a lady of the Tartar Duku family, and was thus a brother-in-law of Yang Chien, founder of the Sui dynasty. His son, Li Yüan, was the father of Li Shih-Min.

Besides Shih-Min, who was the second son, Li Yüan had

[1] There is a conflict of evidence on Li Shih-Min's age. The commentator of the *Tzŭ chih t'ung chien*, Hu San-Sheng, who lived in the Mongol period, A.D. 1260–1340, says that he was fifty-three at his death in A.D. 649. But the text of the *Tzŭ chih t'ung chien* itself states that he was sixteen in the year A.D. 615. As the Chinese reckon a child to be one year old at birth, this would mean that he was born in A.D. 600 and was forty-nine years old when he died. I have followed the older authority.

four children by his consort the Lady Tou,[1] but only three of these played a part in the history of the time—the eldest and youngest sons, Li Chien-Ch'êng and Li Yüan-Chi, and his daughter, the Lady Li.

Shih-Min, as the second son of a great family, received the education and upbringing of his class. This included classical Chinese literature and calligraphy, at which the youth excelled. Chinese calligraphy is more than a neat accomplishment. It is reckoned as one of the arts ranking with painting or poetry. Shih-Min was a famous calligraphist, and many specimens from his pen, engraved on stone tablets, still exist. Rubbings of these are widely sold in China as models upon which the student should base his style.

Besides the scholarly education to which the Chinese ruling class have always paid so much attention, the boy was trained in the warlike pastimes which the Tartar conquest had made popular in China. Shih-Min perhaps inherited from his grandmother's family his passionate love of horses. This taste is attested by the famous bas-reliefs, formerly guarding the approach to his tomb, with their vivid portrait sculptures of his six war-horses killed in battle beneath him.[2] Shih-Min was also a superb archer, the most famous of his age, an accomplishment to which he was to owe his life on several occasions.

When the boy was still in his early 'teens his father was appointed governor of Shansi, with headquarters at T'ai Yüan Fu, the post being one of the principal frontier commands bordering the country of the Turks, then the dominant and rising power in the Mongolian steppe. It was in this elevated, bracing mountain country, far from the luxury of the extravagant Sui court, that Shih-Min passed his formative years, among scarred frontier troops, learning endurance on hunting expeditions and warfare in border alarms.

---

[1] Tou Shih. Her personal name is not mentioned.
[2] Four of these reliefs are now in the Shensi Provincial Museum at Ch'ang An (Hsi An Fu). The other two are in Philadelphia.

The first important campaign in which he distinguished himself occurred in the year A.D. 615, when he was fifteen years old. The emperor, Yang Ti, of the Sui dynasty, son and successor of Yang Chien, came up to the cooler climate of the Shansi mountains to pass the summer in a palace which he had built near T'ai Yüan Fu. This was in the year in which Li Yüan had been made governor of the province. Yang Ti, after some stay in his palace, passed beyond the Great Wall to make a tour of the northern frontier. Up to this year the Sui dynasty had been on friendly terms with the khan of the Turks, indeed the Princess I Ch'êng had been given to the khan in marriage. But Yang Ti, who had begun to fear the power of the Turks, had recently attempted to stir up dissension among the lesser khans. His efforts failed in their purpose, only serving to anger Sibir Khan, the paramount chief, who was well aware of Yang Ti's intrigues.

Hearing that the emperor had unwisely passed to the north of the Great Wall, Sibir Khan, gathering a force of several thousand horsemen, made a sudden swoop in the hope of capturing the entire imperial party. He would almost certainly have succeeded had not the Princess I Ch'êng, his Chinese wife, sent the emperor a secret warning. This gave Yang Ti time to fly post haste to Yen Mên, a fortress and gate of the Great Wall, in which he was immediately besieged by the Turkish host.

The position of the emperor was now extremely hazardous. Yen Mên was a small place, in which, with the inhabitants, refugees, huge imperial train and guards, there were now no less than 150,000 people, without any adequate supply of provisions. Of the forty-one fortified posts in the district the Turks quickly captured thirty-nine, while Yen Mên itself was incessantly attacked so that "arrows fell like rain". Yang Ti, who at best was an unbalanced character, seems to have lost his nerve. Clasping his youngest son in his arms, the emperor spent his time "weeping till his eyes were swollen".

His generals and ministers offered a variety of advice, but

the distracted monarch could not make up his mind. The generals urged him to choose a few thousands of the best troops and cut his way out through the besiegers on some dark night. The ministers, who risked being left to their fate if this plan was adopted, tried to persuade their sovereign to publish a decree promising to discontinue the unpopular Korean war, which was rapidly exhausting the strength of the dynasty. If this were done, they declared, the troops would fight with renewed ardour.

The best advice came from Hsiao Yü, younger brother of the empress, who was a descendant of the former southern imperial house of Liang. He suggested that a message should be sent secretly to the Princess I Ch'êng, Sibir Khan's Chinese wife, who, as her previous warning proved, was at heart always Chinese in sympathy. Apprised of the emperor's plight, she might be able to contrive some means of raising the siege. Yang Ti, desperately afraid, acted upon this advice, also promising to give up the Korean war, and reward with official rank every man who defended Yen Mên.

Meanwhile Li Yüan, as governor of the province, had been informed of the Turkish invasion and had despatched all available troops to the emperor's assistance. Shih-Min accompanied the expedition, which was in charge of a subordinate general. This commander, however, doubted whether he could raise the siege with his small force. He asked the advice of his staff, and it was then that the young Shih-Min gave early proof of his aptitude for war. "The Turks", he said, "would never have dared to besiege the emperor in Yen Mên if they had not already known that our force was too insignificant to embarrass them. Consequently we can only succeed by making them believe that the main imperial army is arriving to raise the siege. To do this we must march by day in a long column, displaying a great number of standards, and when camped at night, light fires over a wide area, keeping up a constant sound of drums. The Turkish scouts, seeing our army covering the roads for many miles, and hearing so much noise at night, will really believe that the main army has arrived to save the emperor. Then they will retire without fighting, as is their custom."

The general followed this plan, and the Turks were in effect deceived. As he received a message at the same time from the Princess I Ch'êng saying that he was menaced from the north by another Tartar tribe, Sibir Khan, believing that he had the imperial army on his hands, abandoned the siege and retreated to his steppes. The emperor hastened to put himself in safety by a swift retreat to T'ai Yüan Fu.

At this time, A.D. 615, Yang Ti, second emperor of the Sui dynasty, had been ten years on the throne, but the extravagance of his conduct and the unpopularity of his tyrannical rule made it unlikely that he would occupy it in peace much longer. Though not without talents, the emperor's character had steadily deteriorated after he ascended the throne. In his later years he became a real megalomaniac. It was above all Yang Ti's reckless expenditure that brought the Sui dynasty to ruin. The empire, barely recovered from the destructive wars of three centuries of partition, was taxed to the limit to provide money for the emperor's gigantic programme of public works.

Discontented with Ch'ang An, his father's capital, Yang Ti rebuilt the city of Lo Yang, in Honan province, which had been largely ruined in the troubles at the end of the Wei dynasty fifty years earlier. It was now reconstructed on a most spacious plan, adorned with palaces more magnificent and costly than any yet seen, with a vast imperial park to the west of the city. This pleasaunce had artificial lakes and small hills covered with forest trees which were dug up and conveyed to the site from distant forests. The huge park, larger than Ch'ien Lung's ruined Yüan Ming Yüan, which still covers the countryside near Peking, was rushed to completion, regardless of cost, by press-ganged labourers, who were treated with the utmost brutality.

Lo Yang, however, was only one of Yang Ti's expenses.

His most useful and lasting monument was the Grand Canal from Hang Chou in Chekiang, across the Yangtze near Yang Chou to the Yellow river, a distance of 500 miles. Though this great work served the uses of peaceful commerce, the emperor had it constructed more for his own pleasure than to benefit his subjects. Its primary purpose was to provide a comfortable route by which the imperial court could travel from Lo Yang to Yang Chou, near Nanking, where Yang Ti had built a new southern capital scarcely less magnificent than Lo Yang.

A fleet of superb barges, decorated and equipped with the utmost splendour, served to convey the court on these journeys, while on either bank of the canal the emperor was protected by a numerous army, for whose support every town within a hundred-mile zone was forced to contribute provisions.

Had Yang Ti been content to reign at home in this dearly bought luxury, his extravagance, though it bore heavily on the people, might have caused no upheaval. Unfortunately his foreign policy was as ambitious, and even more costly, than the internal administration. Ambassadors were sent to all the kingdoms of Central Asia to obtain acknowledgment of Yang Ti's suzerainty. As the envoys did not dare to return unsuccessful, they gained their ends by bribing the petty kings with enormous sums of money. The vain monarch was perfectly content when he had purchased these empty promises at a fabulous cost.

The emperor's crowning folly, which finally ruined the dynasty, was the Korean war. There was no reason whatsoever for this expedition. Korea[1] had been a province of the Han empire, and Yang Ti, who considered himself to be by far the greatest ruler China had ever had, was determined to

[1] The Korean peninsula was then divided between three kingdoms. Of these Kao Li, from which the name Korea is derived, was the most powerful. It occupied not only the northern half of the peninsula but also the region now called South Manchuria, or Liao Tung, up to the Liao river on the west. Yang Ti attacked this kingdom.

reduce this country to its ancient obedience. In three successive years, A.D. 611, 612 and 613, the emperor hurled the strength of the empire against the Korean king, and each time he failed dismally. The first expedition, which he commanded in person, was held up at the siege of Liao Yang (near the modern Mukden) till the onset of the bitter northern winter forced the Chinese to retire. In the next year an army under the chief generals of the empire, which had failed to take the Korean capital, was cut to pieces on its retreat at the crossing of the Yalu river. When Yang Ti once more took command of the third invasion he was interrupted when besieging Liao Yang by the news of a dangerous revolt in China proper.

The disasters of the Korean war, coming on top of all Yang Ti's colossal programme of public works, had beggared the empire. The oppressive taxation drove the despairing people to banditry, while the soldiers, unwillingly pressganged to fill the ranks of the army, deserted in thousands to swell the forces of the malcontents. In A.D. 611 these deserters were so numerous in Shantung province that they could defy the regular imperial forces. Under a leader of capacity, named Tou Chien-Tê, they allied themselves with the bandits, becoming year by year more formidable.

The rebellion which recalled Yang Ti from Korea was even more serious. The leader, Yang Hsüan-Kan, was a member of the aristocracy, a man of ability with a winning personality. As has often been the case in the rebellions of China, Yang Hsüan-Kan was driven to revolt by the fear that his life was in danger. Yang Ti had once made a remark which Yang Hsüan-Kan took as a hint of his future doom. When the emperor had become involved in the tiresome siege of Liao Yang, Yang Hsüan-Kan raised the standard of rebellion at the city of Li Yang.[1] The rebel was at once joined by one Li Mi, who was destined to play a major part in the troubles of that age. Li

[1] Near Ta Ming Fu in Hopei province. Li Yang does not now exist. In the seventh century it was an important crossing of the Yellow river.

Mi also came of a good family. He had been a page at court, till one day Yang Ti was heard to remark, "that black-a-vised boy has a strange look". This ill-omened observation had been taken as a hint by Li Mi's family, who withdrew the boy from a court where the monarch's displeasure was apt to lead to a sudden curtailment of the offending subject's life.

Realising that he could never find fortune at the Sui court, Li Mi, who was endowed with restless ambition and many of the qualities of a great leader, readily joined Yang Hsüan-Kan, with whom he was well acquainted. As chief adviser to that rebel he proposed a plan of campaign which showed great strategic insight. "The emperor", he said, "is now in Korea with the pick of the army. If we occupy the gates of the Great Wall we can cut off all his supplies and interrupt his communications with China. As the season is now far advanced he and the army will be starved to submission before his supporters in China can come to his rescue. This is the best plan. The second plan is to raise what troops we can, and occupy, with the least possible delay, the province of Kuan Chung.[1] With this inexpugnable base we can at leisure conquer the rest of the empire, which is weary of the Sui dynasty. There is a third plan, inferior to the others. We may seize the capital (Lo Yang) and then, having the families of the aristocracy and the treasure of the empire in our hands, we can readily win wide support. But this plan admits of no delay, for if the imperial troops arrive before we take the city, we are lost beyond hope."

Yang Hsüan-Kan, who wanted quick results, lacking the patience and foresight of a great commander, opted for the third and worst plan.

The dangers inherent in this scheme, which Li Mi had foreseen, proved only too real. During the absence of the emperor, Lo Yang had been committed to the care of his

---

[1] Kuan Chung was the old name for the province now called Shensi. The name, meaning "Between the Passes", sufficiently indicates the character of this easily defended region.

grandson and heir, Yang T'ung, Prince Yüeh. Though his troops were frequently beaten by the rebels in the open field, Prince Yüeh managed to defend the immensely strong walls until two imperial generals, Yü-Wên Shu and Ch'ü-T'u T'ung, arriving post haste with troops from Korea, made it impossible for the rebels to continue the siege.

Then, too late, Yang Hsüan-Kan tried to carry out Li Mi's second plan, and seize Shensi: but as even now he could not be persuaded to realise the vital importance of speed, he was overtaken, totally defeated, and killed near Shan Chou on the Lo Yang-Ch'ang An road, in the autumn of A.D. 613. Li Mi was taken prisoner, but managed to escape after making his guards drunk. For some years he led the roving life of an outlaw, till opportunity once more came his way.

Yang Ti returned in triumph to Lo Yang, but his presence failed to check the rising tide of disorder which soon swelled up into open revolt in every province of the empire. The rebellion of Yang Hsüan-Kan occurred two years before Yang Ti's unfortunate experience at Yen Mên. During those two years, which the emperor passed at Lo Yang, the condition of his empire steadily deteriorated. The extreme severity of the laws against bandits only served to multiply their numbers, for as soon as one horde was dispersed, several others rose in its place.

The mentality of the imperial madman is best illustrated by a sample of his legislation. In A.D. 615 he decreed, as a measure to suppress banditry, that the entire rural population must take up its residence in the cities, only going out to work the fields by day. The villages were to be occupied by troops, so that all persons found outside the city walls at night could be apprehended as robbers. Such absurd laws, obviously incapable of application, only served to infuriate the people; while the bandits, joined together in formidable armies, swept the countryside.

But Yang Ti, living withdrawn amid the delights of his parks and palaces, paid little heed to the affairs of state. He flew into a violent rage if his attention was called to the growth of the rebellions. At last his ministers, realising from some tragic examples that it was folly to provoke him with the truth, soothed the all-powerful tyrant with grotesquely mendacious accounts of the state of the country. On one occasion, some rumour of the menacing progress of the rebellions having reached him, Yang Ti asked Yü-Wên Shu, President of the Board of War, whether the revolt was dangerous. Yü-Wên unhesitatingly replied, "They are only a few bands of petty thieves who will soon be dispersed". This thundering lie so tickled the sense of humour of another minister present, that he was forced to dodge behind a column, lest the emperor should perceive his uncontrollable mirth. Yang Ti, in fact, did notice his strange conduct, and the minister was only able to explain his behaviour by pretending a sudden indisposition.

On returning from his alarming adventure at Yen Mên, the emperor promptly broke the promise he had made to discontinue the Korean war, and decreed a fresh conscription for another invasion of the contumacious kingdom. This order precipitated a general revolt in every part of the empire. Already a rebellion of the people of Kiangnan (the country south-east of the Yangtze) had been suppressed by the general, Wang Shih-Ch'ung, who had resorted to the most despicable treachery. He issued a proclamation saying that all rebels who submitted would be pardoned and that the rigorous laws would be modified. When more than 30,000 insurgents, who had only taken up arms in desperation, had surrendered on these terms, Wang surrounded these unfortunates with his troops, and massacred them to the last man. Needless to say, the other rebels were only rendered the more desperate by this gross treachery. Henceforward they would never submit, no matter what terms were offered to them.

The emperor, who, since he was no longer willing to listen to the reports of his ministers, remained in ignorance of these events, decided in the year A.D. 616 to return to Yang Chou, his southern capital. Yang Ti seems to have had a curious prediliction for the south, though his family was of northern origin (Shensi) and his mother of Tartar blood. He could speak "the language of Wu", the dialect of the Yangtze delta, and had acquired a taste for the sophisticated customs and vices which had flourished in the old southern empire. While ordering fresh levies for the Korean war, he determined to spend another year at his beloved Yang Chou, in spite of the earnest remonstrances of the entire court, which was convinced that if the emperor went south, nothing could stop the spread of the rebellions in the northern provinces.

The tyrant not only refused to listen to this advice, but decapitated the more importunate officials. Even after the emperor had embarked he was implored to return by a group of people who lined the banks of the canal, wailing and prophesying woe if he persisted in his design. The incensed monarch's reply to their petition was to order his guards to massacre these loyal, though imprudent subjects. Then, moving in his fleet of gorgeous barges, attended by the picked troops of the empire, who rode along either bank, the emperor journeyed south through a country already seething with revolt.

All the evil consequences which the ministers had predicted followed swiftly upon this fatal voyage. Li Mi, emerging from his hiding-place, put himself at the head of a large host of rebels who were in arms to the east of Lo Yang, and, receiving constant reinforcements on his march, boldly advanced upon the capital. Tou Chien-Tê, the bandit leader in Shantung, acquired new strength, and soon dominated the north-east plain, where early in the next year he proclaimed himself king, giving his new dynasty the name of Hsia.

In that year, A.D. 617, the Sui empire dissolved into irremediable chaos. Revolts led by men of influence and standing broke out everywhere. The banditry of previous

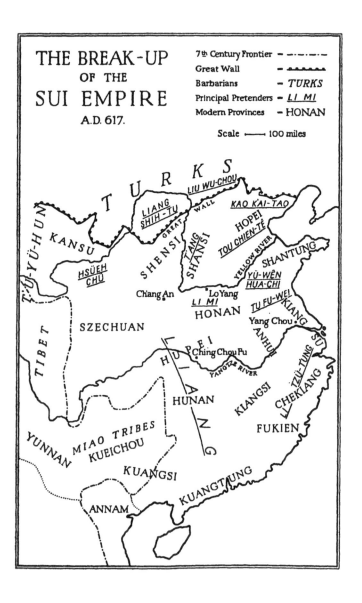

THE BREAK-UP
OF THE
SUI EMPIRE
A.D. 617.

7th Century Frontier — – ·· – ·· –
Great Wall — ▲▲▲▲▲
Barbarians — *TURKS*
Principal Pretenders — *LI MI*
Modern Provinces — HONAN

Scale ⊢——⊣ 100 miles

TURKS

LIU WU-CHOU
LIANG SHIH-TU
KAO K'AI-TAO
TÜ-YÜ-HUN
KANSU
GREAT WALL
SHENSI
T'ANG SHANSI
HOPEI
TOU CHIEN-TÊ
YELLOW RIVER
SHANTUNG
HSÜEH CHÜ
YÜ-WÊN HUA-CHI
Ch'ang An
Lo Yang
LI MI
HONAN
TU FU-WEI
KIANGSU
TIBET
SZECHUAN
Yang Chou
ANHUI
HUPEI
Ching Chou Fu
YANGTZE RIVER
YANGTZE
HUNAN
KIANGSI
TZU-TUNG
CHEKIANG
FUKIEN
YUNNAN
MIAO TRIBES
KUEICHOU
KUANGSI
KUANGTUNG
ANNAM

years was succeeded by a general partition of the empire. As these rebels all aspired to the imperial throne, and mostly adopted the imperial title, it will be convenient to give a brief account of them and the areas they occupied.

(1) In the extreme north-west corner of China the province now called Kansu passed into the hands of one Hsüeh Chü.

(2) A military officer named Liang Shih-Tu rebelled in the north of Shensi and proclaimed himself emperor. He was supported by the Turks, who gave him the title of khan.

(3) In north Shansi another rebel, Liu Wu-Chou, assumed the rank of emperor, receiving Turkish support.

(4) In the far north of Hopei (Chihli), Kao K'ai-Tao, calling himself prince of Yen, held court at Yung P'ing Fu.

(5) To the south of Yen, Tou Chien-Tê reigned in the coastal plain, later fixing his capital at Kuang P'ing Fu in southern Hopei.

(6) Li Mi assailed Lo Yang in alliance with less well-organised rebels who ravaged the province of Honan.

(7) Tu Fu-Wei, a sixteen-year-old shepherd-boy, made himself head of a rebellion as early as A.D. 614. He controlled the lands between the Huai river and the Yangtze.

(8) South China extended a warm welcome to Hsiao Hsien, a member of the former southern imperial house of Liang. He was accepted without opposition in Hupei, Kiangsi, Hunan, and Kuangtung. He ruled this large empire from Ching Chou Fu on the Yangtze in Hupei.

In other parts less well-organised rebels roamed the country, almost the only part of China remaining unaffected being Szechuan, too remote to feel the weight of Yang Ti's oppression.

The greatest of all the rebellions was that raised by Li Shih-Min in his father's province of Shansi, but the origin and progress of this, which ended in the foundation of the T'ang dynasty, will be related in detail in the next chapter. Here only the tragic fate of the Sui house remains to be told. Yang Ti was not insensible to the perils which menaced his grandson and heir, Yang T'ung Prince Yüeh, in Lo Yang. He despatched the general, Wang Shih-Ch'ung, who had so cruelly massacred the Kiangnan rebels, with a large army to attack Li Mi, who, having mastered all the northern part of Honan, was now besieging the capital. Lo Yang, indeed, was reduced to serious straits. Li Mi had defeated the troops of Prince Yüeh outside the city and plundered the great granaries. By distributing the grain to the populace he gained the goodwill of the people, who freely brought provisions to his army. The rebel leader had also received the support of many influential men, attracting to his standards all the adventurous spirits who found Yang Ti's tyranny intolerable. Among those who now joined Li Mi the most noteworthy were Wei Chêng and Hsü Shih-Chi. The former, an ex-Taoist priest, was a man of rare ability, who became one of Li Mi's counsellors. Hsü Shih-Chi, better known to history as Li Shih-Chi (the change of surname dated from his adherence to the T'ang cause), was then only seventeen years old. Even at this early age his outstanding ability gained a command in the rebel army for one who was destined to be a very famous general.

Although Wang Shih-Ch'ung and the imperial army reached Lo Yang, Li Mi defeated the relieving force in open battle, and forced it in turn to take refuge inside the walls of the city. The position of Lo Yang was therefore still most precarious. The rebel generals now urged Li Mi to leave Lo Yang alone, and occupy Shensi, thus putting into practice the plan which he had once proposed to Yang Hsüan-Kan. Li Mi was forced to abandon this plan for fear that his soldiers, who were from the eastern provinces, would not be willing to follow him to Shensi, far from their homes. In this decision Li Mi made a mistake; for, as he proved unable to capture Lo Yang, his inaction was in the end fatal to his cause.

But in this year Yang Ti's generals were no more successful against the other rebels than at Lo Yang. An army, sent to suppress Tou Chien-Tê, was not only totally defeated by that rebel in a battle fought in a fog, but the surviving Sui troops also made common cause with the rebels. The territory north of the Yellow river was henceforward entirely dominated by rebel forces.

The emperor had spent this disastrous year secluded in his palace at Yang Chou, scarcely troubled at all by the deepening shadows which were fast closing over the dynasty. Accompanied by troops of women, he spent his days in the delightful gardens of his southern palace, feasting, drinking and watching theatrical entertainments, seeking to forget the loss of an empire in the pleasures of the senses. Nevertheless, his privacy was from time to time disturbed by the importunities of his ministers and the growing murmurs of the army. Neither the courtiers nor the soldiers shared the emperor's fondness for the southern capital.

The ministers, mostly members of the northern aristocracy, had left their families and possessions in the north, where they were exposed to all manner of perils from one or other of the victorious rebel armies. The imperial guard were all men of the north, recruited in Shensi, the home province of the Sui emperors. The troops now wearied of the south, where, cut off by hundreds of hostile miles from their villages and families, they seemed destined to a permanent exile. Indeed, the emperor, when he could be roused to give any consideration to the fate of the dynasty, had expressed the opinion that it was useless to hope to reconquer the north. Instead he toyed with the idea of fixing his permanent capital at Nanking, and contenting himself with the southern part of the empire. The short-lived Sui reunion of China had already foundered, even before the dynasty finally succumbed.

Yang Ti's new policy was not revealed to the army, but the discontent of the soldiers was appeased for a time by a singular expedient. The emperor, learning that their chief grievance was the long separation from their families, conceived the simple plan of providing them with new families in the south. Orders were given that every soldier must take a wife from a family resident in Yang Chou. This remarkable mass marriage seems to have contented the troops for the moment, though history does not record the opinion which the maidens of Yang Chou formed upon the matter.

But by the spring of A.D. 618, even the charms of the young women of Yang Chou could not silence the discontent in court and camp. The events of the preceding year had made it plain that, while Yang Ti reigned, there could be no possibility of the Sui dynasty recovering the northern provinces. But the ministers and generals, not less than the soldiers, were opposed to any permanent exile in the south, such as the emperor contemplated. Plots and evasions became frequent. In spite of the death penalty pronounced against deserters, soldiers, and even high officials, were daily abandoning the doomed monarch. Yang Ti appears to have realised that the end was near. One morning, as he was combing his hair before a mirror, he exclaimed to the empress, "Such a beautiful head! who would dare to cut it off?" The answer to this question was not to be long delayed.

Among the ministers at court were the two sons of the general, Yü-Wên Shu, who had so boldly lied to his sovereign about the progress of the rebellions. Yü-Wên Shu was of Tartar descent, of the same clan as the former imperial house of Northern Chou, which had been dethroned by the first Sui emperor. The general had recently died, leaving three sons—Yü-Wên Hua-Chi, Yü-Wên Chih-Chi and Yü-Wên Shih-Chi. The last, an able general, and later a notable at the T'ang court, took no part in the conspiracy which his elder brothers fomented. But Yü-Wên Hua-Chi was a brutal and debauched character, who, as a youth, had enjoyed the unworthy favour of the emperor.

Whether because he felt that the time was now ripe to give full rein to his natural ambition, or because he was actuated by some motive of revenge for the fall of his ancestral house, he became the leader of the extreme malcontent party at Yang

Chou. The avowed aim of the conspiracy was to compel the emperor to take the northern road, relieve beleagured Lo Yang, and re-establish the capital in the original home of the dynasty at Ch'ang An.

When, on a dark night, the mutineers, having slain the loyal guards, broke into the palace, these legitimate aims were forgotten. The emperor, startled by the tumult, hid with his youngest son in a secluded room, but his refuge was betrayed by one of the palace women. Dragged forth from his hiding-place, Yang Ti was held under guard till dawn when, Yü-Wên Hua-Chi having seized the city and overcome all opposition, the emperor was carried in his chair to the Hall of Audience, where his former favourite awaited him.

The insolent rebel at this spectacle shouted out roughly, "Why are you carrying that thing about?" Then, ordering the monarch to be seated on a chair in front of him, Yü-Wên Hua-Chi proceeded to accuse him of his many crimes and follies. But the soldiers, whose blood lust had been aroused, were impatient of formalities. Before the rebel leader had finished his accusations, one of the mutineers drew his sword and with one blow decapitated the young prince, a mere child, Yang Ti's favourite son, who had accompanied his father ever since the mutiny began. The blood of this wretched boy splashing upon his father's robes incited the soldiers to complete their work, but the emperor, an actor even in this extremity, exclaimed, "The Son of Heaven has his own way of dying. Do not shed my blood, fetch poison". The appeal was refused, but the soldiers instead of slaying their sovereign with the sword, strangled him on his throne with his own scarf.

This deed consummated, the mutineers made a general massacre of the princes of the imperial family, and the ministers and generals who had remained faithful to Yang Ti. Yü-Wên Hua-Chi, after permitting the empress to give Yang Ti and his son a hasty burial in the grounds of the palace, carried off the treasure and harem of the murdered emperor, and set out for the north with his mutinous army, along the Grand Canal.

With this sanguinary tragedy the strange reign of Yang Ti came to an end, leaving China, more divided than ever, a prey to a dozen contending aspirants.

CHAPTER II

THE FOUNDATION OF THE T'ANG DYNASTY
A.D. 617–18

During the year A.D. 616 Li Yüan had been actively engaged in warfare with the Turks, who, since the siege of Yen Mên, had kept up a series of border raids and sudden forays. In addition, the duke of T'ang had been ordered to co-operate with other governors in the seemingly hopeless task of suppressing the bandits and rebels who infested the northern provinces.

In all these campaigns Shih-Min, although only sixteen years old, took a prominent part. In seventh-century China youths were considered old enough to engage in politics and war at an age which we now regard as very immature. It is noteworthy that Shih-Min was not the only boy of his generation who signally distinguished himself while still in his 'teens. Tu Fu-Wei, the rebel leader in the Huai valley, was at the head of a large army before he was seventeen. Hsü Shih-Chi (Li Shih-Chi) was one of Li Mi's generals at the same age. Among the Sui officers defending Lo Yang was Lo Shih-Hsin, who at the age of thirteen led a cavalry charge against an army of bandits.

It was an age of youth. The wars and tumults of the time had weakened the heavy control of the older generation. The Confucian maxims enjoining unquestioning submission of youth to age were but little observed. The T'ang dynasty was founded by youths triumphing over the fears and caution of a less inspired generation; following a dismal period of disunion and weakness it dawned as an era of confidence and hope.

Early in A.D. 617, Li Shih-Min, realising that the Sui dynasty was definitely on the decline, began to consider the possibility of a revolution. Among the officers stationed at

T'ai Yüan Fu was Liu Wên-Ching, who commanded the guard at the imperial palace where Yang Ti had spent the previous summer (A.D. 615). This officer was related by marriage to the rebel Li Mi; consequently an order now arrived from the court for the arrest of Liu, who was to be held in prison till the question of his complicity in Li Mi's rebellion was investigated.[1] Liu Wên-Ching was a close friend of Shih-Min, who came often to visit him in prison. Liu, who now had no hope of making a career in the Sui service, took advantage of these visits to urge Shih-Min to plan a revolt. Shih-Min already entertained the same ideas; he now began to canvass his friends, and secretly enlisted soldiers. He did not, however, mention these activities to his father, Li Yüan.

Li Yüan, duke of T'ang, was an easygoing aristocrat, not remarkably intelligent, a weak character. He lacked tenacity, foresight and resolution. Had he not been the father of Shih-Min there was no man living in China less likely to win his way to the throne. Shih-Min, who perfectly understood his father, knew that he could never be persuaded to take decisive action unless presented with a *fait accompli*. Therefore he kept his plans to himself until the moment was ripe.

At this time a curious prophecy was current in all parts of China, to the effect that after the fall of the Sui dynasty, the imperial throne would pass to a family of the Li surname. There is no doubt that this prophecy, which proved so true, was not invented in later years, but really was current under the Sui emperors, for Yang Ti had one important official family named Li exterminated, because he believed this clan to be the one indicated by the prophecy. The idea had ob-

---

[1] Rebellion and conspiracy to rebel were capital crimes under the laws of all Chinese dynasties. Furthermore, the crime usually entailed the penalty of death on all members of the rebel's family, which, in accordance with Chinese social custom, was regarded as the unit, of which the individual was merely a part. Relatives by marriage and maternal relatives were included in the sentence, though in their case the penalty was reduced to banishment, imprisonment, confiscation of property or heavy fines. Liu Wên-Ching was at least liable to these lesser penalties.

tained such a hold on the popular imagination that a group of rebels in Kansu selected a man named Li to be their leader, although he was not the originator of the rebellion. Other prominent rebels who owed much of their success to their names were Li Tzǔ-T'ung, in south-east China, and Li Mi, who was at first the most popular candidate for the honours designated by the prophecy.[1]

Shih-Min and his supporters may have been influenced by this saying; the young man certainly used it as an argument when he approached his father with the momentous suggestion. He began by pointing out the sad state of the empire and the utter hopelessness of the Sui cause. Then he suggested that his father, threatened by the tyranny of Yang Ti on the one hand, and the rising power of the rebels on the other, should save himself by "following the wish of the people, raise a righteous army, and convert calamity into glory".

The worthy governor was greatly shocked at his young son's proposition. He exclaimed, "How dare you use such language! I will have you arrested and handed over to the magistrates!" He even picked up a pen to sign the order. Shih-Min was not impressed by this paternal bluster. Making no apology for his words, he replied, "I only spoke because, as I see it, this is the true state of our affairs to-day. If you arrest me, I am quite ready to die". His father testily replied, "How could I think of having you arrested? Never dare to speak like that again".

The boy was not deceived by this show of bad temper, which he rightly interpreted as the instinctive reaction of a weak character faced with a serious decision. He re-opened the subject the next day. "At present", he said, "the rebels are increasing every day, they have spread over the whole

[1] Such prophecies are not uncommon in Chinese history. A similar one was current at the end of Li Shih-Min's own reign (see chap. x). In modern times there has been the *Song of the Cakes* in which the whole history of the Manchu dynasty and subsequent events is said to have been forecast in oracular form. According to one account the author of this interesting political horoscope was Liu Po-Wên, the minister who built Peking for the Ming emperor, Yung Lo.

empire. Do you, Sire, suppose that you can carry out the orders of the emperor and suppress them? Even if you could succeed, you would still be suspected, and accused of some crime. Everyone says that the Li name is destined to obtain the empire, and for that reason the emperor butchered the whole family of Li Chin-Ts'ai, although they were guilty of no crime. If you really put down the rebellions your services would be beyond recompense, and therefore you would go in peril of your life. The way to escape this danger is to do what I said yesterday. It is the only way, make no doubt of that."

Li Yüan sighed, then replied, "All last night I thought over your words. There is much truth in them. Now if our family is ruined and our lives forfeit, it will be all your fault; but if we mount to the throne it will be equally thanks to you".

Shih-Min, however, knew his father's character. Li Yüan might be induced to approve of the plan, but it did not follow that he would act upon it. The boy therefore contrived an intrigue which would commit his cautious father beyond escape.

Through the agency of Liu Wên-Ching, Shih-Min had made friends with P'ei Chi, eunuch-superintendent of the imperial palace at Fên Yang, near T'ai Yüan Fu. P'ei Chi became a member of the conspiracy, and his aid was now most useful. Instigated by Shih-Min, who had studied his father's pastimes to some purpose, P'ei Chi made a selection of the most beautiful damsels from the harem of the palace, which was under his control, and presented Li Yüan with these choice flowers from the emperor's private garden, without telling the unsuspecting governor whence they came.

A few days later the eunuch invited Li Yüan to a banquet, and when the wine had flowed freely, P'ei Chi, feigning a tipsy confidence, remarked, "Your second boy (Shih-Min) is secretly enlisting soldiers and purchasing horses, no doubt for 'the Great Affair'. Now that I have given your Grace some of the ladies from the Fên Yang palace I am afraid that if this news leaks out we will all face a capital charge. It is really a very serious matter. I think we should all act together, what is your Grace's opinion?"

Li Yüan, astounded, could only stammer out, "So my boy planned all this! If things are as you say, there is no going back, and I must give my consent".

The final argument was supplied by the emperor himself. An officer from the court arrived at T'ai Yüan Fu with an order for Li Yüan, who was directed to travel to Yang Chou forthwith, to answer for his conduct in failing to suppress the rebels. No one could doubt that the governor had incurred the fatal suspicion attaching to all who bore the name of Li. This news was decisive. Li Yüan knew what his fate would be, if, when he reached the court to report his ill-success against the rebels, the further capital charge of violating imperial concubines came to light. It was even doubtful whether he could reach the southern capital at all, across hundreds of miles of rebellious provinces.

Vehemently urged to revolt by Shih-Min, P'ei Chi and all his officers, the wavering governor only hesitated long enough to give his eldest and youngest sons, Chien-Ch'êng and Yüan-Chi, time to escape from the city of P'u Chou Fu, in the south of the province, where they were then residing. This city was held by the well-known Sui general, Ch'ü-T'u T'ung, who was loyal to Yang Ti. As soon as these young men had reached T'ai Yüan Fu, Li Yüan assembled his officers, and after going through the last formality of asking their advice, proclaimed his intention to revolt.

The revolution was accomplished without difficulty. Certain officials who had not joined the conspiracy attempted to organise resistance, but the precautions which Shih-Min had taken rendered their efforts futile. The city passed easily into the hands of the insurgents. A greater danger came from a roving band of Turks, who, attracted by the news of the tumult, attempted to capture the city. But though they in-

vested the walls for some days, they lacked the means to force
so strong a position, and after plundering the neighbourhood,
made off in search of easier booty.

The plan of campaign, in the framing of which Shih-Min
bore a chief part, had for its objectives the conquest of
Shensi and the capture of Ch'ang An, the capital of that
province. This plan, it will be remembered, was one of the
three which Li Mi proposed to the rebel Yang Hsüan-Kan,
though Li Mi himself did not adopt it when he had the
opportunity. It is a notable proof of the abiding strategic
importance of Shensi that most of the great conquerors in
ancient China used this country as the cradle of their empires.
Shih Huang Ti, of Ch'in dynasty, the first unifier, Kao Tsu,
the founder of the Han dynasty, and Yang Chien the founder
of the Sui, all used Shensi as their base. With the slow change
in the centre of gravity of the Chinese state, which has now
moved southward, the strategic importance of the north-west
has declined, and the dwindling population and increasing aridity of this country have robbed it of its ancient
strength. But in the seventh century Shensi was the heart
of China.

To penetrate Shensi the T'ang army had to pass the Yellow
river, which could only be reached by an advance down the
valley of the Fên, a tributary which drains the Shansi plateau.
The Fên valley was strongly defended by several cities still
loyal to the Sui cause. The first of these obstacles was the
city of Fên Chou, fifty miles from T'ai Yüan Fu. Shih-Min
and his eldest brother, Chien-Ch'êng, were sent against this
place with the advance guard. Fên Chou made only a feeble
resistance, falling after a few days' siege. The strict discipline
of the T'ang army, which paid for its provisions and require-
ments, made a favourable impression on the inhabitants of
the surrounding country, who submitted without difficulty.

Before advancing farther, Li Yüan was anxious to protect
his base, T'ai Yüan Fu, by making peace with the Turks.
Sibir Khan was not unwilling to come to terms; indeed he

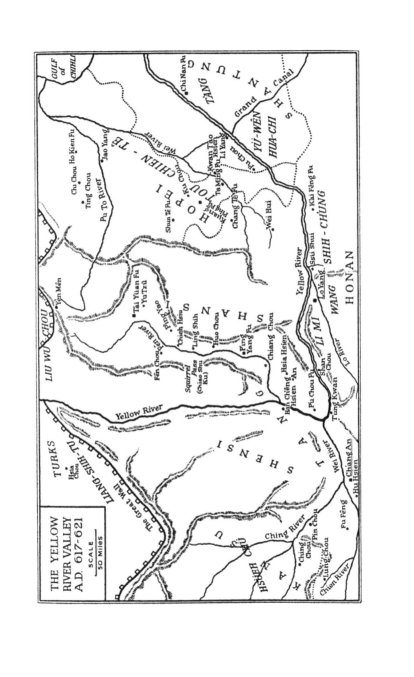

THE YELLOW
RIVER VALLEY
A.D. 617–621

SCALE
50 Miles

suggested that Li Yüan should at once take the imperial title. The Turk was always ready to support Chinese pretenders who would weaken the power of the Sui dynasty. He had already set up two puppet emperors, Liang Shih-Tu and Liu Wu-Chou, who had accepted Turkish suzerainty. But the duke of T'ang realised that it would not do to appear as a Turkish vassal of this type. He therefore adopted the expedient of declaring Yang Ti deposed, recognising as emperor Yang Yu Prince Tai, a grandson of Yang Ti. This young prince was the nominal governor of Ch'ang An, the objective of the T'ang army.

In the seventh month of the year A.D. 617, in the middle of summer, the T'ang army, about 30,000 strong, passed unopposed through the Squirrel pass (Ch'iao Shu Ku), a position of great natural strength which, had it been guarded, would have checked all advance into the lower Fên valley. The Sui generals, realising too late their error, hastily gathered 20,000 men to garrison Huo Chou, a city at the southern end of the pass. Another Sui army was stationed at P'u Chou Fu in the angle where the Yellow river makes the great bend to the east, a city which guards the approach to the crossing at T'ung Kuan, the gateway of Shensi.

The T'ang army was now held up by lack of supplies and the heavy rains of midsummer. During this delay negotiations were opened with Li Mi, but that rebel, though he promised to do nothing to hinder the T'ang march, would not commit himself to open support, preferring to cherish independent ambitions.

The rains continuing unceasingly, scarcity of provisions in the T'ang camp became acute. At the same time the news that Liu Wu-Chou, the pretender in north Shansi, was raiding the border and menacing to attack T'ai Yüan Fu itself filled the irresolute Li Yüan with alarm and uncertainty. Supported by P'ei Chi and others of his staff, he decided to retire to protect T'ai Yüan Fu. At this crisis the persistence and vision of Shih-Min alone prevented what would have been a ruinous mistake. Vehemently he insisted that to retreat now would be fatal. The Sui commanders would have time to assemble a far superior army, while a retirement would dishearten the T'ang troops, encourage their enemies, and above all remove any possibility of entering Shensi by surprise. He further maintained that though Liu Wu-Chou might raid as far as T'ai Yüan Fu, he could not hold the country so long as Ma I and other border forts were in T'ang hands.[1]

In spite of these trenchant arguments Li Yüan refused to reconsider his decision, and the troops had actually started on the march back, when Shih-Min, still unwilling to allow this disastrous move, came by night to his father's tent. At first refused admission, he made so great a clamour outside that Li Yüan was compelled to let him in. The youth once more urged his thesis, declaring that all would be irretrievably lost if the retreat continued. Li Yüan objected, with the evasion of the real issue habitual to his weak character, that the orders had already been given and the troops were on the march. Shih-Min, seeing that his father was weakening, promptly offered to go himself in pursuit with counter-orders. Then with a laugh and a shrug, Li Yüan yielded, remarking, "Whether we win or lose will be your responsibility; call them back if you wish". Shih-Min and his elder brother, Chien-Ch'êng, instantly rode after the army and gave orders to cease the retreat. His judgment was strikingly confirmed a few days later by the arrival of ample supplies from T'ai Yüan Fu with the news that the threatened invasion by Liu Wu-Chou had never eventuated.

In the eighth month, the rains being over, the T'ang army advanced against Huo Chou, a city built in a narrow neck of the Fên valley, which here is bordered by steep mountains. Li Yüan was afraid that the Sui general would remain on the

[1] Ma I, or "Horse Town", was a famous border fortress, where, as the name suggests, the Tartars came to trade horses with Chinese merchants. It appears to have been about forty miles north-west of the Yen Mên pass in the neighbourhood of P'ing Lu Hsien, north Shansi.

defensive, effectively blocking the T'ang advance. Shih-Min, who knew the Sui general to be a brave but unsubtle commander, suggested a plan to draw the enemy out to battle. While the T'ang army remained at a distance, a few horsemen were sent ahead to the foot of the city wall, where they began to mark out the ground for siege trenches, working in a leisurely manner as if confident that they would not be molested by the garrison. As Shih-Min had expected, the Sui general considered this apparent confidence as a reflection on his courage. Enraged at such contemptuous treatment of a strongly held fortress he made a sortie at the head of the full strength of his garrison.

The T'ang army had been divided into two corps, the larger under Li Yüan and Li Chien-Ch'êng was drawn up in sight of the town outside the east gate. The cavalry under Shih-Min worked round to the south, remaining out of sight of the city till the battle had been joined. The Sui forces, not troubling to ascertain whether there were any T'ang troops in ambush, advanced resolutely upon the main body, which yielded gradually before the weight of their attack. When the Sui forces had thus been led some distance from the city, Shih-Min at the head of the cavalry suddenly appeared on their flank and rear. The unexpected charge of these troops, augmented by the counter-attacks of the main T'ang force on their front, threw the Sui line into confusion.

Shih-Min, plunging into the mêlée, inflicted great slaughter "till his sleeves were running with blood" as the historian puts it. At the height of the battle a cry that the Sui commander had been captured was raised, and this completed the defeat of the Sui army, which broke into flight.

Their position on the flank enabled Shih-Min's cavalry to outstrip the enemy, so that fugitives and pursuers arrived at the foot of the wall together. The inhabitants, seeing what was going to happen, had already shut the gates, thus barring out the flying soldiers. The Sui commander, who in reality had not been taken prisoner, arrived at the east gate and shouted orders for it to be opened. But his tone of authority only served to identify him to a band of pursuers, who rode up before the gate could be opened, and cut off his head. Profiting by the panic of the defenders the T'ang forces carried the city by assault as the day ended.

The fall of Huo Chou opened up the lower Fên valley to the T'ang advance. The surviving Sui troops had been incorporated in the victorious army, which occupied P'ing Yang Fu, the second city of the province, without resistance. Chiang Chou, the next place, was defended by an officer of note, Ch'ên Shu-Ta, a son of the last emperor of the southern Ch'ên dynasty, which the Sui had overthrown. This city was captured after some days of siege, Ch'ên Shu-Ta taking service with the T'ang army.

The T'ang army now entered the south-west corner of Shansi, the angle of the Yellow river bend. In this angle stands the strong city of P'u Chou Fu, which covers the crossing places of the river. P'u Chou Fu was garrisoned by a large Sui army under Ch'ü-T'u T'ung, one of the foremost generals of the empire. Instead of trying to take this strong position the T'ang leaders left a covering force to watch Ch'ü-T'u T'ung, while the main army crossed the river farther up stream, opposite the city of Han Ch'êng Hsien.

This plan was the more likely to succeed as the Shensi bank in this neighbourhood was dominated by a bandit chieftain, with whom Li Yüan entered into negotiations. The bandit welcomed these overtures, and crossed the river with a few attendants to swear allegiance to the duke of T'ang. With the co-operation of this irregular, who was appointed a general, the advance guard crossed the river unopposed and constructed an entrenched camp to cover the passage of the main body. Ch'ü-T'u T'ung, when he discovered that he had allowed the T'ang army to slip past, made a night attack with part of his army on the T'ang covering force, hoping to brush aside this corps and fall upon the main army before it could finish crossing the river. Although his initial attack was successful, a timely T'ang reinforcement turned the Sui flank. Ch'ü-T'u T'ung was defeated and forced back to P'u Chou Fu, where he was besieged.

The more cautious advisers of Li Yüan were anxious to capture that city before invading Shensi, but Shih-Min, who realised that speed was essential, urged an immediate advance on Ch'ang An, which, he declared could easily be taken if the Sui armies were allowed no time to recuperate and raise fresh levies. His view prevailed: while sufficient forces were left to blockade P'u Chou Fu, the main army took the Ch'ang An road. No sooner had the T'ang army begun its march than many cities sent in their submission, while volunteers flocked to the T'ang camp "like folk going to market".

Li Yüan despatched Chien-Ch'êng with 10,000 men to blockade T'ung Kuan, the key of Shensi, where the main road from the east passes through a narrow gap between the Yellow river and high mountains. When this place was taken no Sui troops from Honan could come to the assistance of Ch'ang An. Shih-Min headed the advance guard, moving along the Wei river, Li Yüan himself following with the main army.

At the outbreak of the T'ang revolution in T'ai Yüan Fu a message had been sent to Chai Shao, Li Yüan's son-in-law, warning him to leave Ch'ang An, where, as an officer of Prince Tai's bodyguard, he was stationed. Chai managed to get away, but as his family could not accompany him without arousing suspicion, his wife, the Lady Li (Li Shih), Li Yüan's daughter, took refuge in the city of Hu Hsien, a few miles south of Ch'ang An, where she remained in hiding. Li Shên-T'ung, a cousin of the duke of T'ang, fled to the mountains, where he enlisted a band of supporters to assist the T'ang invasion. The Lady Li did not consider that her sex should prevent her from furthering the cause of her family. She engaged the support of a bandit chief, a former Central Asiatic merchant, and leading this force to the support of Li Shên-T'ung, combined with him in an attack on Hu Hsien. The city was taken after a brief struggle, and this success rallied all the bandits of the countryside to the T'ang standards. These bands, which were led by proscribed members of the official class, were formed into a regular army by the Lady Li, who soon dominated the country south of Ch'ang An, capturing the smaller cities in the Wei valley.

While his valiant sister was engaging in these exploits, Shih-Min had advanced along the north bank of the Wei to a point only ten miles distant from Ch'ang An. The T'ang army encountered no real resistance on this march, while the number of new adherents who came daily to the camp swelled the army to a strength of 90,000 men. Among these who joined Shih-Min at this stage were Chang-Sun Wu-Chi, his wife's elder brother, and Fang Hsüan-Ling, a very able official who became his chief civil adviser.

After joining forces with his sister's army, henceforth honoured with the title of the "Heroine's Legion", Shih-Min invested the western capital with an army which now numbered 130,000 men. Messages were sent to Li Yüan urging him to come up to receive the surrender of Ch'ang An, which was not likely to stand a long siege. In the tenth month, when winter was beginning, Li Yüan arrived before the city with the main T'ang army, now no larger than Shih-Min's swollen advance force. After a short siege of only a few days' duration, the city was carried by storm and the objective of the first T'ang campaign was achieved.

Ch'ang An, then one of the most populous and magnificent cities in Asia, had recently been rebuilt by the founder of the Sui dynasty, who had made it his capital. Yang Ti's preference for Lo Yang and the south had not yet had time to rob Ch'ang An of its importance, or to lead to any diminution in its wealth. Under the T'ang dynasty it was destined to become the most famous city in Asia, the metropolis of the eastern world. The city stands in the valley of the Wei, ten miles south of the river, and about twenty miles north of the rugged Nan Shan mountains, a range plainly visible from the city in clear weather.

To-day the undulating plain between Ch'ang An and the mountains is bare, even desolate; only a few sparse trees marking a tomb relieve the yellow monotony of the loess fields. Of the parks and gardens, temples and palaces which surrounded the greater seventh-century city, little trace remains. Beyond the eastern gate the small Pa river which comes down from the mountains to join the Wei is till spanned by the famous Tung Pa bridge, a magnificent stone bridge, frequently mentioned in T'ang literature. Three miles south of the present wall the Ta Yen pagoda, which in T'ang times, according to tradition, was inside the south gate, still dominates the shrunken city.

Ancient Ch'ang An was indeed far larger than the city of to-day. Although little of it remains, a full description has been preserved in Chinese literature.[1] The city, as rebuilt by the Sui emperor, was, like its successor Peking, divided into several distinct cities, each surrounded by its own wall. The city of Ch'ang An proper formed a rectangle, six miles long by five across, having an area of thirty square miles. On the east it extended as far as the banks of the Pa river, which is two miles at least beyond the present walls. The city was traversed from north to south by a great thoroughfare, the Street of Heaven, which was a hundred paces wide, while other important streets crossed this at right angles. The city was laid out in a symmetrical plan, similar to the design which the Ming builders of Peking employed eight hundred years later.

In the centre of the north wall the Palace and Imperial cities formed an enclave. The Imperial City, the more southerly of the two, contained the government offices and the residences of nobles and officials. The common people were not allowed to reside in this enclosure, which had an area of about three square miles. To the north of the Imperial

[1] The *Ch'ang An chih* and the *T'ang liang ching ch'êng fang k'ao*.

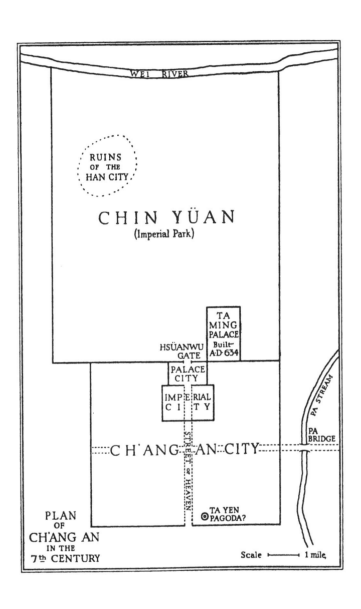

WEI RIVER

RUINS
OF THE
HAN CITY.

CHIN YÜAN
(Imperial Park)

TA
MING
PALACE
Built
A·D·634

HSÜANWU
GATE

PALACE
CITY

IMPE︙RIAL
C I︙T Y

STREET or HEAVEN

CH'ANG··AN··CITY

PA
STREAM

PA
BRIDGE

TA YEN
PAGODA?

PLAN
OF
CH'ANG AN
IN THE
7ᵗʰ CENTURY

Scale ⊢————⊣ 1 mile

City was the Palace City, equivalent to the Forbidden City of Peking. This area was slightly smaller than the Imperial City, being about two square miles. It was the palace and residence of the Sui and early T'ang emperors, before Shih-Min built the Ta Ming Kung.[1] The Palace City continued to be used throughout the dynasty on ceremonial occasions such as enthronements.

The north gate of the Palace City, the Hsüan Wu gate, later renamed the Yüan Wu gate, led into the Chin Yüan or Imperial Park, beyond the walls of the city. This pleasaunce, enclosed by the Sui emperors, had an area of no less than sixty-three square miles; on the north it was bounded by the banks of the Wei river, and it included within its boundaries the ruins of the old Han city of Ch'ang An. The great park contained an infinity of pavilions, small lakes, gardens, and miniature palaces, a delicious landscape garden on the largest scale. Such was Ch'ang An, a vast and splendid capital, by far the greatest and wealthiest city in Asia.

On capturing Ch'ang An, Li Yüan had issued strict orders that neither the Sui Prince Tai, whom he affected to recognise as emperor, nor the inhabitants were to be harmed. Even the Sui officials were left in peace, except for those responsible for desecrating the tombs of the Li family, action which they had taken on hearing of Li Yüan's revolt. These officials were decapitated. Among those taken prisoner was a certain Li Ching, with whom Li Yüan had quarrelled. The duke of T'ang ordered Li Ching to be put to death, but the victim indignantly exclaimed, "You pretend to be the leader of an army pledged to redress the wrongs of the people and restore tranquillity to the state, and yet your first act is to seek revenge for a private quarrel by slaying an innocent man!"

Shih-Min, who was witness of this scene, interceded in Li Ching's favour, obtained his pardon, and took him into his

[1] In A.D. 634 Shih-Min added the Ta Ming Kung, "Great Brilliant Palace", which was in effect another Palace City built beyond the north wall into the Imperial Park. It had an area of just under three square miles. This palace became the habitual residence of the later T'ang emperors.

own suite. In the event Li Ching was to be one of the most famous generals of the T'ang dynasty.

As Li Yüan was not yet prepared to assume the imperial title, the youthful Yang Yu Prince Tai, Yang Ti's thirteen-year-old grandson, who had been the nominal governor of Ch'ang An, was proclaimed emperor. Li Yüan was rewarded with the title of prince of T'ang, and became minister with plenary powers, and generalissimo, having charge of all affairs, civil and military. No one, we may be sure, had any doubt as to Li Yüan's ultimate intentions, but Chinese etiquette and sense of legality required a gradual approach to the throne, lest posterity should reproach the first T'ang emperor with the name of usurper.

This arrangement endured six months. In the early summer of the next year, A.D. 618, when news of Yang Ti's tragic death had been received, the final act was staged. The boy emperor was induced to offer the crown to Li Yüan. When the prince of T'ang had made the three refusals demanded by Chinese etiquette, and the Sui monarch had thrice insisted, Li Yüan formally assumed the imperial dignity. The Sui prince retired into peaceful obscurity. He did not live to enjoy this sheltered existence for long, but died in the next year, A.D. 619. The cause of his early demise is not stated by the historian; whether it was natural, or assisted, must remain unknown.

After Li Yüan had ascended the throne with the accustomed ceremonies and rejoicing, titles and rewards were distributed to all who had played a part in the great undertaking. Chien-Ch'êng, Li Yüan's eldest son, was proclaimed crown prince, while Shih-Min to whose genius and resolution the victory was due, was rewarded with the title of Prince Ch'in. The disposition of the crown in favour of Chien-Ch'êng, who had done little to deserve it, and the exclusion of Shih-Min, the real founder, from the succession contained the seeds of trouble which was later to produce an evil fruit. For the time this question was not acute. The T'ang dynasty so far only ruled in less than two provinces, Shansi and the Wei valley in Shensi. The rest of the empire remained to be conquered.

By the summer of A.D. 618 China was divided between twelve claimants: Li Yüan, and eleven others. There was no reason to suppose that Li Yüan was likely to triumph over all his fellows for, if none were more formidable than the T'ang emperor, some were at least his equal in power and already ruled over a far wider extent of territory. To the eight rebels who had been in the field against Yang Ti the year before (see chap. 1, p. 25) three more, besides Li Yüan, had been added. In the south-east, along the coast from the Yangtze to Fukien, the country had passed into the hands of a certain Li Tzŭ-T'ung.

Yü-Wên Hua-Chi, the regicide, at first recognised a surviving Sui prince as puppet emperor, but four months later murdered that shadow monarch also, and usurped his title. His headquarters were Ta Ming Fu, in Hopei.

Wang Shih-Ch'ung, the general despatched by Yang Ti to succour Lo Yang, at first acknowledged the Sui Prince Yüeh as legitimate emperor of the dynasty.

There ensued a desperate and confused struggle for the mastery. No claimant was able to depend on the neutrality, still less the friendship, of any other. An attack on one rival was certain to invite an onslaught by some other at the least guarded point; if two rivals combined to destroy a third, they immediately proceeded, the task achieved, to attack each other. No mercy was shown to fallen leaders. Each "emperor" considered his rivals as rebels, executed the captives, and exterminated their families. In this intricate and desperate warfare, where security could only be attained by complete victory, defeat meant death, and even surrender purchased no safety, Shih-Min, almost alone, sustained the cause of the T'ang. Li Yüan from the moment of his enthronement resigned all military operations to the direction of his younger son, occupying his days in Ch'ang An with the civil administration, from which he sought relief, at frequent intervals, in his favourite recreation of hunting.

Upon Shih-Min, a youth of eighteen, devolved the double task of conquering the rival "emperors" and parrying the raids of even more formidable external foes—the Turks. Sibir Khan had watched the collapse of the Sui empire with complacency. Nothing but good, from the Turkish point of view, could come from chaos and partition in the civilised empire within the Wall. The frontiers would be unguarded, opening a delightful vista of opportunity for plundering forays. Weak Chinese pretenders, such as Liang Shih-Tu and Liu Wu-Chou, would seek Turkish support, and as Turkish vassals could be used to hamper any consolidation of a new Chinese power. Finally there was always the chance that the weakness and disunion of the Chinese claimants would open a way for a grand invasion, the conquest of all or part of China, and the foundation of a Turkish dynasty.

The Turkish menace hung, a black, portentous cloud in the northern sky. In all Shih-Min's campaigns this danger was always present, a constant source of weakness and anxiety.

CHAPTER III

THE CONQUEST OF WESTERN CHINA
A.D. 618-20

The first campaign which Shih-Min undertook as commander-in-chief followed immediately after the occupation of Ch'ang An. It was directed against Hsüeh Chü, the pretender who was recognised as emperor in Kansu province. Hsüeh Chü, who had invaded Shensi by the valley of the Wei river, had hoped to capture the prize of Ch'ang An before the T'ang army could arrive. Although disappointed in this hope, he had already arrived at the city of Fu Fêng, sixty miles to the west. Fu Fêng sent a message promising submission to the T'ang dynasty and begging for relief. Shih-Min, entrusted with the task of raising the siege of this place, was completely successful. In a sharp action beneath the city walls Hsüeh Chü's forces were defeated and driven to retreat into Kansu.

The T'ang army did not pursue this campaign further. The eastern border was as yet insecure, consequently Shih-Min did not dare to lead the strength of the army into the remote highlands of the west, especially in the depths of winter. During this campaign Shih-Min was joined by Hsiao Yü, who governed a district in this area. Hsiao Yü will be remembered as Yang Ti's brother-in-law, who had offered the best advice when that emperor was besieged in Yen Mên. Hsiao Yü became an influential civil minister at the T'ang court.

It has already been pointed out that in seizing the hill-girt province of Shensi the T'ang leaders were conforming to an ancient strategic plan, which had been followed by all the great conquerors of the past. The control of this province gave the new dynasty a sure base from which expeditions for the conquest of the other provinces could be launched.

Judging by the course of the subsequent campaigns it would seem probable that Shih-Min, who was now in charge of all military operations, had studied the military history of the warring states period of the Chou dynasty, 400–223 B.C. At that time the contesting kingdoms strove with varying success to achieve one or other of two rival political and strategic concepts. Ch'in, the ultimate victor, a state which occupied the province of Shensi, aimed to accomplish what was called the "horizontal" plan that was to conquer a belt of country from Shensi eastward along the valley of the Yellow river to the sea, and so cut off the rival states in the north from all possibility of co-operation with their allies in the south.

These states for their part sought to put into effect what was called the "vertical" plan, and establish a north-to-south chain of allied kingdoms which would form a barrier against the eastward progress of Ch'in. A study of the map of North China will show that these rival plans embody abiding strategic verities conditioned by unchanging geographical facts, which will remain true in all ages. Similar plans were framed in the civil wars of 1923–30, and during every contest between the western hill provinces and the great eastern plain, the "horizontal" and "vertical" plans of the ancient Chou strategists reappear in all essentials unchanged.

Geography and the lessons of history thus forced Shih-Min to adopt the "horizontal" plan, since his base, like the kingdom of Ch'in, was Shensi province. His opponents, less educated or less quick-witted than he, were slower to understand that only the rapid consummation of the "vertical" strategy could save them from ultimate defeat.

In the early spring of A.D. 618 Shih-Min was occupied in the east. Ch'ü-T'u T'ung, the Sui general commanding at P'u Chou Fu, was induced to submit after the fall of Ch'ang An, and this obstacle to an eastward advance being removed, Shih-Min and his brother Chien-Ch'êng moved into Honan along the Lo Yang road. Without encountering serious opposition the T'ang army reached the neighbourhood of that capital, which was still being besieged by Li Mi. Had

Li Mi been willing to submit to the T'ang there is no question that the combined armies could have carried the city by storm, but Li Mi was too ambitious to accept a subordinate rôle. His attitude was so ambiguous that Shih-Min decided to retreat, giving his opinion that even if Lo Yang could be taken, it would be difficult to hold the city while campaigns in the far west, which was still unpacified, would require the full strength of the army.

Although for the moment abandoning any designs on Lo Yang, the T'ang army took care to seize and garrison the cities along the main road to the west of the capital, securing the route for a future invasion.

Shih-Min's decision not to embark on large scale operations in Honan was justified by the news which he heard on returning to Ch'ang An. Hsüeh Chü from Kansu had made a fresh advance, and had reached Pin Chou, sixty miles northwest of Ch'ang An. While on the way to check this invasion Shih-Min was incapacitated by an attack of fever. He was forced to resign the command to Liu Wên-Ching, to whom he gave strict orders not to engage battle. Shih-Min had a reason for enjoining inaction. He knew that the enemy, who were a long way from their base, were having difficulty in obtaining supplies. He therefore intended to play a waiting game till he could force Hsüeh Chü to engage battle under unfavourable circumstances.

Unfortunately Liu Wên-Ching and the other generals imagined that Shih-Min held their ability in low esteem, and was acting upon the defensive only because he himself was too ill to take command. Piqued by what they felt to be a boy's unreasonable contempt, they ignored Shih-Min's instructions, and gave battle to Hsüeh Chü near Pin Chou. The T'ang army suffered a disastrous defeat from which the generals themselves escaped with difficulty. Shih-Min gathered the fugitives and fell back on Ch'ang An. Liu Wên-Ching and his associate generals were deprived of their commands and rank.

The defeat of Liu Wên-Ching left the Kansu pretender free to advance on the T'ang capital. Hsüeh Chü's death, when already on the march, averted the immediate danger; for his son and successor, Hsüeh Jên-Kuo, did not press the campaign in this direction. Instead, he endeavoured to consolidate his position in the west. A T'ang force was driven into Ching Chou, on the Kansu-Shensi border, and the city besieged. Another force, sent to extricate the first, was itself defeated and compelled to seek safety in the same city, where the starving garrison, after eating their horses, were forced to subsist on a meal made by crushing the bones of these animals.

Hsüeh Jên-Kuo scored a further success by capturing the strong fortress of Lung Chou, which was betrayed to him by an officer who had made a false submission to the T'ang in the hope of finding an opportunity of delivering the city to his real master. The progress of the enemy was not arrested till Shih-Min, who had recovered from the fever, advanced in the later autumn to the vicinity of Lung Chou, where he made an entrenched camp. There he remained inactive for more than sixty days, waiting till the coming of winter caused a shortage of provisions in the enemy army. Hsüeh Jên-Kuo, whose rule was harsh and tyrannical, did not enjoy his father's popularity in Kansu. When the scarcity in his army became acute, several officers with their troops deserted to the T'ang.

When Shih-Min judged that these desertions had sufficiently weakened both the strength and morale of the enemy, he detached a portion of his army to make a new camp at the springs of the Ch'ien river (Ch'ien Shui Yüan), the very place where Liu Wên-Ching had been defeated a few months previously. As he had expected, the Kansu army, seeking an easy success, made haste to attack this camp, and were so intent on their attack that they failed to observe the movements of the T'ang main body. Shih-Min evacuated his original camp and led his troops by a detour through the hills to a position which menaced the rear of the Kansu army. The enemy, discovering their dangerous predicament, endeavoured to retreat, but being now taken between two fires were utterly defeated. The T'ang army drove the fugitives to the walls of Hsüeh Jên-Kuo's capital, a city on the Ching river near Ching Chou, Kansu.[1] The Kansu pretender rallied the fugitives with the intention of giving battle once more, but his followers were in no mood for further fighting. At the approach of the T'ang army so many deserted that Hsüeh Jên-Kuo was forced to retreat into the town without fighting. As soon as the siege was formed, the soldiers of the garrison profited by the night to slip over the walls and surrender, till in a few days Hsüeh Jên-Kuo, deserted by all his followers, was compelled to make an unconditional submission. In accordance with the custom of the time he was taken to Ch'ang An and decapitated in the market place. So ended the first of Shih-Min's rivals, and by his defeat all the north-west of China was added to the T'ang domain.

While this campaign had been occupying the T'ang armies in the west, important developments had occurred in Honan, where Li Mi was besieging Lo Yang. His strife with the Sui general, Wang Shih-Ch'ung, was now interrupted by the approach of a common enemy, the regicide Yü-Wên Hua-Chi, who had come north with the mutinous imperial army after the massacre at Yang Chou. The Sui officials in Lo Yang, hard pressed by famine, with no hope of relief in any direction, conceived the plan of "pardoning" Li Mi, so that he might fight Yü-Wên Hua-Chi. By this plan two dangerous enemies would be weakened while Lo Yang was given a chance to revictual.

The scheme appealed to Li Mi, who, for his part, reflected that once he was allowed into Lo Yang he could make short work of any who still supported the hopeless cause of the Sui dynasty. Pardoned and appointed grand-general by the Sui

[1] Shê Chih, which does not now exist.

Prince Yüeh,[1] Li Mi marched away east to meet Yü-Wên Hua-Chi at the city of Li Yang, on the Yellow river near Ta Ming Fu. Here Li Mi twice defeated the regicide, the second time so severely that Yü-Wên Hua-Chi was driven across the river with only a remnant of 20,000 men. Had not Li Mi himself been wounded in this battle, a misfortune which delayed the pursuit, the regicide would not have escaped. Even as it was Yü-Wên Hua-Chi realised that all hope was gone. After reaching the temporary haven of Ta Ming Fu he abandoned himself to a life of wine and debauch, in the midst of which he one day exclaimed, "Death is certain. Can I not be emperor if only for a day?" Forthwith he gave orders to slay the shadow Sui monarch whom he had set up at Yang Chou, and proclaimed himself emperor.

Li Mi's victories in the east were very unwelcome news to Wang Shih-Ch'ung who, with his army, was still at Lo Yang. His reputation had suffered greatly from his repeated defeats at Li Mi's hands. It was bitter for him to see his old adversary not only pardoned but appointed to the highest posts. Wang feared, with reason, that if Li Mi entered Lo Yang in triumph after his return from the east, he himself would be the first victim of the ex-rebel's all-powerful influence. To protect himself he decided to prevent Li Mi from entering the city. His intrigues came to the ears of those Sui officials who favoured Li Mi and feared Wang Shih-Ch'ung. They decided that Wang, whose services would no longer be required, and who could not be expected to work in harmony with Li Mi, had better be removed.

Their plans were not well laid and leaked out. Wang Shih-Ch'ung acted with speed and determination. At the head of his troops he attacked the palace, overpowered the guards, and dragged his principal enemies from the very

---

[1] Yang T'ung Prince Yüeh was recognised as emperor in Lo Yang after Yang Ti's death. He is known in history as the Emperor Sui Kung Ti, a title also given to his brother Yang Yu, whom Li Yüan made emperor for a few months in Ch'ang An. To avoid confusion I have used the original titles of these two princes.

presence of Prince Yüeh to instant execution. He then made a massacre of all the officials opposed to his party, and had himself appointed generalissimo and minister with plenary powers, the recognised first step to usurping the throne. Prince Yüeh "had but to sit on his throne with folded hands", as the historian puts it.

On hearing the news of this revolution, Li Mi, then marching back to Lo Yang, threw over his allegiance to the Sui prince, and prepared to renew the siege of the capital. Wang Shih-Ch'ung, realising that Lo Yang was in no condition to withstand a fresh blockade, decided to risk everything on one battle. After impressing upon his troops the desperate plight of the city, and the absolute necessity of victory, he marched out to confront Li Mi. That rebel, over-confident since his victory over Yü-Wên Hua-Chi, believed that success was certain. Disregarding the wise advice of his generals, who were in favour of delay, he made a rash attack upon the army of Wang Shih-Ch'ung. But the Sui army, keyed up by their desperate situation, fought with unusual valour, and achieved a complete victory. Most of Li Mi's principal generals were slain, while he himself, escaping with difficulty from the rout, fled with such troops as remained to him, less than 20,000, to submit to the T'ang emperor.

Li Yüan felt distrustful of a submission which was manifestly only the result of defeat and ruin. Although Li Mi was invited to Ch'ang An and given rank and titles, he was deprived of the command of his army. Li Mi, for his part, felt slighted at the T'ang court. He had still many partisans in the eastern part of Honan, who after his defeat were left in much uncertainty. While some submitted to Wang Shih-Ch'ung, the most important, Hsü Shih-Chi (Li Shih-Chi), followed his chief's example and swore allegiance to Li Yüan. The T'ang dynasty thus acquired a detached territory in the eastern plain. For this service Hsü Shih-Chi was rewarded with the imperial surname of Li, and it is as Li Shih-Chi that he is known to history.

Li Mi, persuaded that his old officers would rise in his favour if he returned with an army to Honan, asked to be given charge of an expedition to the east, which he said could easily be brought under the authority of the T'ang emperor. Li Yüan consented after much hesitation. Many at the court were strongly opposed to the plan. "To send Li Mi to Honan", said one, "is like loosing a tiger on the mountain, or throwing a fish back into the river. He will inevitably revolt." The prediction might perhaps have proved untrue if Li Yüan, with typical indecision, had not acted in such a way as to rouse Li Mi's fears. When the general was already east of the T'ung Kuan pass, at the head of his army, Li Yüan decided to recall him. When Li Mi received this order he was alarmed and angered. Aware that he had so far been perfectly loyal to his new master, he suspected that some intrigue had been set on foot against him, and that if he returned to Ch'ang An he would be put to death. Besides these fears, his pride made it difficult, after several years of independent leadership, to obey the vacillating orders of one whose ability to command was far inferior to his own.

Instead of returning to the court, he slew the imperial messenger and raised his own standard in revolt. But fortune had now finally deserted the adventurer. The T'ang troops stationed in the cities of western Honan, on hearing of the revolt, ambushed Li Mi's army in a defile among the loess hills of that country. In the battle Li Mi himself was killed, and with his death the rebellion collapsed.

Li Shih-Chi did not take part in the revolt of Li Mi. The territories along the lower course of the Yellow river which he had presented to the T'ang dynasty formed a detached area which was menaced on the west by Wang Shih-Ch'ung, on the north by Yü-Wên Hua-Chi and the emperor of Hsia, Tou Chien-Tê. To succour these places the T'ang court despatched an army under Li Shên-T'ung Prince Huai An, Shih-Min's uncle. Prince Huai An and Li Shih-Chi had at first considerable success in this region. Ta Ming Fu was wrested from the regicide Yü-Wên Hua-Chi, who was forced to take refuge in the smaller city of P'u Chou (not to be confused with P'u Chou Fu, in Shansi). There he was closely besieged.

The progress of the T'ang armies in this country aroused the hostility of a far more formidable foe, Tou Chien-Tê, emperor of Hsia, whose territory already covered the greater part of the eastern plain north of the Yellow river. Tou Chien-Tê, hearing of the T'ang successes against Yü-Wên Hua-Chi, decided to demand his share of the spoils. The regicide, who could not hope to withstand his enemies for long, offered to submit to the T'ang dynasty, supposing that Prince Huai An, as the weaker party, would be glad of his assistance against Tou Chien-Tê. But the prince preferred to leave the prey to the emperor of Hsia rather than make a composition with the regicide, who was held in universal detestation.

Although Tou Chien-Tê had been one of the first to rebel against Yang Ti's tyranny, he had professed the greatest horror at the news of the massacre at Yang Chou. He put his court into mourning for the sovereign against whose authority he had been for many years in open rebellion. With these sentiments it was not surprising that he attacked P'u Chou with determination, and carried the city after a short siege. The regicide was taken prisoner, together with the treasure and harem of the fallen Sui emperor. Tou Chien-Tê immediately executed Yü-Wên Hua-Chi, his brother Yü-Wên Chih-Chi, and all those who had been implicated in the tragedy of Yang Chou. The Empress Hsiao, who Yü-Wên Hua-Chi had carried off at his departure from Yang Chou, received kindly treatment from the emperor of Hsia, who later managed to send her to the Turkish khan, where she received shelter from the khan's Chinese wife, the Sui princess, I Ch'êng.

In the spring of A.D. 619 Wang Shih-Ch'ung made it clear that he too must be regarded as a claimant to the empire and no longer a loyal subject of the Sui dynasty. He had already obtained the title of prince of Chêng; now he presented his sovereign, Prince Yüeh, with a peremptory demand that he should yield the throne. Yang T'ung Prince Yüeh had courage and ability worthy of a happier destiny. He flatly refused to surrender his heritage. But Wang Shih-Ch'ung was not deterred by his failure to obtain the formality of his sovereign's consent. He imprisoned Prince Yüeh and appropriated the imperial ornaments, after which he was proclaimed emperor, taking the name of his principality of Chêng for the new dynasty.

The change was not popular in Lo Yang, where Wang's arbitrary methods were resented by the polished courtiers of Yang Ti's former capital. A plot to assassinate the usurper and restore Prince Yüeh was formed. Unfortunately the conspirators were careless, and information of their designs came to the knowledge of the new emperor. After decapitating all suspected of complicity in the plot, Wang Shih-Ch'ung decided to prevent further conspiracies by removing the person in whose interest they might be formed. A cup of poisoned wine was sent to the imprisoned Prince Yüeh. The unfortunate young man, when he realised the grim nature of his visitor's mission, asked for time to take leave of his mother, but his request was inhumanly refused. Then, falling on his knees before the altar of Buddha, the last ruler of the Sui dynasty uttered the memorable prayer, "May I never, in any future life, be reborn a prince or an emperor". The poison not taking effect as rapidly as the assassins wished, they hastened his end by strangling him with a scarf.

The rival pretenders in central and eastern China had hitherto been too occupied with their own ambitions to check the progress of the T'ang dynasty in the west and north. The T'ang leaders for their part had been absorbed in the task of consolidating their position in Shensi and Kansu. Li Yüan for these reasons had not paid sufficient attention to the latent menace of Turkish hostility. Accepting the treaty made in A.D. 617 with Sibir Khan, he had ignored the danger of an attack by Liu Wu-Chou, the pretender in north Shansi who had accepted Turkish suzerainty. It was from this quarter that the T'ang dynasty had now to resist an onslaught more determined and sustained than those it had so far encountered.

When Sibir Khan accepted the offer of T'ang friendship in A.D. 617 he was following his policy of supporting as many Chinese claimants as he could find in the hope that their dissensions would pave the way for a Turkish conquest. The rapid progress of the T'ang armies under Shih-Min was unwelcome to the Turk, who began to fear that the T'ang dynasty was growing too powerful. To redress the balance Sibir Khan decided to give active support to his two vassals, Liang Shih-Tu, who held the country north of Shensi province in the "loop" of the Yellow river, and Liu Wu-Chou, who reigned in north Shansi. In the spring of A.D. 619 the main strength of the Turkish hordes crossed the Yellow river "loop" to assist Liang Shih-Tu, while Liu Wu-Chou was ordered to attack T'ai Yüan Fu.

This formidable invasion was about to break in along the whole line of the northern T'ang frontier, when Sibir Khan died. He was succeeded by his younger brother Chur Khan, who was not prepared, on the morrow of his accession, to undertake a major campaign. While consolidating his position on the insecure Turkish throne he contented himself with encouraging the two Chinese pretenders. Liang Shih-Tu harried the border cities without much success. The operations of Liu Wu-Chou, on the other hand, rapidly developed into the most serious menace that had yet threatened the T'ang dynasty.

When the T'ang court was established at Ch'ang An, T'ai Yüan Fu and the province of Shansi had been left in the care of Li Yüan-Chi Prince Chi, Shih-Min's youngest brother,[1]

---

[1] The third brother was Hsüan Pa. Beyond the single fact of his name nothing concerning him is mentioned. It is therefore most probable that he had died in early youth.

who, as it proved, was a most unsuitable choice. Yüan-Chi's age is not stated, but as Shih-Min himself was only nineteen at this time, Yüan-Chi cannot have been more than seventeen years old. At that age Shih-Min had planned and directed the T'ang revolution; but Yüan-Chi had few qualities in common with his elder brother. Finding himself the master of a province, with wide powers, he gave himself up to a life of pleasure and outrageous violence, which did the greatest harm to the T'ang cause in its original home itself.

Arming the women of his palace, the young prince forced them to engage in sanguinary, and sometimes mortal, gladiatorial combats for his amusement. When passing through the streets of the city he would take snap shots with his bow and arrows at the citizens, in order "to see if they could dodge the arrows". At night he would sally out accompanied by a troop of libertines, and entering at will into any private dwelling, spend the night there in debauch. Like his father, Li Yüan-Chi was passionately devoted to hunting, often saying, "I can go three days without food, but not one without a hunt". On this pastime he lavished the revenues of the province.

The people and officials of T'ai Yüan Fu, outraged by this barbarous behaviour, sent a petition to the emperor, who had the sense to respond by promptly relieving the young savage of his post. Unfortunately Yüan-Chi knew how to play upon the weakness of his father's character. By a show of contrition he obtained his reinstatement at T'ai Yüan Fu. The emperor's weakness was to have dangerous consequences. Liu Wu-Chou, who had observed Yüan-Chi's conduct, came to the conclusion that the people of Shansi were not likely to regret a change of masters. Early in the summer of this year (A.D. 619) he invaded the province in great strength.

Yüan-Chi, who had given his officers little reason to respect his judgment, sent an inadequate force against the invaders, in spite of the protests of the officer placed in command. This officer, convinced that his small force could not hope to gain the battle, and knowing that if he was defeated he would be executed by the young tyrant, escaped from this dilemma by joining the invaders, and leading them to the capture of Yü Tzŭ, a city twenty miles east of T'ai Yüan Fu.

Sung Chin-Kang, who commanded the army of Liu Wu-Chou, next besieged T'ai Yüan Fu itself, while detached forces, roving over the plateau, captured P'ing Yao and Chieh Hsiu. The latter city is an important strategic point which commands the northern mouth of the Squirrel pass (Ch'iao Shu Ku) the narrow defile through which the Fên river comes down from the T'ai Yüan plateau. In consequence, the T'ang army from the south of the province, hurrying up to the relief of T'ai Yüan Fu, found its advance blocked at this point. The generals rashly gave battle, but Sung Chin-Kang, who had placed part of his troops in ambush, scored another victory, driving the T'ang army back into the pass.

After this check the command was given to P'ei Chi, the eunuch, a foolish choice, for which Li Yüan was responsible. P'ei Chi, on joining the army, made a new attempt to take Chieh Hsiu, for without this city in his hands he could not advance on to the plateau. He encamped before the walls, but his position was so unskilfully chosen that the enemy were able to cut off his water supply. Sung Chin-Kang waited till the T'ang army, suffering from thirst, had dispersed in search of water, when he made a sudden sortie, which caught the improvident eunuch general unawares. The T'ang army suffered a disastrous defeat, P'ei Chi himself only escaped by covering the seventy miles to P'ing Yang Fu in a day and a night.

Following this calamity every city in the province north of P'ing Yang Fu surrendered to Sung Chin-Kang. The crowning misfortune came when the incompetent Li Yüan-Chi, the cause of all these disasters, fled panic-stricken by night from T'ai Yüan Fu itself, which, on hearing of the prince's desertion, promptly surrendered. Li Yüan was furious at this news, for the city had a strong garrison and provisions for a long siege. The fall of this place might mean the loss of all Shansi. Nothing now arrested the advance of Sung Chin-Kang. P'ing Yang Fu, the second city of the province, was taken, and the smaller places in the south-west of Shansi fell one after another into his hands. It seemed as if the triumphant advance of the T'ang army through this same region two years before was now to be repeated—this time by their enemies.

The ill-advised strategy of P'ei Chi contributed in no small measure to these enemy successes. In the hope of checking the progress of Sung Chin-Kang, the T'ang general ordered the rural population to burn their crops, now ready for harvest, and assemble in the cities. This policy meant ruin and starvation for the peasantry. Their resentment was so keen that a revolt broke out, the rebels capturing the town of Hsia Hsien which they handed over to Sung Chin-Kang.

The loss of Shansi seemed so final that Li Yüan, always easily discouraged, abandoned all hope of recovering the province, proposing in council to make the Yellow river the frontier of his empire, and renounce all ambitions for the conquest of eastern China. This pusillanimous proposition was vigorously combated by Shih-Min. He pointed out that Shansi had been the base from which the T'ang dynasty had drawn its strength in the opening phase of the revolution. From this country they had advanced to capture Ch'ang An. If Liu Wu-Chou was to be left in possession, he too would use the resources of Shansi to organise a further invasion of the T'ang territories.

Li Yüan, as usual, yielded to the arguments of his younger son. Instead of evacuating the country east of the Yellow river, Shih-Min was appointed to command a new army with full authority to carry on the war against Liu Wu-Chou. It was already late in the year when Shih-Min at the head of these fresh troops crossed the Yellow river north of P'u Chou Fu. His first act was to abolish the unwise regulations with which P'ei Chi had alienated the peasantry. The news that Shih-Min was in command was the most potent factor in restoring the confidence of the people and the army. Before long Shih-Min's camp was abundantly supplied with provisions.

The new commander-in-chief was not prepared to take the offensive in the depths of winter. Before undertaking major operations he wished to restore the morale of the army, badly shaken by the disasters of the previous summer. To this end he engaged the enemy raiding parties in frequent skirmishes. On one of these expeditions Shih-Min met with an adventure which nearly proved fatal. He had left the camp, attended by a squadron of light horse, to reconnoitre the enemy position. As the country was cut up by deep defiles, his force gradually dispersed till the prince was accompanied by only one officer. He had ridden to the top of a mound to get a view of the country, when a large band of enemy horsemen, emerging from a defile, surrounded the position.

Shih-Min and his companion would have been surprised beyond any hope of escape had it not been for a stroke of luck, which the popular imagination later attributed to divine intervention. The officer in attendance, who had dismounted and was lying on the grass, was suddenly startled by a snake, which, in pursuit of a field mouse, passed close in front of his face. Leaping up with a shout, he caught sight of the enemy, who were more than one hundred strong. Shih-Min and his companion owed their lives to the prince's skill at archery, for when Shih-Min had picked off the officer leading the enemy, the rest fell back, enabling the prince to escape to his camp.

Operations on a larger scale began with an attack on the rebels in the town of Hsia Hsien. The T'ang force which had been detached for this expedition encountered a vigorous defence from the enemy general, Yü-Ch'ih Ching-Tê, by whom it was severely defeated. Shih-Min did not allow this battle to go unavenged. While another T'ang force engaged Yü-Ch'ih Ching-Tê around Hsia Hsien, the prince himself, by a forced march, outflanked the enemy, and at the city of An I totally defeated Yü-Ch'ih Ching-Tê, who had difficulty in escaping from the field. After this victory most of the generals were in favour of pressing the offensive against Sung Chin-Kang's main force, but Shih-Min did not consider the moment opportune.

Instead, he remained inactive till the spring. His reason for this delay was the difficulty which the enemy encountered in maintaining their supplies. In the depths of winter they were unable to find sufficient forage for the horses or food for the soldiers. Shih-Min decided to wait till a long and hungry winter had weakened their cavalry, when he could force them to engage battle in circumstances which favoured the T'ang army. His own camp was plentifully supplied by means of the Yellow river and its tributary, the Wei, which enabled him to draw provisions for men and beasts from Shensi. Liu Wu-Chou, fearing that this delay would prejudice his plans, attempted to create a diversion elsewhere in order to draw the T'ang army out to battle. He sent raiding parties over the mountains into south-east Shansi, which had hitherto been undisturbed. At first he met with some success, capturing two small cities. Shih-Min, however, refused to be drawn, and the raiders were driven out of the south-east by the local T'ang garrisons.

Towards the end of spring, in the fourth month, the army of Sung Chin-Kang, having exhausted its supplies, was forced to retreat. This was the opportunity for which the prince had waited so patiently. He started in pursuit, and after a forced march came up with the enemy rearguard at Ling Shih, a town at the southern mouth of the Squirrel pass (Ch'iao Shu Ku).

His object was to engage and defeat the enemy before they could pass this defile. As has already been mentioned the

Squirrel pass, by which the Fên river descends from the plateau of T'ai Yüan Fu, is a position of great natural strength, where for nearly twenty miles the river and road wind together through a narrow ravine bordered by steep cliffs of rock and loess. If the position is held strongly no army coming from the south could force its way up on to the plateau.

The swift pursuit of the T'ang army took the enemy by surprise; the rearguard was scattered and the T'ang cavalry launched in pursuit. Shih-Min, pressing to the utmost the attack upon the retreating enemy, broke through the defence and prevented any rally. The army of Sung Chin-Kang was given no chance to reform. Pausing neither for food nor rest, the T'ang army drove the enemy headlong through the defile, fighting ten separate engagements, after covering nearly seventy miles in twenty-four hours. After a prodigious slaughter of the flying mob, the prince drove Sung Chin-Kang out of the northern mouth of Squirrel pass into the city of Chieh Hsiu. Then the T'ang army, exhausted by these efforts, was allowed to encamp. The generals, who feared that the prince would be exposed to danger in this furious chase, had begged him to take rest, but Shih-Min, who had waited months for this moment, replied, "Opportunity comes seldom and is easily missed. Superiority, acquired with difficulty, can be lost in a moment". During this pursuit Shih-Min took no food for two days and did not put off his armour for three. When at last the army encamped, only one sheep could be found for the prince and his staff. This they cut up with their swords and shared between them.

Chieh Hsiu, the city in which Sung Chin-Kang, with the remnant of 20,000 men that remained to him, had taken refuge, is a square, solidly walled city, standing on the edge of the plateau about two miles from the Fên river. This place was the next objective of the T'ang army. If Sung Chin-Kang retreated farther he would be defenceless in the wide T'ai Yüan plateau, but if he remained in the city, he could be

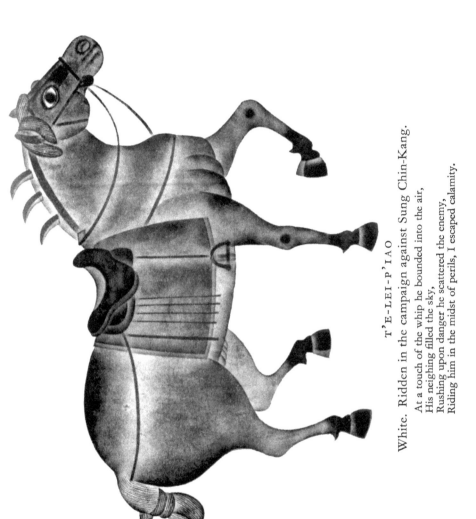

PLATE I

T'E-LEI-P'IAO

White. Ridden in the campaign against Sung Chin-Kang.

At a touch of the whip he bounded into the air,
His neighing filled the sky,
Rushing upon danger he scattered the enemy,
Riding him in the midst of perils, I escaped calamity.

blockaded by a part of the T'ang army, which was now greatly superior in numbers. Faced with these alternatives, Liu Wu-Chou's general decided to risk a last battle in the hope of recovering control of the Squirrel pass. Leaving the general Yü-Ch'ih Ching-Tê in charge of the city, Sung Chin-Kang led out his army and formed a line of battle with his rear protected by the city wall.

As this formation prevented Shih-Min from employing his customary outflanking manoeuvre, he ordered Li Shih-Chi, who had joined the army earlier in the year, to engage the enemy with the infantry, while Shih-Min held off with the cavalry until he judged that the enemy were tiring. Then giving the order to charge, the prince swept through the weary ranks of Sung Chin-Kang's smaller force, which broke into flight. The enemy commander with a few attendants managed to escape from the field, but the army, relentlessly pursued, was dispersed and destroyed. Yü-Ch'ih Ching-Tê, who had witnessed the rout from the walls of Chieh Hsiu, decided to surrender, yielding the fortress to Li Tao-Tsung Prince Jên Ch'êng, a cousin of Shih-Min, a young commander who was to achieve great fame in later years.

The rout of Squirrel pass and the battle of Chieh Hsiu were decisive. The army of Liu Wu-Chou had ceased to exist. The pretender himself fled from T'ai Yüan Fu to the Turks; but as he had ceased to be of use to Chur Khan, he was put to death not long afterwards, and his faction died with him. Sung Chin-Kang met with no better fate. More resolute than his chief, he had attempted to raise a fresh army, but meeting with no success he endeavoured to escape to the north-east, only to be killed on the road. T'ai Yüan Fu and every other city which had been held by Liu Wu-Chou surrendered without opposition on the approach of the T'ang army.

In this campaign Shih-Min had given outstanding proof of his military genius, and it was now that he collected round him a brilliant staff of subordinates who in later years carried the T'ang standards to victory across the vast deserts of

Central Asia. Besides Li Shih-Chi, already well known, the Shansi campaign proved the merit of Li Tao-Tsung Prince Jên Ch'êng, Yü-Wên Shih-Chi, a brother of the regicide—but one who had taken no part in the massacre at Yang Chou—and Yü-Ch'ih Ching-Tê, who though he had fought for the enemy was now granted a command in the T'ang army and became the captain of Shih-Min's personal guard.

After the fall of T'ai Yüan Fu, Shih-Min left the task of pacifying the frontier to his generals, marching south, where his genius and determination were urgently needed to repair the disasters which had befallen the T'ang arms in eastern Honan (see chap. IV). On his way he passed Hsia Hsien, the city which had rebelled against P'ei Chi's harsh legislation and welcomed the invaders. The prince summoned the rebel city to surrender, and when the inhabitants rashly refused, he ordered the army to take the place by storm, and exterminate the citizens for the double crime of revolting and now refusing to return to their lawful allegiance. These orders were carried out. The massacre of the people of Hsia Hsien is one of the few bad acts recorded against Shih-Min. Although the laws and customs of the time were not opposed to such severity against contumacious rebels, the historians consider that in this action Shih-Min did not live up to his character. He himself regretted his cruelty, and in after life, when faced with a similar situation in Korea, ransomed the inhabitants himself, although by the laws of war they were the prey of his soldiers.

The victorious conclusion of the Shansi campaign, which not only restored the lost T'ang territories, but eliminated another rival emperor, produced a profound impression even in distant parts of China. Already the rebels who had overthrown the Sui officials in eastern Shantung had acknowledged Li Yüan as emperor. Their example was now followed by Tu Fu-Wei, the young leader who dominated the Huai valley in the east, and by Kao K'ai-Tao, who, calling himself prince of Yen, ruled the north-eastern part of Hopei province from

Yung P'ing Fu. Tu Fu-Wei, invested with the title of prince of Wu, was given plenary authority to conquer and administer the lands south of the Huai. Before the end of the year he had justified this trust by capturing Nanking from Li Tzǔ-T'ung, an "emperor" who ruled the south-east coast. Szechuan had already been conquered by the T'ang prince Chao (Li Hsiao-Kung), son of Shih-Min's uncle, Li Shên-T'ung Prince Huai An.

There still remained Hsiao Hsien, the ruler of the middle Yangtze and southern provinces, and two, more formidable, foes in the north—Tou Chien-Tê, emperor of Hsia in the eastern plain, and Wang Shih-Ch'ung, the new emperor of Chêng at Lo Yang. These two, menaced by the rising power of the T'ang dynasty, were driven to form an alliance which should oppose its united strength in a final struggle for mastery.

CHAPTER IV

THE BATTLE OF SSŬ SHUI
A.D. 620-1

The early part of the year A.D. 619 had been unfortunate for the T'ang arms not only in Shansi but also in Honan. Wang Shih-Ch'ung had profited by the defeat of Li Mi to extend his authority eastwards. By the end of the year he had occupied K'ai Fêng Fu with other cities to the east of that place, and was threatening the districts along the lower course of the Yellow river, which had recently submitted to the T'ang emperor. Even more serious was the progress made by Tou Chien-Tê, emperor of Hsia. After he had destroyed the army of the regicide Yü-Wên Hua-Chi, Tou Chien-Tê turned his attention to the cities north of the Yellow river which Prince Huai An had brought under the authority of Ch'ang An.

Moving down the great northern road the army of Hsia captured Kuang P'ing Fu, where the emperor of Hsia fixed his capital, then Chang Tê Fu, farther south, and by autumn was advancing on Wei Hui. If this city fell into enemy hands all communication between the T'ang territories in the eastern plain and Ch'ang An would be interrupted. Prince Huai An and Li Shih-Chi, the T'ang generals, were then at Li Yang, forty miles north-east of the threatened city. The T'ang forces were greatly inferior in numbers to the army of Hsia, consequently there could be no question of meeting the enemy in open battle. Instead Li Shih-Chi made harrying attacks on the flank of the enemy columns until Tou Chien-Tê sent reinforcements to drive him off.

The T'ang strategy failed in its purpose, the deliverance of Wei Hui, for Tou Chien-Tê decided to attack Li Yang first, and crush the T'ang eastern army before advancing south. This change of plan took the T'ang generals by surprise. The army of Hsia carried the city by storm, taking prisoners all the prominent T'ang leaders in the east. Apart from Li Shên-T'ung Prince Huai An, the prisoners included a sister of the T'ang emperor; Wei Chêng, and the father of Li Shih-Chi. Li Shih-Chi himself, fearing that his father would be injured, was induced by motives of filial piety, which no Chinese could ignore, to surrender to the emperor of Hsia. Tou Chien-Tê acted with unusual humanity towards these captives. Prince Huai An and the princess were kept in honourable captivity. Li Shih-Chi, whose ability was much esteemed, was given the post of garrison commander at Li Yang, though his father was retained at the Hsia court as a hostage for his loyalty. Wei Hui and all the smaller cities of the region surrendered to the emperor of Hsia on hearing the news of this disaster.

Li Shih-Chi only served his new master by compulsion and with regret. He eagerly sought some opportunity to return to his old allegiance without involving his father in danger. Open revolt was for this reason out of the question. Instead, Li Shih-Chi devised an elaborate plot. Pretending to espouse the cause of his new sovereign, he proposed an invasion of Honan, declaring to Tou Chien-Tê that the T'ang areas in the east of that province and in southern Shantung could be conquered without difficulty. He planned to attack the camp of the Hsia emperor when the army reached Li Yang, slay Tou Chien-Tê, and release his own father. Li Shih-Chi believed that in the confusion which would follow such a bold stroke it would be easy for him to make himself master of all the Hsia territory. With this magnificent service to his credit he would have no difficulty in obtaining pardon for his enforced desertion of the T'ang cause.

Although Tou Chien-Tê fell into the trap and marched down to Li Yang to invade the eastern T'ang districts, the plot miscarried through the precipitate action of some of Li Shih-Chi's supporters. The surprise having failed, there was nothing to do but escape. Li Shih-Chi managed to get away on a fast horse, making his way across country till he reached

T'ang territory. Li Yüan pardoned his temporary desertion, sending him to join Shih-Min, who was then engaged in the Shansi campaign described in the preceding chapter. Tou Chien-Tê, who had a chivalrous character, refused to put the hostage to death. "Li Shih-Chi", he said, "is a loyal servant of the T'ang dynasty. Is that a crime for which his father should be executed?"

While the emperor of Hsia was extending his territory and winning the allegiance of the people by such acts of moderation, Wang Shih-Ch'ung, the new emperor of Chêng, seemed determined to alienate all his supporters by his arbitrary actions. In this year he lost two men of mark, Ch'in Shu-Pao and Lo Shih-Hsin. They had first become prominent as Sui officers against the bandits of Shantung, when Lo Shih-Hsin, then aged thirteen, had gained great fame by his intrepid behaviour. Both had subsequently submitted to Li Mi and, after his defeat, to Wang Shih-Ch'ung. The latter treated them with such scant courtesy that both left his service to join the T'ang. Lo Shih-Hsin was appointed to the command of a border district in western Honan. There he made frequent harassing raids upon the territory of his former sovereign, on one occasion even penetrating by night into the outer defences of Lo Yang itself.

These tactics were effective in one respect. They weakened the morale of the Chêng army, which began to desert whenever opportunity occurred. Wang Shih-Ch'ung, to prevent these defections, took hostages from his generals and officials, who were made responsible for their subordinates. The suspects and hostages were compelled to dwell in the inner or Palace City, where there were soon as many as thirty thousand people confined. Drastic laws were enacted against all who attempted to desert. The offender was not only himself punished with death, but his family also was exterminated. These severities only increased the number of fugitives, for when one person fled, his family and friends hastened to follow him lest they be put to death. Discontent spread far and wide through the dominions of Wang Shih-Ch'ung.

This was the state of Honan when Li Shih-Min, famous from his recent victories in Shansi, came south to take command of the T'ang army which was preparing to invade the empire of Chêng with Lo Yang as objective. The overthrow of Liu Wu-Chou and the consolidation of the T'ang empire in the west had left Shih-Min free to pursue his "horizontal" strategical design. Moving eastward along the Yellow river, he wished to secure a belt of country stretching from the border of Shensi to the sea on the south Shantung coast. China would then be cut in half, and the pretenders in the north could not communicate with possible allies in the south. Tou Chien-Tê would be ringed round with T'ang territories, and his ultimate defeat made certain. Already the allegiance of Tu Fu-Wei had forged one important link in this encircling chain. The defeat of Wang Shih-Ch'ung would make the ring complete.

Marching eastward from Shan Chou, an important point on the great western road from Lo Yang to Ch'ang An, Shih-Min encountered no real resistance till his army was approaching Lo Yang. Wang Shih-Ch'ung, who was already looking for assistance elsewhere, did not wish to risk a battle. Frequent skirmishes took place, in one of which Shih-Min becoming separated from his supporters had a narrow escape from capture, returning alone to the camp so covered with dust that the sentries could not recognise him, and would not admit him till he spoke, and was known by his voice.

Meanwhile the T'ang army had encamped close to Lo Yang, and was daily harrying the supply trains with which Wang Shih-Ch'ung sought to provision the city for the inevitable siege. The Chêng emperor, though he still avoided battle, led out a strong force, and parleyed with the T'ang prince across the water of the Lo river. Wang Shih-Ch'ung proposed a partition of the empire, by which the T'ang dynasty should renounce all ambitions in the east. Shih-Min sent his general, Yü-Wên Shih-Chi, to reply that no such conditions could be discussed, but if Wang Shih-Ch'ung surrendered at once, the T'ang prince would guarantee his life. The emperor of Chêng indignantly rejected this offer.

The T'ang court was more anxious to conciliate Tou Chien-Tê, lest the powerful ruler of Hsia should come to the rescue of Chêng. There was the greater danger of this as Chêng and Hsia had never engaged in serious hostilities with each other, and were equally menaced by the rising T'ang power. These negotiations were not conclusive. The emperor of Hsia could easily perceive the latent menace to his territory involved in any T'ang conquest of Honan, but he was not yet ready for an open breach, so as some evidence of goodwill he released the T'ang princess captured at Li Yang.

If Tou Chien-Tê had hoped that the T'ang army would fail in the war with Chêng, and so save him the risk of joining in the campaign, he was doomed to disappointment. By the end of the year (A.D. 620) so many of Wang Shih-Ch'ung's cities in eastern and southern Honan had surrendered, that the Chêng emperor was virtually confined to Lo Yang itself. Alarmed at this general defection, Wang adopted more aggressive tactics. One day Shih-Min, accompanied by Yü-Ch'ih Ching-Tê and 500 horsemen, was riding round the advanced T'ang positions on an inspection. To get a wider view of the country he rode up on to the vast tomb mound of the Wei emperor, Hsüan Wu, which still stands on the slopes of Pei Mang Shan, a hill overlooking the city.

Wang Shih-Ch'ung, seeing the prince so lightly attended in this advanced position, made a sudden sortie at the head of 10,000 men. Although the swift advance of the Chêng troops surrounded the tomb mound, Shih-Min and Yü-Ch'ih Ching-Tê cut their way through the enemy to safety. Ch'ü-T'u T'ung arrived with large reinforcements at this moment, and the action became general. Shih-Min vigorously counter-attacked and drove the Chêng force back to the walls

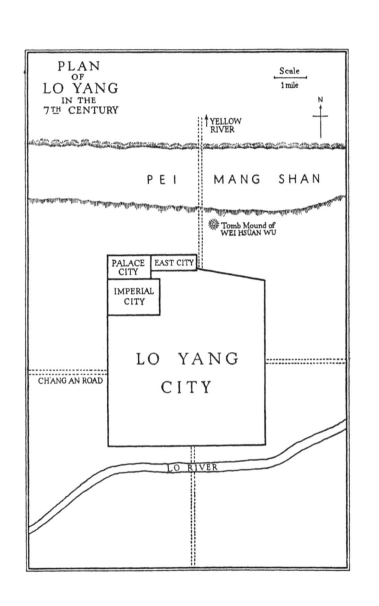

PLAN
OF
LO YANG
IN THE
7TH CENTURY

Scale
1 mile

N

YELLOW
RIVER

P E I   M A N G   S H A N

Tomb Mound of
WEI HSÜAN WU

PALACE
CITY

EAST CITY

IMPERIAL
CITY

LO YANG
CITY

CH'ANG AN ROAD

LO RIVER

with a loss of 1000 dead and 6000 prisoners. This unfortunate end to the sortie made Wang Shih-Ch'ung more chary of rash attacks.

In the next month the loss of the city and pass of Ssŭ Shui caused far graver injury to the cause of Chêng. This city, fifty miles east of Lo Yang, commands the road to the east, which at this point leaves the tumbled loess hills of western Honan to enter the vast expanse of the eastern plain. When this city, abandoned through the folly of Wang Shih-Ch'ung's eldest son, fell into T'ang hands, the communications between Chêng and Hsia were interrupted. Already Wang Shih-Ch'ung had sent an embassy to Tou Chien-Tê suggesting an alliance and common action against the T'ang power, and these pleas were now reinforced by the logic of events. Hsia had never ceased to make attacks on the T'ang city of Yu Chou[1] which was held by the general Lo I, who had submitted to the T'ang dynasty.

When the emperor of Hsia called upon his ministers for their advice, he found the court in favour of war. "If", they said, "we permit the T'ang dynasty to crush Chêng, we will be unable to withstand its power, and our future ruin is certain. Whereas, if we succour the Chêng empire, we may defeat the T'ang. Then we will be in a position to absorb the weak Chêng empire and can at leisure complete the conquest of all China."

Tou Chien-Tê decided to follow this advice. While mobilising his full strength, he sent an embassy to Shih-Min requiring him to raise the blockade of Lo Yang and quit the territories of Chêng. To this embassy Shih-Min made no reply.

The news of Tou Chien-Tê's intervention having reached Lo Yang, Wang Shih-Ch'ung, who had remained inactive since the battle at the tomb of Wei Hsüan Wu, decided that

---

[1] Yu Chou was on the site of modern Peking. As the latter name is so definitely associated with the capital built by the Ming, it has seemed better to use the ancient name in this case.

PLATE II

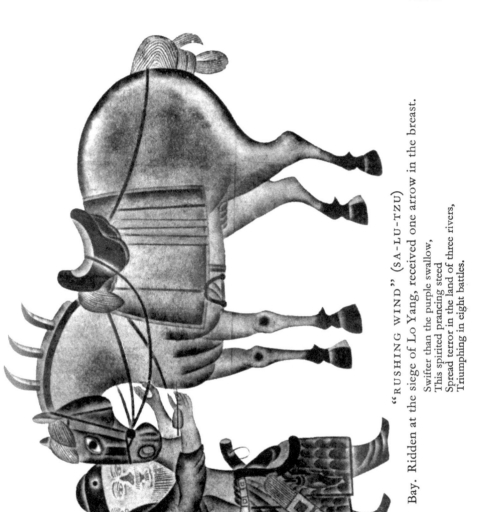

"RUSHING WIND" (SA-LU-TZU)

Bay. Ridden at the siege of Lo Yang, received one arrow in the breast.

Swifter than the purple swallow,
This spirited prancing steed
Spread terror in the land of three rivers,
Triumphing in eight battles.

he might now risk a more offensive attitude. His first sortie made some headway against Ch'ü-T'u T'ung, but when Shih-Min came up with his bodyguard of 1000 heavily armed horsemen, the Chêng troops gave way and were driven into the city with a loss of 6000 killed. This victory, and the capture of a large convoy of provisions which Wang was endeavouring to bring into the city, made Shih-Min decide to convert the blockade of Lo Yang into a close siege. Permission for this move having been obtained from Ch'ang An, in the second month of A.D. 621 Shih-Min gave orders for a general advance to siege positions.

Wang Shih-Ch'ung, who had had bitter experience of siege conditions in Lo Yang when Li Mi was investing the city, made a last effort to frustrate the T'ang plan. He marched out with his entire field force, which still numbered about 20,000 men. The T'ang army was drawn up to receive them on Pei Mang Shan, the long bare ridge which overlooks the city on the northern side. This was the site of Li Mi's disastrous defeat by Wang Shih-Ch'ung in A.D. 618. The memory of that victory inspired the Chêng army to make a desperate effort.

Shih-Min established his headquarters on the tomb mound of Wei Hsüan Wu, the site of the battle two months before. The battle was very fiercely contested; Ch'ü-T'u T'ung, who led the first T'ang attack, was repulsed. Shih-Min re-established the line by repeatedly charging the Chêng army at the head of the heavy cavalry. In the mêlée his horse was killed under him, and the prince was forced to fight on foot till remounted by one of his officers. Wang Shih-Ch'ung stubbornly maintained the battle till noon, when despairing of victory he fell back within the walls of Lo Yang. Nevertheless the Chêng loss did not exceed 7000 killed, and these casualties were not much greater than those of the T'ang army.

Well contested though the battle was, the army of Chêng henceforward made no attempt to break out. The siege was pressed by every device then known to the science of war.

Catapults, hurling a heavy stone two hundred paces, bombarded the walls. Eight-fold bows, a kind of multiple crossbow, which could shoot an arrow 500 yards, were directed against the defenders when they showed themselves above the parapets. The city was assaulted on all four sides both by day and by night. But the immense walls resisted the bombardment, and the defenders were not discouraged. The successful defence of Lo Yang against Yang Hsüan-Kan and Li Mi had proved that the Sui capital was not easily forced.

The T'ang generals, dismayed by this strenuous resistance, and by the severity of the midwinter cold, urged Shih-Min to raise the siege. When the prince peremptorily refused, furthermore declaring that anyone who advocated such a course would be executed for mutiny, the generals secretly sent word to the court, and induced the emperor to order a retreat. But Shih-Min was not so easily dissuaded. He sent his own messenger to Ch'ang An, who prevailed upon the vacillating Li Yüan to issue counter-orders permitting the siege to be continued.

While these intrigues were taking place outside the city the defenders were suffering acutely from famine. Of the 30,000 suspects whom Wang Shih-Ch'ung had imprisoned in the Palace City, not more than 3000 survived. Even the highest officials were to be seen with sunken cheeks and swollen bodies wandering about the streets in search of scraps of food, while the corpses of those less fortunate and influential encumbered the public roads. Nevertheless, buoyed up by his one remaining hope, the assistance of Tou-Chien-Tê, Wang Shih-Ch'ung rejected all suggestions of capitulation and doggedly held on.

He had reason. The emperor of Hsia was at last on the march. In spite of a flank attack from Shansi, by which the T'ang court endeavoured to distract him from his purpose, Tou Chien-Tê, leaving strong garrisons in his home cities, passed the Yellow river with a huge army, estimated to exceed 300,000 men. Capturing the smaller cities which lay in his path, the emperor of Hsia moved westward along the road to Lo Yang, his supply trains coming up the Yellow river by boat.

Shih-Min was now faced with the most critical military decision of his life. The army of Hsia was more numerous than his own, well armed, and hitherto successful. It had defeated T'ang generals such as Prince Huai An and Li Shih-Chi. Nor was this armament his only foe. The army of Wang Shih-Ch'ung, though cooped up in Lo Yang, was not impotent. The investment of Lo Yang had to be maintained by large forces. The newly captured cities in Honan were not to be trusted. These places had surrendered to the T'ang dynasty when Shih-Min's star seemed to be in the ascendant, but if he retreated, or was beaten, they would instantly embrace the cause of the victors.

To await the approach of Tou Chien-Tê at Lo Yang meant certain destruction. Caught between two fires the T'ang army could not hope to conquer. Nor could Shih-Min obtain reinforcements which would equalise the struggle. The Turks, inspired by all the enemies of T'ang, were more hostile than ever, raiding the frontier, watching for their opportunity. Two courses remained open for the T'ang commander-in-chief. The first, which was vehemently urged by generals of the older, experienced, generation such as Ch'ü-T'u T'ung, was to raise the siege, abandon Honan, and retire to defend the passes leading into Shensi.

The adoption of this plan meant the final abandonment of all hope of conquering eastern China and reuniting the empire. Once Tou Chien-Tê had occupied Honan he would absorb the exhausted Chêng empire, consolidating his rule over all the central and eastern plain, then the most populous and fertile part of China. Such T'ang supporters in the south-east as Tu Fu-Wei, isolated by the advance of Hsia, would be forced to submit to the new power or face certain defeat. Retreat would be fatal to the dream of unity, perhaps in the end fatal to the T'ang dynasty itself.

And yet, resistance, the only alternative plan, contained even greater dangers. To keep Lo Yang under siege and still defeat the vast host of Hsia with a smaller army seemed impossible, and the penalty of failure was more terrible. If the T'ang army was routed in Honan, there would be no obstacle to prevent Tou Chien-Tê from following up his victory by an invasion of Shensi, the capture of Ch'ang An, and the extinction of the T'ang dynasty. Nevertheless, it was this, the more hazardous policy, but which held promise of the greater prize, that the young general determined to follow, in the face of the repeated warnings of his older advisers.

Fifty miles east of Lo Yang, the confused loess hills which stretch eastward along the south bank of the Yellow river from the Shensi border end abruptly at the stream of Ssŭ Shui. The stream flows in a flat valley about a mile broad, bordered to the west by the loess hills which end in a steep slope. To the east the stream has in past ages scoured out a low, vertical cliff, on the top of which the great plain begins; flat, featureless, dotted at intervals with villages in groves of trees. The stream itself, receding from this cliff in the course of time, now flows in the centre of the sunken valley, with a stretch of flat land on either bank. The road from the east to Lo Yang and Shensi descends into the ravine, crossing the stream at the little city of Ssŭ Shui, before entering the hills by a narrow defile among precipices.

This was the position which Shih-Min chose as the best place to await the advance of Tou Chien-Tê. The T'ang army had a double task. Not only must Tou Chien-Tê be blocked at Ssŭ Shui, but Wang Shih-Ch'ung, starving and desperate, had to be held in Lo Yang. The advance of the one, or the escape of the other, would be equally fatal to Shih-Min's plans. He had therefore to leave the strength of the army, under his younger brother Yüan-Chi and Ch'ü-T'u T'ung, to blockade the wide compass of Lo Yang's walls, while he himself, with only 3500 men, all picked troops, rode east to Ssŭ Shui. If Wang Shih-Ch'ung noticed some diminution in the number of his enemies, he judged it too small to justify a sortie by his starving troops.

There was already a T'ang garrison at Ssŭ Shui, but its numbers are not stated by the historians. Even with this reinforcement it is not likely that the T'ang army can have exceeded 10,000 men, but they were picked troops under a commander of genius. The prince's first operation at Ssŭ Shui was intended to raise the morale of his troops and show them that he was not overawed by the vast numbers of the Hsia host. At the head of 500 horsemen he crossed the stream, climbed the cliffs beyond, and rode out into the plain a distance of seven miles towards Tou Chien-Tê's camp. Leaving part of his forces posted in ambush under Li Shih-Chi and Ch'in Shu-Pao, the prince rode on with only four or five horsemen, among whom was his faithful Yü-Ch'ih Ching-Tê, until he was within a mile of the Hsia camp. As Shih-Min was remarking to Yü-Ch'ih Ching-Tê, "You with the spear and I with my bow are a match for a million of them", they encountered a party of enemy scouts who, not expecting any T'ang troops so close to their lines, at first took the prince and his escort for foragers from their own camp. Shih-Min speedily disillusioned them by shouting out, "I am the Prince Ch'in",[1] at the same time he loosed an arrow which pierced the officer commanding the enemy party. As he had intended, this daring action roused the enemy camp, from which five or six thousand horsemen came dashing out.

Shih-Min's followers changed colour at this alarming spectacle, but the prince remarked, "You go off first; Ching-Tê and I will act as rearguard". When the foremost pursuers were within bowshot Shih-Min picked off their leader, and while the others hesitated to come within range of his terrible arrows, he and Yü-Ch'ih Ching-Tê retreated farther. Three times the enemy horsemen closed in on the prince, but on every occasion he took such toll with his bow that the

[1] Shih-Min had been made Prince Ch'in at the accession of the T'ang dynasty and was generally known by this title.

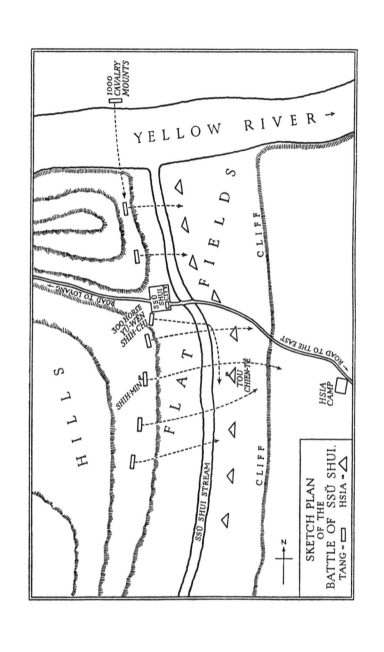

1000 CAVALRY MOUNTS

YELLOW RIVER →

FIELDS

CLIFF

ROAD TO LOYANG

SSŬ SHUI CITY

300 HORSE
YÜ-WEN
SHIH-CHI

SHIH-MIN

ROAD TO THE EAST

TOU CHIEN-TÊ

HSIA CAMP

HILLS

FLAT

SSŬ SHUI STREAM

CLIFF

N

SKETCH PLAN
OF THE
BATTLE OF SSŬ SHUI.
TANG = ☐ HSIA = △

pursuers dared not press on. In this way Shih-Min decoyed them past the ravine where Li Shih-Chi and the 500 T'ang horse were concealed. These troops, suddenly issuing from their ambush, fell upon the startled Hsia cavalry, slaying more than 300 men and capturing several high officers.

After returning to Ssŭ Shui, Shih-Min sent a letter, couched in the style of sovereign to subject, to Tou Chien-Tê. The emperor of Hsia was advised to keep to his own country and leave Chêng to its fate, lest he should meet with misfortunes which he would have reason to repent too late. Tou Chien-Tê replied by making a fruitless assault on Ssŭ Shui city. Finding the position too strong to be forced, he returned to encamp on the open plain. The days lengthened into weeks, and still the huge army of Hsia remained inactive before this Chinese Thermopylae. Shih-Min, except to send parties of cavalry to harass the enemy convoys, rested passively on the defensive.

He had nothing to lose by delay. Lo Yang was slowly starving, the army of Hsia incapable of rendering relief to the doomed city. In all his campaigns Shih-Min paid the greatest attention to the time factor. Few generals have been so skilful in making time and weather fight on their side. It was not only Lo Yang which suffered from this delay. The army of Tou Chien-Tê met with increasing difficulty in maintaining its supplies. The T'ang convoys came down the river laden, with the advantage of the strong summer current. But the Hsia boats had to toil upstream fully loaded, and only benefited by the current when returning empty. The great size of the Hsia army was a further difficulty, making demands upon Tou Chien-Tê's treasury which were increasingly difficult to meet.

The generals of the Hsia council, impressed by this disadvantage, and seeing the futility of trying to force a position like Ssŭ Shui, suggested an alternative plan to their chief. "Across the river", they said, "is the T'ang province of Shansi, lightly garrisoned, almost undefended, and open to attack. Why not withdraw from our present position, leaving a sufficient force to prevent pursuit, and invade this province? The T'ang army will then be obliged to go to the defence of their own territory, the siege of Lo Yang will be raised, and we can re-occupy Honan at our leisure."

Tou Chien-Tê was inclined to follow this advice, when the ambassador of Chêng, who realised that his master could not hold out more than a few weeks at most, came in tears to press the urgency of Lo Yang's plight.

Tou Chien-Tê had a chivalrous character. He was unwilling to adopt a plan which would expose him to the reproach of abandoning his ally to pursue conquests for his own profit. He therefore listened to Wang Shih-Ch'ung's ambassador and rejected the advice of his own council. That night his consort, the Lady Tsao, a woman of unusual penetration, urged him to follow the generals' plan. "Shansi is empty", she declared, "we will meet no resistance. With the Turks already harrying their northern frontier, the T'ang army will have no choice but to raise the siege of Lo Yang and retire to defend Shensi. Whereas if we go on camping here we will waste money and discourage the soldiers to no purpose."

Tou Chien-Tê must have known that his wife was right. But he had made up his mind and would not be shaken. He merely replied, "This is not a matter women can understand. I came to save Lo Yang, which can scarcely hold out from dawn to dusk. If I abandon this purpose and go elsewhere, is it not a breach of faith?" Instead of invading Shansi the Hsia emperor prepared to make a grand assault on the T'ang position.

Early in the fifth month, the beginning of summer, Shih-Min, who guessed that the enemy would soon be forced to take the offensive, made his own preparations. He crossed the river with part of his troops and 1000 horses, which, with their grooms, were left on the north bank, in order to deceive Tou Chien-Tê into the belief that Shih-Min had divided his army to guard against an invasion of Shansi. The prince led back all the troops from the north bank under cover of darkness. The device worked. Tou Chien-Tê, believing that Shih-Min's force was weakened by this partition, decided that the opportunity to force Ssǔ Shui had at last arrived. He broke camp and marched down into the sunken valley of the Ssǔ Shui stream.

The emperor of Hsia did not assault the T'ang position. He hoped to induce Shih-Min to fight in the open. Therefore the Hsia army was drawn up in a line extending from the banks of the Yellow river along the valley of the Ssǔ Shui, for nearly seven miles. The army did not cross the stream, leaving that as a natural moat in advance of their position. Shih-Min, whose forces were drawn up on the heights west of the valley, rode to a point which commanded a wide view. After studying the enemy dispositions, he said to his officers, "The enemy come from the eastern plains, and have never fought in hill country. Now that they have come down into the ravine they are in a bad position. Their purpose in approaching is to defy us, and by coming so close it is clear that they despise our power. We will stand firm, and let their courage cool. Presently, drawn up in battle array as they are, their troops will become thirsty. Then they will begin to fall out in order to find water and their formation will be relaxed. At that moment, if we attack, they will be caught in the ravine and routed. I promise you that before evening the victory will be ours".

Tou Chien-Tê, who was anxious to make the T'ang army engage, confident that with his superior numbers he would be easily victorious, sent 300 horse across the stream to insult the T'ang lines, with a herald who challenged Shih-Min to send an equal force against this squadron. The prince, who only wanted a pretext to delay the general action, while keeping the Hsia army under arms in the hot June sun, sent 200 lancers to engage the enemy squadron. The action was indecisive, the two forces wheeling and charging about the flat meadows on the banks of the Ssŭ Shui river, until both retired exhausted to their respective armies.

A Hsia officer, who had a very beautiful horse which had come from Yang Ti's stables, next rode up and down below the T'ang positions displaying the merits of his steed, challenging the T'ang officers to attack him. Shih-Min observing this horse remarked upon its beauty, whereupon Yü-Ch'ih Ching-Tê asked permission to go and capture it. The prince would not agree, saying, "What, for one horse risk the life of a good officer!" But Yü-Ch'ih, paying no attention, dashed down the slope with two companions. Before the Hsia army could realise what was happening, the three T'ang officers had captured horse and rider and were safely back in their own lines.

Shih-Min had already sent orders to bring over the 1000 horses from the north bank of the Yellow river. He was waiting for these to arrive before joining battle. As the morning wore on to noon, the Hsia army, which had been drawn up under arms since dawn, became wearied. Some sat down on the grass, while others went to the stream for water, or wandered back to bring up food. This was the opportunity for which Shih-Min was waiting. The horses from the north bank had now arrived, and all the cavalry could be mounted. The prince called Yü-Wên Shih-Chi and ordered him to take 300 horse and ride along the Hsia front, from their right flank, moving up the valley of the Ssŭ Shui stream. "If the enemy stand firm, leave them alone and ride back to our lines", he commanded. "But if they start falling back as you approach, and get confused, then charge them."

When Yü-Wên Shih-Chi's squadron drew near to the Hsia line, the enemy soldiers, dispersed and out of formation, showed a confused movement, some falling back, and others trying to form up. Shih-Min, watching, exclaimed, "Now we can attack". The prince put himself at the head of the cavalry, and followed by the whole T'ang army, swept down

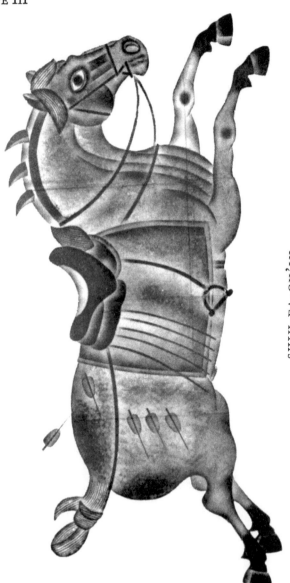

PLATE III

SHIH-FA-CH'IH

Chestnut. Ridden in the battle against Tou Chien-Tê. (Ssŭ Shui.)
Wounded by four arrows from the front and one from behind.

By the Ch'an and Chien there was no peace,
With halberts and battle axes I extended my power,
In a red sweat this horse charged forward
Under the green banner we returned singing the song of victory.

the steep slopes, across the flat land and the shallow stream, to charge the disordered Hsia army.

The emperor of Hsia was holding council in his tent when the news of the T'ang attack was brought. He ordered his cavalry to make a counter-attack to give the infantry time to form up. Unfortunately the generals were all at the council and could not get back to their posts in time. The impetus of the T'ang onslaught had thrown the Hsia army into confusion, in which the orders of the generals never reached the soldiers. Tou Chien-Tê attempted to control the situation, but finding himself in danger of capture fell back to the low cliff which formed the eastern boundary of the Ssŭ Shui valley. With their backs to this natural wall the Hsia troops rallied for the moment. The battled was undecided when Shih-Min's young cousin, Li Tao-Hsüan Prince Huai Yang, a youth of eighteen, charged furiously through the Hsia line till he emerged behind the enemy, when, turning round, he cut his way back to the T'ang host. Repeating this exploit, he once more hacked a corridor through the enemy army till "His armour was thick with arrows like the quills of a porcupine". This time, though his horse had been killed, he was remounted by Shih-Min, who led the cavalry after him into the heart of the mêlée.

While the dust "filled the sky" veiling the confused battle from the enemy commanders, the T'ang prince and his cavalry cut their way through the enemy till they gained the high ground behind the army of Hsia. There they displayed the T'ang standards, and at this sight, which seemed to menace the only way of escape, the Hsia army broke into flight. The rout was disastrous. The T'ang army chased the flying mob for ten miles, slaying as they went. Though the killed did not number more than 3000, Shih-Min took 50,000 prisoners, while the rest of the huge army of Hsia dispersed over the country-side. The fate of Tou Chien-Tê himself completed the disaster to his cause. Carried away in the press of the rout, he was thrown from his horse while being pursued by two T'ang officers. As they were about to spear him, Tou Chien-Tê cried out, "Do not slay me. I am the emperor of Hsia, and can richly reward you". The T'ang officers thereupon dismounted and secured this valuable captive, whom they led back to Shih-Min.

The capture of Tou Chien-Tê prevented any rally of his army. Only a few hundreds of horsemen escaped to Kuang P'ing Fu, the Hsia capital. The vast army of Hsia had ceased to exist. After this prodigious victory, which eliminated all danger from the east, Shih-Min led back his army and captives to Lo Yang. Some of the Hsia officers were sent into the city to make known the extent of the disaster, and Tou Chien-Tê himself was brought to the foot of the walls to inform his ally that all was lost. Wang Shih-Ch'ung, mounting the ramparts, heard from the lips of the deliverer in whom his hopes had reposed the melancholy tale of defeat. Unable to restrain their emotion, the two emperors, who met for the first time in these tragic circumstances, broke down and wept.

After a brief discussion, the council of the Chêng emperor urged Wang Shih-Ch'ung to make an unconditional surrender. There was no possibility of further resistance in starving Lo Yang. There remained no hope of escape to another refuge, or of relief from any other ally. At the head of his entire court, with his coffin at his side, Wang Shih-Ch'ung in mourning robes led the dismal procession out of the gates of Lo Yang to make submission to the conqueror. When the fallen emperor of Chêng was brought into his presence, freely perspiring with the emotion of such a moment, Shih-Min said to him, "You always used to say, I hear, that you 'would like to meet that "boy"'. Now you see the 'boy', how are you going to behave?" Wang Shih-Ch'ung bowed his head and made apologies.

Except for certain Chêng officials, who were regarded as traitors to the T'ang dynasty, and were decapitated, none of the inhabitants of Lo Yang suffered any harm. Only some of the magnificent palaces, which Yang Ti had erected at the cost of so much suffering, were, by Shih-Min's orders, burned. The prince remarked that this luxury, purchased as it was by the life's blood of the people, was the real cause of the downfall of the Sui dynasty. As a warning to the age and an example to posterity such buildings should be destroyed. The records of the Sui empire were found to have been burnt by Wang Shih-Ch'ung, though vast spoils and treasures still remained from Yang Ti's extravagant court.

The fall of Lo Yang ended this war. The empire of Chêng had ceased to exist, and that of Hsia was occupied without resistance. The remnants of Tou Chien-Tê's army, after looting the treasury of Kuang P'ing Fu, yielded the town to the T'ang troops and dispersed. The great battle of Ssŭ Shui brought all North China from Tibet to the sea under the authority of Ch'ang An. Only the southern pretenders, Hsiao Hsien and Li Tzŭ-T'ung, remained outside the new empire.

Shih-Min on his return to court made a triumphal entry into Ch'ang An. Clad in a suit of golden armour, the conqueror rode through the city, followed by two captive emperors and their courts, twenty-five of his own generals, and 10,000 heavy armed horsemen. Such were the fruits of the famous battle of Ssŭ Shui which, since it established the T'ang dynasty on an unshakable basis, and made possible the reunion of China, may well be reckoned as one of the decisive battles in the history of the world.[1]

[1] Li Shih-Min's victory was not the first decisive battle to be fought on the banks of the Ssŭ Shui. It was on this same ground that Han Kao Tsu, founder of the Han dynasty, won a battle (in 203 B.C.) which was the turning-point in the war with his rival to the throne. Thus, by a strange coincidence, the two greatest Chinese dynasties were consolidated by victories won upon the same spot.

CHAPTER V

PACIFICATION AND CONSOLIDATION
A.D. 622–4

Although the battle of Ssŭ Shui really established the T'ang dynasty in an unassailable supremacy, there still remained a considerable military task to be accomplished before the whole of China was pacified and consolidated under the authority of Ch'ang An.

The south still flaunted its independence, fortified by the long tradition of partition which seemed to make a northern conquest unlikely. Hsiao Hsien, emperor of Liang, was the most notable pretender in these provinces. Descendant of the earlier emperors of Liang, who had reigned in the south from A.D. 503–55, he was no mere upstart adventurer, claiming the crown by virtue of military strength. Hsiao Hsien posed, and was accepted, in the south as the legitimate heir of an old dynasty, restored after a period of usurpation. His authority had been acknowledged over a very large area, the provinces of Hupei, Hunan, Kiangsi, Kuangtung and Kuangsi, in so far as these two latter were colonised by the Chinese.

Hsiao Hsien did not rule the south-east coast. After the murder of Yang Ti, that area, comprising the south part of modern Kiangsu province, Chekiang and Fukien, had fallen to one Li Tzŭ-T'ung, who at first placed his capital at Nanking.

In the summer of A.D. 621 orders were given for a general offensive against Hsiao Hsien, emperor of Liang. The T'ang dynasty had already acquired the great inland province of Szechuan, which submitted without offering resistance soon after the fall of Ch'ang An. They thus controlled the upper waters of the Yangtze and Han rivers, which gave them the very great advantage of having the current with them in any operations against the territories of Liang, farther down stream.

Hsiao Hsien realised the danger to which his estates were exposed by the T'ang occupation of Szechuan. As early as A.D. 619 he had been defeated in an unsuccessful attempt to force the Yangtze gorges and invade the province. Since then he had been too occupied suppressing minor revolts against his authority in Hunan to undertake major operations against his dangerous neighbours.

This inaction was most prejudicial to the cause of Liang, for it allowed the T'ang generals to make lengthy and undisturbed preparations for the conquest of the lower river country. No warfare along the Yangtze river is possible without the command of the river in the naval sense. To secure this the T'ang generals constructed a large war fleet of junks manned by Szechuanese watermen, who, since the upper river is the most dangerous stretch of the Yangtze, are the most skilful and intrepid navigators of all the riparian people. When all was ready the joint expedition was placed under the supreme command of Li Ching[1] with Li Hsiao-Kung Prince Chao as admiral in command of the fleet. Prince Chao, a cousin of Li Shih-Min, was the son of Li Shên-T'ung Prince Huai An.

The emperor of Liang, though aware of the T'ang preparations, did not believe that any invasion would be possible until the winter was far advanced, as the gorges and rapids would not be safely navigable until the low-water season had come.[2] Prince Chao and Li Ching, who knew that Hsiao Hsien's main strength was far away to the south,

---

[1] Li Ching will be remembered as the man against whom Li Yüan had a spite, and who was pardoned at the intercession of Shih-Min at the fall of Ch'ang An (see chap. II).

[2] At the present time, since the formation of the Hsin T'an rapids in 1896, dangerous only in low water, there is little to choose between the perils of navigation in summer and winter. But for junks the low-water season, before the formation of this very difficult rapid, was considerably safer than in summer, when the gorges are filled with a furious rush of wildly churning water. In winter the gorges are tranquil and afford few perils.

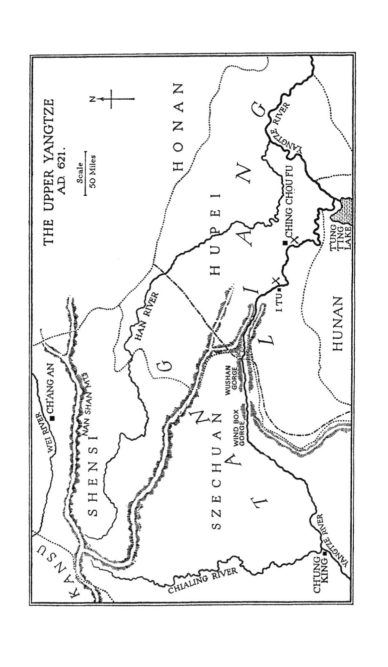

THE UPPER YANGTZE
A.D. 621.

Scale
50 Miles

N

HONAN

HUPEI

LIANG

YANGTZE RIVER

CHING CHOU FU

TUNG TING LAKE

ITU

HUNAN

HAN RIVER

WUSHAN GORGE

WIND BOX GORGE

SZECHUAN

LIANG

SHENSI

NAN SHAN MTS

WEI RIVER

CH'ANG AN

KANSU

CHIALING RIVER

CHUNG KING

YANGTZE RIVER

and would take many weeks to reach the Yangtze, decided to risk the perils of high-water navigation in order to achieve that most valuable of all advantages in war, surprise. Ching Chou, the Liang capital, might thus be taken before the Liang army from the south had reached the Yangtze valley.

It was in the tenth month, late autumn A.D. 621, when, though the falling river was still high, the dangers of the gorges were in some measure reduced, that Prince Chao with the fleet of 2000 war junks took the van, leaving Li Ching to follow with the army when the fleet had secured the passage of the narrow places. The surprise was complete. Prince Chao's fleet crossed the rapids in safety; nor was the passage of the sombre gorges which divide Szechuan from Hupei disputed. Hsiao Hsien's failure to guard this, one of the most easily defended positions in the world, which nature alone has rendered very difficult of access, was a monumental folly, fatal to his cause. Sailing triumphantly out into the flat valley of the middle Yangtze, Prince Chao seized the city of I Tu below the first gorge, a point only fifty miles above Ching Chou,[1] the Liang capital.

The court of Liang, perturbed at the news of this unlooked-for invasion, hastily despatched the fleet up-river to block the advance of Prince Chao. The two fleets met in battle a few miles west of I Tu. Prince Chao skilfully used the advantage of the current which his up-stream position gave him. Breaking through the Liang fleet he inflicted a crushing defeat, taking more than 300 of their ships and making a slaughter of more than 10,000 men. Nothing now stood between the T'ang forces and the enemy capital. As soon as Li Ching with the army had passed the gorges and joined the fleet, the united T'ang forces moved rapidly down river, arriving before Ching Chou, well in advance of the Liang

[1] Ching Chou still exists, though the alteration in the course of the river has reduced its importance. It now lies ten miles from the river bank, the present-day port being Shasi, a town well known to foreign merchants.

southern army, which had to toil wearily up-stream against the force of the strong Yangtze current.

Throughout this campaign the two T'ang commanders, though northerners, showed a remarkable grasp of the alien strategy of southern river warfare, in which the strong currents and seasonal fluctuations of the South China rivers have in all ages been factors of the highest importance.[1]

At Ching Chou the T'ang army found another Liang fleet awaiting them. Realising that any delay would be favourable to the enemy, who were anxiously awaiting the slow advance of their southern reinforcements, Li Ching at once gave battle. The story of I Tu was repeated before Ching Chou; the whole Liang fleet was captured or burnt, and the army driven routed into the walls of the city, which was then closely besieged. Ching Chou, being a strong city with a large garrison, it was feared that the siege would not be successful before the Liang southern army arrived. Li Ching therefore devised a stratagem by which he hoped to delay these advancing succours. Taking all the captured Liang ships, he cut them loose, so that, carried away by the current, they drifted down river.

The commanders of the Liang southern army, ignorant of the real situation up-river, could not conceal from their troops these grim evidences of disaster, which, floating down the broad waters of the Yangtze, seemed to tell of the total defeat of their sovereign and the fall of his capital. Discouragement and apprehension spread rapidly among the troops, while the generals hesitated to advance farther. One of these generals was Kao Shih-Lien, maternal uncle of Li Shih-Min's consort, the Princess Chang-Sun. Kao had only submitted to Liang, because holding a position under the Sui dynasty in Annam, he found himself cut off in that remote appanage of the empire when the dynasty collapsed.

---

[1] Even the advent of steam has not eliminated these considerations. While a steamship can descend the 1400 miles from Ch'ungking to Shanghai in seven or eight days, the fastest vessel cannot make the reverse journey against the current under sixteen or seventeen days.

The call to come north at the head of his troops provided him with an opportunity to submit to the new dynasty with which he was connected by marriage. Kao Shih-Lien did not hesitate to avail himself of this chance.

While, paralysed by dissension and disaffection, the Liang army made no progress, Ching Chou, briskly assailed by the T'ang army, seemed unlikely to stand a long siege. Hsiao Hsien, despairing at the unaccountable delay of his army, which he feared had deserted to the enemy, lost all hope. He decided to surrender to the T'ang prince, although he was fully aware that such a step would cost him his life. The Liang emperor in this extremity showed a moral courage of which in his somewhat unjust administration he had hitherto given little proof. "Heaven", he said, "does not favour Liang. Why for the sake of one man such as I should my people suffer further miseries?"

He ordered the gates to be set open, and led out his court to submit to the T'ang generals. When brought into the presence of Prince Chao he still urged that the citizens of Liang be spared. "I alone should suffer death, the people have done you no injury, you should therefore leave them in peace", he said.

The T'ang generals wisely followed this generous advice, realising that a display of clemency would win the unresisting submission of all the wide domains of Liang, whereas if Ching Chou was abandoned to the soldiers, the other cities of the provinces would make a desperate stand in fear of a similar fate. This policy was fully justified by results. The southern cities, hearing of the capture of their sovereign and the lenient treatment of Ching Chou, made haste to surrender at the approach of the T'ang forces. Even the great southern Liang army which had at last slowly pushed up the Yangtze towards Ching Chou, laid down its arms without fighting. Li Ching, travelling through the south as imperial commissioner, obtained the submission of even the remotest provinces of Liang, Annam and the valley of the West river.

The conquest of the south was completed in the last month of this victorious year (A.D. 621) by Tu Fu-Wei, the young viceroy of the south-east. He invaded the territory of Li Tzŭ-T'ung, the emperor of the south-east coast, whom he defeated in battle not far from Nanking. Li Tzŭ-T'ung was himself made prisoner, and this disaster put an end to the resistance of his subjects. Tu Fu-Wei added the coastal provinces to the T'ang empire without further fighting. Li Tzŭ-T'ung, sent to Ch'ang An, was at first spared, as he was not considered a formidable figure. But he unwisely tried to escape to the south, and being recaptured on the road, was brought back to Ch'ang An and decapitated in the market-place.

This fate had already befallen Tou Chien-Tê and Hsiao Hsien. The fate of the fallen emperor of Hsia provoked a rising in the north-east, his old country, which constituted the last serious internal menace which Shih-Min had to face. The people of the eastern plain remained uncompromisingly hostile to the T'ang dynasty, even when Ssŭ Shui had ruined their hopes. The death of their well-liked sovereign and the fate of Wang Shih-Ch'ung bred a distrust of T'ang promises which encouraged the irreconcilable element to make another bid for independence.

Wang Shih-Ch'ung had been brought to Ch'ang An after the fall of Lo Yang. In view of the promise Shih-Min had once made to spare his life if he surrendered, and as he was not considered a dangerous pretender for whom the people of Honan would rise in revolt, Li Yüan granted the ex-emperor of Chêng his life. He and his son were degraded to the rank of common people, and exiled to a distant part of Szechuan province. The road the captives had to follow was long and difficult. The officer charged with escorting them to their place of banishment felt resentful at his wearisome task, which would take months of travel through inhospitable mountains. When the party reached a secluded village in the mountains south of Ch'ang An, this officer forged a decree ordering the execution of the captives, and when he had put the unfortunate Wang Shih-Ch'ung and his son to death, returned to court with a story that the prisoners had tried to escape. When the real facts were known the murderer was punished by being deprived of his office and made ineligible for further employment. But this lenient sentence did not reflect great credit on the good faith of the T'ang emperor.

The prisoners taken at Ssŭ Shui, released at Ch'ang An, had witnessed the tragic fate of Tou Chien-Tê, and heard the story of Wang Shih-Ch'ung's treacherous murder. On their return to their villages in the east they recounted these tales, and were heard with indignation by the disbanded soldiers and retired officers of the Hsia army. In all such revolutions the fall of one party turns into the street a host of officials and officers who served the fallen court. There was therefore no lack of malcontents in the territory which had belonged to the emperor of Hsia. Before many months had passed a group of officers had raised a revolt, led by one Liu Hei-T'a, a former general of Tou Chien-Tê's army.

The T'ang court had not appreciated the strength of the hostility still felt by the people of the eastern plain. They were completely surprised by the vigorous support which the rebels obtained. Within a few weeks the rebel leader had taken several cities, and defeated a T'ang force near Chi Chou, Hopei (Nan Chi Chou). The court, realising that the affair was serious, ordered the former viceroy of the east, Prince Huai An, to suppress the rebellion in conjunction with Lo I, governor of Yu Chou (Peking). Li Shên-T'ung Prince Huai An had been in captivity at Kuang P'ing Fu until the victory of Ssŭ Shui brought his release. He was not an outstandingly skilful general, but on this occasion he met with ill-luck which could scarcely have been foreseen.

It was already midwinter when the T'ang army met Liu Hei-T'a in battle near Jao Yang in Hopei, on the Hu T'o river thirty miles south east of Ho Chien Fu. Prince Huai An had 50,000 men, considerably more than his opponent. As

the T'ang army was superior, Prince Huai An had no hesitation in ordering an attack, especially as snow was falling,
driven by a light wind towards the rebel army. Prince Huai
An hoped to profit by this circumstance, which would
embarrass the enemy. But on this day the stars in their
courses fought for Liu Hei-T'a. At the height of the battle
the wind changed, starting to blow violently in the opposite
direction, driving the snow into the faces of the T'ang
soldiers. Liu Hei-T'a profited by this good fortune, winning
a complete victory. The T'ang army lost two-thirds of its
strength, only Lo I's corps drawing off intact to Yu Chou
(Peking).

The loss of this battle was disastrous to the T'ang cause.
Liu Hei-T'a occupied all the cities in the north-east except
Yu Chou. He was further reinforced by the revolt of Kao
K'ai-Tao, prince of Yen, who had formerly been an inde-
pendent pretender, and had then submitted to the T'ang
dynasty. The Turks, pursuing their policy of helping the
weaker parties, hastened to send assistance to the rebels.
Marching south, Liu Hei-T'a defeated Li Shih-Chi near
Kuang P'ing Fu. After capturing that city he retook Chang
Tê Fu and Wei Hui, and so re-established the old empire of
Hsia.

These calamities forced Li Yüan to turn to Li Shih-Min,
the guiding genius of the T'ang cause, without whom everything always went awry. Appointed grand-general of the
empire, ranking above all princes and ministers, with plenary
powers as commander-in-chief and viceroy of the east,
Shih-Min led the picked troops of his army along the eastern
road. In the first month of A.D. 622 he crossed the Yellow
river, and at the mere rumour of his approach the rebels
abandoned Wei Hui and Chang Tê Fu, falling back to
protect Kuang P'ing Fu, where they had established their
capital. The aim of Shih-Min's strategy was to crush the
rebels between his own force, coming from the south, and the
northern army under Lo I, which was moving southwards

from its base at Yu Chou (Peking). When these two T'ang armies could make contact along the great northern road, which runs north from the Yellow river through Kuang P'ing Fu to Yu Chou and Korea, the rebels would be pinned against the sea coast, cut off from their only allies, the Turks.

To counter this menace Liu Hei-T'a was forced to divide his army. After some hesitation he left his generals to oppose Lo I, taking command himself of the army which was covering Kuang P'ing Fu. When Shih-Min's forces approached this place, the small town of Ku Chou, ten miles north-east of Kuang P'ing Fu, surrendered to the T'ang commander. Shih-Min promptly put in a garrison, as Ku Chou is a point of strategical importance. With this city in his possession the T'ang prince could command the road from Kuang P'ing Fu to the north-east, towards Ho Chien Fu, from which district the rebel army drew their supplies.

Liu Hei-T'a also realised the importance of Ku Chou. He made a determined effort to recapture the city, but while he was occupied in this attempt, Shih-Min slipped round north of Kuang P'ing Fu and captured the next large city on the northern road, Shun Tê Fu. By this movement Kuang P'ing Fu was surrounded. To complete the T'ang success, news came that Lo I had beaten the northern rebel army and was marching south to join Shih-Min. Meanwhile Liu Hei-T'a was attacking Ku Chou with the greatest fury. The city was strongly defended by a water moat fifty paces wide. To overcome this obstacle Liu Hei-T'a started to construct causeways, which, when complete, would enable him to use his rams on the wall.

Shih-Min could not yet spare the troops to make a full-scale attempt to relieve the place, as the investment of Kuang P'ing Fu occupied large forces. Though more than one effort was made, the T'ang army was unable to force the enemy siege lines and succour the town. A council was held at which Li Shih-Chi was of opinion that if Liu Hei-T'a completed his causeways, the town would fall. He believed, however, that if the garrison could be reinforced, Ku Chou could still hold out for some time. Lo Shih-Hsin, the young general who had left Wang Shih-Ch'ung to join the T'ang army, offered to force his way into the town with a small reinforcement of picked troops. This could be done, he said, if the garrison co-operated by making a sortie. The raiding party would attack at the same time and cut a way through to the city.

Shih-Min decided to attempt this plan, which was communicated to the garrison by signalling from a mound inside the T'ang lines.[1] The raid proved successful, the garrison co-operating as arranged, by making a sortie. In the confusion the former garrison commander cut his way out to the main T'ang army, while Lo Shih-Hsin and his men gained the city. Shih-Min intended to make a grand assault on the rebel position within a few days, when his main force would have assembled. It was thus only necessary for Lo Shih-Hsin to hold Ku Chou a short time.

Unfortunately the weather turned unfavourable. It was now the depths of winter. A great northern gale sprang up bringing blinding snowstorms, which raged unabated for a week. To attack in the teeth of such a wind was to court the disaster which had overtaken Prince Huai An. Shih-Min was obliged to await better weather, but before the change came, Ku Chou fell. Liu Hei-T'a would have liked to enlist the heroic Lo Shih-Hsin in his service, but as the young man steadfastly refused to entertain such an idea, he was ordered to execution. Lo Shih-Hsin was then in his twentieth year. A few days later Shih-Min led the whole army to the attack, broke through, and forced Liu Hei-T'a to relinquish Ku Chou. But for Lo Shih-Hsin he came too late.

Although Liu Hei-T'a had been forced to give up this prize, he was not yet beaten. He encamped in the vicinity,

[1] This fact proves that the T'ang army could use some sort of "morse" code system. A complicated combined action could not have been pre-arranged otherwise, especially as the T'ang plan had to be kept secret from the enemy.

guarding the north-east road to Ho Chien Fu. The T'ang army was divided into two camps, Li Shih-Chi to the north of the Ming river, Shih-Min and Lo I to the south. The position of the T'ang camps made it impossible for Liu Hei-T'a to communicate with Kuang P'ing Fu, or assault one T'ang camp without being exposed to attack from the other. Shih-Min prepared to pass the winter here, knowing that his own strength would not diminish with time, while that of the rebels depended on a run of success.

Liu Hei-T'a, who appreciated this fact, was anxious to force a battle. The difficulty he encountered in getting supplies was another incentive to action. While the T'ang army could draw on the resources of a whole empire, the rebels depended on the district of Ho Chien Fu, the only one which still remained entirely in their hands. As at Ssŭ Shui, and in the Kansu and Shansi campaigns, Shih-Min made delay and famine fight for him, forcing the enemy to engage when the moment which he had chosen arrived. This moment was the spring, when the weather could not by some strange trick change the fortune of the day, as at Jao Yang, and when the enemy's supplies would be at their lowest. Meantime Shih-Min harried the enemy convoys which came up the river and burned their wagon trains.

Liu Hei-T'a made one attempt to force the T'ang army to fight, by attacking Li Shih-Chi's camp. But he found that the army from Shih-Min's camp so threatened his flank that he was obliged to break off the action. In this engagement Shih-Min and his young cousin, Prince Huai Yang (Li Tao-Hsüan), had a narrow escape, being surrounded till extricated by Yü-Ch'ih Ching-Tê and the heavy T'ang cavalry. The two armies remained inactive for more than two months, while Shih-Min waited for warm weather.

During this delay the prince made certain preparations. He set his engineers to work higher up the Ming river, building a dam to take the whole flow of the river, but so constructed that it could be swiftly demolished and the flood water released. He gave orders that if the rebel army crossed the river to attack, the dam was to be broken. Shih-Min had no doubt that the enemy, when his supplies were exhausted, would give battle. Liu Hei-T'a had no hope if he ordered a retreat. He had no base to retire upon, and his army, convinced that defeat was certain, would melt away.

Not long after, the rebel general, seeing the end of his supplies in sight, decided to risk all on a battle. Crossing the river he drew up his force in line, his army being about 20,000 strong. Shih-Min accepted the challenge. The T'ang cavalry charged the rebel line and at first drove the enemy cavalry back upon their infantry. Liu Hei-T'a rallied his men and put up a stubborn resistance. Shih-Min gave orders for the dam to be broken, but it was dusk before the rebel army began to give way. At last, as day closed, one of the rebel generals said to Liu Hei-T'a, "Our troops are exhausted, and cannot break the T'ang line. If you remain here you will perish in the rout. It would be best to fly while our line still holds; perhaps elsewhere we can raise another army". The rebel general took this unworthy advice, quietly riding off with a handful of his staff, unnoticed by the army which he had abandoned to its fate.

Liu Hei-T'a, if he deserted his army, did so at the right moment. Hardly had he quitted the field, than the waters of the Ming, released from the broken dam, swept down upon the doomed army in a roaring flood. With the T'ang army before them and the flooded river behind, the rebel army dissolved in panic. 10,000 fell by the sword and almost all those who escaped the T'ang arms were drowned in the waters of the Ming river. The army of Liu Hei-T'a was annihilated.

The leader of the rebellion escaped to the Turks; while the authority of the T'ang emperor was once more admitted throughout the north-east. Shih-Min moved through the southern districts of Shantung, where a local revolt in support of Liu Hei-T'a still remained unsuppressed. The fear of his name alone sufficed to bring these districts back to their allegiance, and such was the impression produced by the victory of the Ming river that Tu Fu-Wei decided he would be safer if he confirmed his allegiance to the T'ang dynasty by visiting the court. When the country was pacified Shih-Min was recalled to Shensi to check, by his presence, the harassing inroads of the Turkish hordes.

Unfortunately the situation in the east changed for the worse once the prince had left these provinces. Liu Hei-T'a gathered a force of Turks, at the head of which he reappeared in Hopei, and soon added reinforcements to his following. The hostility of the eastern provinces was still unappeased. The jealousies among the T'ang generals left in the country facilitated a recrudescence of the rebellion. Ho Chien Fu fell once more into the hands of Liu Hei-T'a, who then moved south, gaining adherents as he went.

At Chi Chou he was met by a T'ang army under the young Prince Huai Yang (Li Tao-Hsüan), who had been given an older, more experienced, general as second in command. This officer, who was jealous of Li Tao-Hsüan's rising reputation, treated the young prince as a boy (he was then nineteen), and hampered his actions. When the armies engaged, this subordinate left Prince Huai Yang unsupported, until, surrounded by enemies, he was slain in the mêlée. The rest of the T'ang army, dispirited by this loss, fled at the attack of the enemy, who were completely victorious. Shih-Min was inconsolable at the death of Li Tao-Hsüan, for whom he had a particular affection. The youth was indeed one of the most attractive figures of the brilliant band who followed Shih-Min's standard.

Liu Hei-T'a, believing that this victory would restore his fortunes, marched south, capturing the cities on his way. Even Kuang P'ing Fu fell into his hands, abandoned by the improvident Li Yüan-Chi Prince Chi, Shih-Min's youngest brother. After this success the rebel turned south-east to besiege Ta Ming Fu, but here fortune finally deserted him.

The city was strongly held, and resisted all the rebel efforts for more than two months. Meanwhile a new T'ang army was approaching, commanded by the crown prince, Chien-Ch'êng.

The crown prince had never distinguished himself in warfare. While Shih-Min fought the wars of the empire, Chien-Ch'êng had spent his time at Ch'ang An. If he now made an unaccustomed appearance in the field, it was due to the advice of Wei Chêng, who had become one of the officers of the crown prince's household, and who, observing the fame of Shih-Min, urged his master to undertake a campaign which would win him some military reputation to offset the brilliant record of the younger prince. Wei Chêng, who had a very shrewd appreciation of the real situation in the east, knew that no great military skill was needed to disperse the heterogeneous rabble which now followed Liu Hei-T'a.

When the army approached Ta Ming Fu, the crown prince, acting on Wei Chêng's advice, published an amnesty, promising free pardon to all who deserted the rebel army; and to prove the sincerity of the offer, he released the political prisoners in the city gaols. Wei Chêng realised that the picked troops of Hsia had perished at the Ming river. Liu Hei-T'a's new following consisted mostly of proscribed criminals who had taken up arms to avoid the penalties which the law imposed on persons guilty of complicity in the late rebellion. He believed that once a sincere amnesty was made public, these people, who only wished to save their lives, would abandon the rebel cause.

His judgment was perfectly correct. The rebels had already suffered a defeat at the hands of the strong garrison of Ta Ming Fu. Now, hearing of the advance of a new T'ang army, against which they could not hope to stand for long, they hastened to avail themselves of the amnesty, and deserted in large numbers. The lack of food in the rebel camp was a further stimulus to the general defection. Liu Hei-T'a, unable to meet the T'ang army, or even to maintain the blockade of

Ta Ming Fu, was forced to retreat. He was held up at the bridge over the Wei river at Kuan T'ao Hsien (on the Shantung-Hopei border), and there the T'ang pursuit came upon him before the bridge could be repaired.

The rebel army was cut to pieces in trying to pass the river, and though Liu Hei-T'a himself escaped, he was a fugitive without supporters. Pursued by the T'ang cavalry he arrived, exhausted and starving at Jao Yang, a city which had risen in his favour. Liu Hei-T'a was now too suspicious of his followers to trust the governor of this place, till with tears in his eyes that official invited him into the town to rest and take food. The rebel leader was justified in his first distrust. No sooner was he inside the walls, while still walking up the street, hastily eating the food which had been given him, than the treacherous governor had him seized, and delivered to the T'ang pursuit. Liu Hei-T'a was executed in the market-place at Kuang P'ing Fu in the first month of A.D. 623. With his death the rebellion which had so long devastated the northeast was finally pacified.

The last sparks of opposition to the T'ang dynasty were extinguished in the next year (A.D. 624); in the north, by the death of Kao K'ai-Tao, who was murdered by one of his generals; and in the south by the failure of the rebellion of a general of Tu Fu-Wei, who attempted to profit by his master's absence at court. This general[1] declared himself independent at Nanking. His forces were defeated at Wu Hu by the river fleet under Prince Chao (Li Hsiao-Kung), who captured Nanking. Li Shih-Chi completed the victory by pursuing the rebel till he met his death near Su Chou, in Kiangsu.

With the suppression of this rising the internal wars, which had raged incessantly since Yang Ti's death, came to an end, and the T'ang dynasty was acknowledged from Tibet to the sea, and from the Great Wall to Annam. Apart from the hostilities with the Turks on the northern frontier, and

[1] Fu Kung-Shih.

colonial wars in Central Asia undertaken in later years, the year A.D. 624 saw the dawn of a great period of peace, which was to last nearly 130 years, nourishing the greatest epoch of Chinese art and culture.

This great achievement, the conquest of a vast empire in less than seven years, was the work of Li Shih-Min; nor can his father, Li Yüan, whom he had made emperor, be said to have contributed in any way to the glorious result. Left to himself, Li Yüan's policy was weak, indecisive, and vacillating. Had it not been for the foresight, the determination, and the courage of Li Shih-Min, the T'ang dynasty would never have triumphed over its rivals, and China would have remained a chaos of warring states.

The military phase of Shih-Min's career was now at an end. There remained the more difficult task of maintaining by wise policy the unity won by the sword, and of re-creating the machinery of civilised government which had perished in a long period of tumult and confusion.

CHAPTER VI

THE HSÜAN WU GATE, A.D. 626

The conquest of the southern pretenders in A.D. 623 completed the pacification of the whole Chinese empire, which was henceforward peacefully united beneath the sway of the T'ang dynasty. For some years after the restoration of internal peace the new dynasty had still to sustain a vexatious war with its northern neighbours, the elusive Turks, now ruled by an energetic sovereign, Qadir Khan. While Shih-Min was occupied in defending the frontiers against this external menace, the security of the state and the hard-won unity of the empire were threatened with destruction by an enemy placed in the very centre of the political system.

Li Chien-Ch'êng, the eldest son of Li Yüan, had been appointed crown prince at the foundation of the T'ang dynasty. Unfortunately he possessed none of the qualities fitting him to rule an empire, nor, apart from the right of birth, had he any claim to a throne which owed its existence and preservation to the genius of his younger brother. There was therefore a latent weakness in the new dynasty. The reigning emperor, Li Yüan, was vacillating, credulous and ageing. At his death the vast empire, conquered by Shih-Min, would pass to Chien-Ch'êng, who had done nothing to acquire such power, and had not the talents to wield it wisely.

If Chien-Ch'êng had been capable of a generous recognition of the obligations he owed to Shih-Min, sought his assistance and cultivated his friendship, it is probable that the younger brother would have served him faithfully, as minister and general, without other ambitions. But the crown prince was by nature jealous and suspicious, a debauchee addicted to the vices for which Shih-Min, the man of action, had neither the time nor the inclination.

The contrast was painfully obvious. Chien-Ch'êng came to
feel that the very existence of his younger brother offered
a silent rebuke to his own unworthy character.

The jealousy of the crown prince was stimulated by the
malicious intrigues of Li Yüan-Chi Prince Chi, the youngest
of Li Yüan's three sons. Yüan-Chi had something of the
energy and leadership of Shih-Min, though lacking his
brother's courage. In his private life he shared the debauched
tastes of Chien-Ch'êng, as has already been recorded in
connection with his conduct as governor of Shansi (see
chap. III). The crown prince and his youngest brother became
fast friends, their relationship cemented by a common hatred
of Shih-Min.

The fresh laurels won by Shih-Min in the campaign against
Liu Hei-T'a inflamed his brothers' growing envy to the
point of active hostility. Towards the end of the year A.D. 622
the two princes began a series of intrigues which aimed to
alienate Shih-Min from the emperor's affection and work his
downfall. The Lady Tou, consort of Li Yüan, and mother of
the three princes, had died before the dynasty was founded.
Her place in the affections of the emperor was eagerly disputed by a large harem of concubines, for Li Yüan had
grown uxorious with increasing age and prosperity. The two
brothers used these women as the channel for their slanderous
accusations. The concubines, flattered, bribed, and gratified
by the two princes, who lived so much at court, were easily
made to dislike the young soldier who was always absent at
the wars, and when he made his brief appearances at Ch'ang
An, spent neither time nor money courting the favour of the
palace ladies.

The queen, Chang Chieh-Yü,[1] was the most active friend
of the crown prince in the inner palace. This lady had con-

---

[1] "Fei", 妃, means an imperial concubine. The title being inferior to
empress could be translated as "princess" but that English word is more
appropriately reserved for the Chinese "kung chu", 公主, applied to a daughter
of the emperor.

ceived a personal spite against Shih-Min, not directly connected with the jealousies of Chien-Ch'êng. After the fall of Lo Yang, Queen Chang Chieh-Yü had, by the favour of the emperor, obtained for her father the gift of a valuable estate in the conquered city. This estate had, however, already been granted by Shih-Min to his uncle, Li Shên-T'ung Prince Huai An, as a reward for his services in the war.

Hearing this, the two princes instigated the queen to accuse Shih-Min of upsetting the decrees of the emperor by assigning to his favourites land which the emperor had already allotted to others. To this accusation, a complete inversion of the real facts, they added the general charge that Shih-Min had kept for himself the spoils of Lo Yang, which should have been paid into the treasury. Li Yüan, always credulous, flew into a rage, and from this time onwards began to suspect Shih-Min. Although the accusation was disproved, the impression produced on the emperor remained.

Queen Chang Chieh-Yü actively fanned the flame of Li Yüan's ill-humour. Every incident which could be turned to Shih-Min's discredit was related in distorted form to the emperor. Tu Ju-Hui, an officer of Shih-Min's household, having occasion to call on the father of the queen, rode into the courtyard on horseback, as his rank entitled him to do. He was at once attacked by the servants, who set upon him, pulling him from his horse, shouting, "Who are you to cross our threshold mounted?" The queen related her own version of this fracas to the emperor, saying that Shih-Min had sent his officers to insult her father. Li Yüan called upon Shih-Min to make an explanation, but refused to believe his account of the affair.

The hold which the intriguing Chang Chieh-Yü had obtained upon his father's affection was naturally a source of sorrow to Shih-Min, who had been very much attached to his mother. He could not conceal the resentment he felt at his father's weakness, and the favour shown to his mother's unworthy successor. On one occasion, at a state banquet,

Shih-Min, seeing this queen seated in the place which his own mother, had she lived, would have occupied, was overcome with bitter reflections. All this glory and pomp, which had been secured by his own achievements, had come too late for his mother to enjoy; instead Li Yüan lavished his favour on unworthy women of no merit. Tears came into his eyes. Throughout the feast he remained silent, plunged in gloom.

Chang Chieh-Yü, ever on the alert to observe faults in Shih-Min's conduct, did not fail to note his despondent attitude, and draw matter for a new insinuation. After the feast she came in tears to the emperor, declaring that the prince's gloomy and menacing manner was a proof of the hatred which he bore to her. She feared that after the death of Li Yüan, Shih-Min would ruthlessly massacre the concubines and their children. At the same time she praised the gentle and decorous conduct of Chien-Ch'êng and Yüan-Chi, adding, with a sigh, that it was to be feared that these princes would never excape the wrath of the evil Shih-Min. The emperor, who could no longer disguise from himself the enmity growing up between his sons, believed the queen's account of Shih-Min's behaviour at the feast, and was much displeased.

It is probable that these court intrigues would have led to some violent tragedy at an early date, had not the exigencies of frontier defence called Li Shih-Min away from Ch'ang An to campaign against the Turks. While the prince passed the greater part of A.D. 623 in north Shansi, blocking by the terror of his name the threatened invasion of these barbarians, the crown prince, as has been recorded in chap. v, undertook the final campaign against Liu Hei-T'a. The absence from Ch'ang An of all the brothers, postponed, for a time, the prosecution of their quarrel.

The next year the crown prince returned to court, his pride swollen by the prestige of his cheaply obtained victory over Liu Hei-T'a. Shih-Min had also returned from the frontiers, where his success in checking the Turks was more generally applauded than the capture of the eastern rebel. The two princes, disappointed to find their hated brother still the idol of the populace and the hero of the army, decided to take extreme measures. Secretly enlisting desperadoes, they sought an opportunity to assassinate Shih-Min without being directly implicated in the crime.

In the summer of A.D. 624 Li Yüan moved to his summer palace, accompanied by Shih-Min and Yüan-Chi, leaving the crown prince in charge of the capital. From this arrangement it may be surmised that the emperor was already afraid to leave Shih-Min and Chien-Ch'êng together in his absence. His fears were only too well founded. The crown prince and Yüan-Chi had decided to avail themselves of this opportunity to kill Shih-Min on the journey. A fortuitous change of plan at the last moment frustrated the plot, and brought the conspiracy to light.

Chien-Ch'êng at Ch'ang An, learning that his father had been informed of the whole plot, was left in a most embarrassing position. At one moment tempted to seize the city, declare the emperor deposed, and usurp the throne, at the next he balanced the wisdom of going straight to Li Yüan and begging for forgiveness. The dangers of the bolder plan were great. As Shih-Min still lived, the army would obey him and support the emperor, for Chien-Ch'êng had few friends among the generals and still less favour with the soldiers. On the other hand, he feared that if he surrendered, his crime would be punished with degradation, or even death.

Finally he chose the more prudent course. Riding to the emperor's camp, Chien-Ch'êng, prostrate at his father's feet, confessed his crime. Li Yüan, his eyes at last opened to the real position, at first proposed to take firm action. The crown prince was confined in the camp while Shih-Min was summoned to the imperial presence. Li Yüan then informed his second son that he had never forgotten that the family owed its elevation to Shih-Min, who had planned the original revolt, and fought every subsequent war to a victorious conclusion. Therefore the succession to the throne was his just due. Chien-Ch'êng, having proved unworthy, would be degraded to the subordinate dignity of prince, with Szechuan province as his appanage. "As the soldiers of that country are weak and unwarlike, he will never be able to menace your power, while if he rebels you can easily suppress him. This is my decision, for unlike Sui Wên Ti (Yang Chien) I will never consent to kill my own son."[1]

Li Yüan-Chi and Queen Chang Chieh-Yü, who had escaped suspicion for their share in the plot, were in despair at this, to them, disastrous development. They left no artifice unused in an assiduous campaign to change the emperor's decision. As Shih-Min, who had never intrigued against his brothers, took no steps to counter their persuasions, Li Yüan, always weak, always willing to accept the advice of the last comer, finally succumbed to this persistent propaganda, and revoked his decree. Chien-Ch'êng was restored to his rank and title; Shih-Min was never appointed crown prince. Apart from the exile of some of the crown prince's unworthy attendants, the whole conspiracy was left unpunished, the weak monarch contenting himself with futile exhortations to his sons to live in harmony.[2]

As might be supposed, the two princes escaping unscathed from the consequences of their plot were encouraged to form fresh conspiracies to compass the death of their brother, who was now aware of the lengths to which their enmity could go. The intrigues with the ladies of the harem were renewed, and Shih-Min's every word and act related to the emperor in a distorted form. The crown prince did not make any

---

[1] Sui Wên Ti or Yang Chien, founder of the Sui dynasty, had his eldest son put to death on a charge of conspiracy, the charge having been invented by the second son, who afterwards reigned as Yang Ti.

[2] Li Yüan was the type of what the Chinese call a "Hao, Hao, hsien shêng", a "Mr. Very well, very well", one who is always ready to persuade himself that all is for the best in the best of all possible worlds.

open attempt on his brother's life; but endeavoured to cause his death in a manner which should appear accidental.

An opportunity presented itself when the three princes had accompanied the emperor on a hunting expedition. Chien-Ch'êng offered Shih-Min a particularly fine horse which, however, had a very vicious temper. It was his hope that Shih-Min would attempt to master this beast and suffer a fatal accident. In fact Shih-Min found the horse quite unmanageable. Three times he was thrown, until Yü-Wên Shih-Chi remonstrated, urging him to abandon the attempt. Shih-Min replied, "Death and life are fore-ordained, so what is the risk". Chien-Ch'êng overheard this remark, which he repeated to Chang Chieh-Yü.

The intriguing concubine was quick to see an opportunity in this apparently innocent saying. She went to Li Yüan, declaring that Shih-Min had said, "I have the Mandate of Heaven and will be lord of the empire, so what is the risk". "*T'ien Ming*", the "Mandate of Heaven", is the Chinese equivalent of Divine Right, the attribute of royalty. Shih-Min's remark in this distorted form thus sounded to Li Yüan like a statement of claim to the throne. In a great rage the emperor summoned Shih-Min and furiously upbraided him. When the prince replied that if he was accused of disloyalty he would willingly stand a trial, confident of his innocence, the emperor angrily refused to continue the discussion.

A call to the defence of the frontier kept Shih-Min away from court throughout the year A.D. 625, postponing a crisis which was now inevitable. On his return to Ch'ang An his brothers were ready with a new scheme. The crown prince had devised a plan which promised certain success. Instead of hostility, he received his brother with professions of friendship, and seemed to seek a reconciliation. A banquet was to be given by Chien-Ch'êng to celebrate Shih-Min's return, and so complete was the pretence, that the prince went to the feast unsuspecting. No open violence was attempted, but Shih-Min was given poisoned wine, from the effect of which he fell to the ground vomiting blood. The presence of mind of his uncle, Prince Huai An, saved his life. Prince Huai An, refusing to allow any member of the crown prince's household to attend the prince, escorted Shih-Min back to his own palace, where thanks to his hardy constitution, fortified by an open air life, he recovered. Had Chien-Ch'êng not made the mistake of giving his brother an overdose of the poison, and so causing acute nausea, he would have accomplished his design.

This second attempt on Shih-Min's life caused a great stir. Although the crown prince could not be convicted of the responsibility, impudently declaring that Shih-Min had been drunk "and could not hold his wine", Li Yüan had no real doubt as to what had taken place. Once more he resolved to make some definite settlement which would dissipate the causes of this deadly quarrel. He now proposed to make Shih-Min paramount viceroy of all the eastern part of China with headquarters at Lo Yang, a partition which would make the prince co-emperor. The decree was promulgated, to the general relief of all Shih-Min's friends, who feared that he would not long survive the murderous plots of his brothers if he stayed in Ch'ang An.

But the news of the emperor's decision caused the most lively anxiety to the two princes. They knew that when once Shih-Min was established at Lo Yang he would be beyond the reach of their enmity. Moreover he would be placed in a situation highly advantageous for a contest for the throne when Li Yüan died. With the pick of the army, and an independent base at the eastern capital, it was certain that Shih-Min could prevail over his unwarlike brother whenever he chose to march on Ch'ang An. The crown prince and Yüan-Chi determined that at all costs this partition must be prevented. Ably assisted by the wily tongue of Chang Chieh-Yü they once more achieved their object. When Li Yüan was told that the followers of Shih-Min had manifested unconcealed delight on hearing of the new partition, and had

openly boasted of their intention to organise revolt as soon
as they reached Lo Yang, the vacillating emperor not only
revoked his partition decree, but decided to arrest Shih-Min
on a charge of treason.

This last folly was prevented by the vehement protests of
Ch'ên Shu-Ta, who not only emphasised Shih-Min's outstanding services to the dynasty, but urged the emperor to
make an adequate settlement on the lines of his earlier
decree. The weak monarch was next assailed by his son Li
Yüan-Chi, who, hoping to strike while the iron was hot,
demanded his brother's instant execution. This unnatural
request Li Yüan still had the firmness to refuse.

That summer (A.D. 626) at Ch'ang An was overclouded by
the lowering menace of the approaching crisis. The success
of the crown prince in frustrating every favourable settlement had increased the strength of his following. All who
believed that the future lay with the acknowledged heir,
whose influence appeared to dominate the foolish emperor,
rallied to the party of the two princes. Only tried friends
remained in the menaced household of Li Shih-Min. Even
among the prince's friends and intimates despondency and
foreboding were undisguised. The open enmity of the heir
of the empire, the weakness and credulity of the reigning
monarch, and the incessant intrigues of the harem were so
many menaces overshadowing the life of Li Shih-Min, and
equally threatening his followers with ruin and death.

These fears were accentuated by the apathetic attitude of
the prince himself. Although he had long known himself
to be the object of his brothers' murderous plots, he had
never made any attempt to convict his enemies, or to defend
himself against their malignant intrigues. It seemed as if this
forbearance had merely served to establish his enemies in so
strong a position that it was now too late to avert the blow.

It was Fang Hsüan-Ling, Shih-Min's principal civil adviser, who first proposed vigorous counter-measures. He
approached the prince's brother-in-law, Chang-Sun Wu-Chi.

Finding themselves in complete agreement, these two, joined by Tu Ju-Hui, came to Shih-Min and urged him to defend himself. Tu Ju-Hui went further. He openly suggested that Shih-Min should slay his brothers before they had time to accomplish their own murderous designs. The prince rejected this advice; he was not yet prepared to commit fratricide merely to forestal the enmity of his brothers.

They, for their part, had no such scruples. Their next plan was to attempt to bribe the captain of Shih-Min's bodyguard, his close friend Yü-Ch'ih Ching-Tê. This faithful officer flatly refused to join their party or touch their money. Instead, he informed Shih-Min of their proposals. The princes, having made a false move by approaching a man of Yü-Ch'ih's type with such an infamous suggestion, to cover up their tracks attempted to assassinate that officer. Yü-Ch'ih Ching-Tê, knowing their plans, left his gate open. The murderers, seeing this, were unable to decide whether it portended gross carelessness or some cunning trap. Therefore they did not dare to enter the house.

Baffled by the loyalty of Shih-Min's officers, the crown prince next tried to have these faithful friends removed from his brother's side. He had Yü-Ch'ih Ching-Tê impeached on a charge of treason. Shih-Min had still sufficient influence to quash these proceedings, but he was less able to prevent his officers being appointed to distant posts in the provinces, a device of Chien-Ch'êng's invention, which threatened to leave Shih-Min unprotected. One of these officers gave him warning of the danger. "Your Highness is letting them pluck all your feathers; if it goes on, how long do you think you can keep on flying?"

He was not the only friend to urge the prince to action. Chang-Sun Wu-Chi, his wife's uncle Kao Shih-Lien, Yü-Ch'ih Ching-Tê, and another officer, Hou Chün-Chi, came night and day to press him to defend himself by slaying the brothers who had already so many times attempted his life. But still the prince refused to take extreme measures.

The delay might well have proved fatal. Chien-Ch'êng and Yüan-Chi had concocted a new plot, which they believed could not fail. Profiting by an incursion of the Turks, the crown prince obtained for Yüan-Chi the command of the army which was to be sent against the invaders. He also obtained an order putting Shih-Min's veteran troops and officers under Yüan-Chi's orders. The princes hoped that when this order had been carried out Shih-Min would be left at their mercy without friends or troops.

Fortunately Shih-Min was not only popular with the army, but admired by the populace at large as the hero of the age. The designs of his enemies could not be formulated without some rumour reaching the ears of those who were devoted to him. One night a certain officer in the service of the crown prince, revolted by the treacherous character of his master, came secretly to Shih-Min's palace. There he related to Shih-Min a conversation between Chien-Ch'êng and Yüan-Chi, which he had managed to overhear. It appeared that the crown prince had said to his brother, "As soon as the troops and officers of Shih-Min's army have left Ch'ang An to join the army against the Turks, I will invite Shih-Min to a farewell banquet, which we will give to you before you leave for the north. The feast will be at a garden outside the city. Desperadoes will be lying in ambush, who will slay Shih-Min at a given signal. We will then immediately report to the emperor that Shih-Min was murdered by mutinous soldiers".

To give colour to this assertion Yüan-Chi was to have all Shih-Min's closest friends put to death at once, as guilty of the crime. If Li Yüan would not accept this explanation of the tragedy, the two princes at the head of the army would return to Ch'ang An, carry out a revolution, and enthrone Chien-Ch'êng as emperor.

Shih-Min could no longer doubt his desperate danger. He summoned his intimate friends to council, and, headed by Chang-Sun Wu-Chi, they unanimously urged him to act first. Shih-Min did not allow himself to be persuaded so easily. He suggested that it would be more honourable to allow his brothers to commit the first act of hostility, after which he could oppose them in the name of law and loyalty to the emperor. Yü-Ch'ih Ching-Tê brushed aside these legal niceties in his forthright manner. "Unless you will protect yourself, we cannot", he said, "and in that case I shall abandon your service."

Chang-Sun Wu-Chi declared that he would be forced to do the same. Shih-Min then asked Yü-Ch'ih what he advised. That officer did not mince his words. "If you have any doubts, you lack wisdom; and if you still hesitate in the face of danger, you have no courage. Take 800 picked men, break into the palace of the crown prince and settle the matter."

Shih-Min then said, "Who else should be killed?"

With one voice all those present exclaimed, "Prince Chi (Yüan-Chi) is evil and unbrotherly". One added that Yüan-Chi had been overheard to say, "One day I shall be the master. When Shih-Min has gone it will be as easy to take the Eastern Palace as turn my hand".[1]

To clinch the argument the officers said to the prince, "What manner of man, in your opinion, was the Emperor Shun?"[2]

"Shun was a sage", replied Shih-Min.

"Yet", they answered, "when his father cast him into a well, he did not remain there till he drowned, but climbed out. Had he not done so, China in later years would not have benefited by his wise government. Is it not said, 'Small wrongs may be endured, but great evils must be resisted'?"

The prince made no direct reply to this appeal to precedent. Instead he called for lots. But before they could be cast, one

---

[1] The eastern palace was the residence of the crown prince. Yüan-Chi's remark was interpreted as meaning that he would use the same methods to get rid of Chien-Ch'êng as they were planning to employ against Shih-Min.

[2] Shun was one of the semi-legendary emperors of the Chinese Golden Age. He is said to have reigned in 2255 B.C.

of the officers of the guard, bursting into the council room, upset the table, throwing the lots to the ground. "Lots", he exclaimed, "may be used to decide a doubtful matter. Here there is no room for hesitation, of what use are the lots? If the answer was unfavourable, would you take no action? It is time to make a plan."

Shih-Min had procrastinated so long in order to test the fidelity of his friends. Assured of their unflinching support, he now threw off all hesitation and became once more the alert, resourceful, commander, planning a victorious battle. Chang-Sun Wu-Chi was sent to fetch Fang Hsüan-Ling and Tu Ju-Hui, who had not been present at this conference, scarcely daring to go near Shih-Min's palace. In fact these two had been so depressed by Shih-Min's apathetic attitude and were now so hopeless of his cause, that they refused the summons, saying, "We have an order from the emperor forbidding us to serve the prince. Should we now disobey and go secretly to him we would be guilty of a capital crime".

When Shih-Min was informed of this reply, the qualities which had made him redoubtable on the battlefield, but which he seemed to have lost in this less honourable warfare of the palace intrigue, flashed out. Drawing his sword he said to Yü-Ch'ih Ching-Tê, "Fang and Tu wish to desert me. Take this to them, and if they will not come bring me their heads".

When Yü-Ch'ih Ching-Tê arrived with this grim message the two statesmen, recognising the voice of the authentic Shih-Min, made no further delay. Singly and secretly, disguised against spying eyes under the robes of Taoist priests, they made their way through the dark city to the palace of Shih-Min. Behind the closed doors of the prince's mansion the night was spent in feverish activity. A memorial was prepared, and sent secretly to the emperor. In this document the crimes and conspiracies of the two princes were fully expounded. Li Yüan, though shocked and alarmed by the accusation, still put off decisive action. He replied that he would investigate the matter the next day, summoning Shih-Min to appear at the morning audience.

The prince, however, was weary of these delays, which only increased the danger of his situation. Li Yüan, he knew from past experience, might promise, but he would never perform. His brothers, he knew, would never relax their implacable enmity. It was useless to assent to some new compromise which would only furnish his enemies with fresh opportunities for plotting. His mind was made up: his plans were ready.

At dawn Shih-Min, attended by Yü-Ch'ih Ching-Tê, Chang-Sun Wu-Chi, and fifty of his picked guards rode out fully armed to the Hsüan Wu gate, the north gate of the Palace City.[1] There he placed his men in ambush in the trees near the gateway. Shih-Min knew that if the crown prince and Yüan-Chi went to court they would enter the Palace City by this gate. Secret though his move was, the spies of Chang Chieh-Yü had none the less learned something of it. She had time to warn the princes that Shih-Min had left his palace with an armed following, and was apparently meditating some strong action.

On hearing this news, Yüan-Chi prudently suggested to Chien-Ch'êng that, pretending illness, or declaring that the guards had prevented them entering the palace, they should not go to court that morning, but await developments. But the crown prince, who remembered the failure of his first plot, and how nearly he had suffered degradation when it was discovered, feared that if Shih-Min saw the emperor alone, he would expose all their iniquities and obtain an order for their arrest. He decided that they must see Li Yüan themselves at any cost. "Our troops are numerous and can overawe all opposition", he said, "We can safely go to the palace and keep watch on the progress of affairs."

[1] The Hsüan Wu gate was later renamed the Yüan Wu gate, and is marked under the later name in the maps appearing in the *Ch'ang An chih* and *T'ang liang ching ch'êng fang k'ao*. It led from the Chin Yüan, or Imperial Park, into the Palace City, which at that time was the residence of the emperor. The Ta Ming Kung had not yet been built (see map, p. 45).

Believing that with their numerous following they were in no danger, Chien-Ch'êng and Yüan-Chi rode lightly attended to the palace, expecting to pass in before Shih-Min had arrived. Outside the Hsüan Wu gate something warned Chien-Ch'êng that all was not well. Perhaps he missed the accustomed guards, or felt some premonition. Checking his horse, he turned abruptly, and started to make off the way he had come. But before he could escape, Shih-Min, giving the shout which acted as a signal to his men, sprang from his ambush. Yüan-Chi was the first to shoot; he loosed three arrows at his brother, but missed every shot. Not so Shih-Min. His long experience at war, and his matchless skill as an archer, stood him in good stead. His first arrow struck Chien-Ch'êng through the heart. Yü-Ch'ih Ching-Tê and the soldiers, at this sight, rushed out of the trees and cut off the retreat of Yüan-Chi, who, wounded by an arrow, fell from his horse. The desperate young man seeing Shih-Min's horse tethered to a tree attempted to mount it, but the horse reared and plunged, scared by the ferocious shouts which Yü-Ch'ih Ching-Tê uttered with this purpose. Yüan-Chi, unable to mount, fled on foot till he fell dead, pierced by an arrow from Yü-Ch'ih Ching-Tê's bow. The followers of the two princes then fled from the scene.

The city was soon in an uproar. The partisans of the crown prince were numerous, and the fact of his death not at first realised. Two thousand of his bodyguard rode up to the Hsüan Wu gate and attacked the palace. In the middle of this tumult, Yü-Ch'ih Ching-Tê, mounting the wall, displayed the severed heads of Chien-Ch'êng and Yüan-Chi, thus convincing the soldiers that they were fighting for a lost cause. At this proof of the death of the princes their followers dispersed, flying from the city to seek refuge in the mountains, or hiding at the houses of relatives and friends.

While these sanguinary events were taking place at the Hsüan Wu gate, the emperor, accompanied by Hsiao Yü and Ch'ên Shu-Ta, was enjoying the freshness of the early summer morning on the lake in the palace grounds. His first intimation of the revolution came when Yü-Ch'ih Ching-Tê, whom Shih-Min had ordered to report events to the emperor, appeared in the imperial presence still in his armour and with his uncleansed sword in his hand. Li Yüan, startled at this alarming apparition, exclaimed, "What has happened? Why do you appear like this before me?"[1]

Yü-Ch'ih Ching-Tê replied, "Prince Ch'in (Shih-Min) knowing that Chien-Ch'êng and Yüan-Chi were meditating rebellion, took soldiers and has had them executed. He sends me to inform you, fearing that you might have heard some disturbance and been alarmed".

The emperor, overwhelmed by this terrible intelligence, could only mutter, "I did not expect to see this day. What must I do now?"

Hsiao Yü and Ch'ên Shu-Ta, both of whom were friendly to Shih-Min, hastened to seize this opportunity. They expounded the wickedness and crimes of the two dead princes, who had contributed nothing to the welfare of the state, contrasting the record of Shih-Min, who had borne the brunt of the wars which had founded the dynasty. On their advice the emperor signed a decree approving Shih-Min's action, and appointing him generalissimo of all troops in the empire. As soon as this news was published the tumults in the city were quickly pacified, and the remaining supporters of the princes went into hiding.

Shih-Min then sought an interview with his father. Li Yüan, relieved perhaps by this solution of his most difficult problem, was most affectionate, exclaiming, "This day has come to clear up all my doubts".

The emperor does not seem to have realised that it was his own weakness and indecision that had made the tragedy inevitable.

Upon the advice of Yü-Ch'ih Ching-Tê, Shih-Min urged

[1] It was a serious crime to appear before the emperor armed, unless on duty in the bodyguard.

the emperor to grant a general amnesty to all those officers and ministers who had served the dead princes, an act of generosity very rare in that age. Of the officials who thus escaped, Wei Chêng was by far the most notable. A man of outstanding moral courage and a blunt tongue, he made no servile submission when brought before Shih-Min. Asked why he had served the crown prince in his plots, Wei Chêng bluntly remarked, "Chien-Ch'êng was foolish. Had he taken my advice the events of to-day would have ended differently".

Shih-Min admired his frankness and knew his talents. To the general surprise he took Wei Chêng into his household and made him a confidential adviser.

One group of people was excluded from the amnesty. According to Chinese custom and law the family share the responsibility of the individual's crime. Therefore the children of the two princes were held equally guilty with their fathers, and in order to prevent any future claim from these descendants, or leave a focus for future conspiracies, the five sons of Chien-Ch'êng and the five sons of Yüan-Chi were put to death. This massacre of innocents, which seems so inhuman to our age and outlook, was an essential corollary of the Chinese clan system. To the men of the seventh century it seemed natural and inevitable.[1]

It may be felt that these executions leave a stain on Shih-Min's reputation and character, but if he is judged by the only just standard, the beliefs and customs of his own time, he will be held to have behaved with extreme leniency in pardoning and employing the officers who had served his enemies.

Li Yüan, having accepted "the solution of all his doubts", soon abandoned all power to his remaining son. Shih-Min was at first appointed crown prince with plenary authority

---

[1] The author and commentator of the *Tzŭ chih t'ung chien*, though deploring the massacre of the inhabitants of Hsia Hsien, mentioned in chap. III, have nothing to say against this slaughter of young children. Machiavelli also, in *The Prince*, advises the extermination of a dethroned sovereign's heirs.

over all affairs civil and military, which he decided before showing them to the emperor. But Li Yüan had no longer any desire even for this shadow of power. Two months after the events at the Hsüan Wu gate, he abdicated in favour of Shih-Min, who now at the age of twenty-six obtained the full and just reward of his arduous campaigns and far-sighted courage.

THE CHARACTER OF LI SHIH-MIN

The tragic story of the quarrel between Li Yüan's sons reveals the defects in Shih-Min's character as clearly as it depicts the criminality of his brothers. The conqueror who had outwitted the most experienced generals of his day and shown deep insight into the minds of his military opponents, had been the helpless and apathetic victim of palace plots, only saved at the eleventh hour by the devotion and despairing vehemence of his supporters. Then, indeed, tardily awaking to his peril, Shih-Min had applied a characteristically swift and drastic remedy.

There is here an apparent contradiction which deserves examination. Shih-Min as the man of action, the general in the field, or the strategist in the council chamber, was resolute, alert and perspicacious. As the courtier attempting to thwart the intrigues of his rivals he was inept, unprepared and obtuse. Shih-Min, in fact, was no politician. This is the more remarkable as skill in the art of politics, in complex intrigues and the adroit manipulation of personal factors, is an outstanding characteristic of the Chinese people. This faculty is developed in early life and constantly exercised in the family life of the widespreading Chinese clan. In households where several generations and many collateral relatives live together under one roof, the individual soon learns the art of intrigue and the higher graces of tact.

Shih-Min conspicuously lacked these very qualities, so highly developed among his countrymen. The singular fact is in some measure explained by the circumstances of his upbringing and early life. From the age of fifteen, when his military career began in the Turkish border wars, Shih-Min had never been absent from the army. His youth and early manhood, for more than twelve years, had been spent in the camp, where he had for long occupied the highest post.

Family life in the ordinary Chinese sense was therefore unknown to him. Accustomed for years to command armies and give orders to his officers, he had no experience of court-craft, no skill in flattering palace ladies and conciliating politicians.

Although it has been convenient to collect the events leading up to the Hsüan Wu gate tragedy into one chapter, it should be emphasised that these intrigues were carried on over a long period of years; years during which Shih-Min was absent on the Turkish frontier for many months at a time. His visits to Ch'ang An were rare and his sojourns at the capital brief. As the military support of the empire his presence was constantly needed on the frontiers. This was inevitable, and Shih-Min could not have evaded these obligations without imperilling the dynasty.

But it is also plain that during those years he took no political steps to counter the machinations of his brothers. He allowed them to gain the emperor's ear through the all-important channel of the imperial concubines. Able men such as Wei Chêng, whose political support would have been invaluable, were permitted to drift into the crown prince's faction, and there is no evidence to show that Shih-Min realised the harm that this indifference to politics was bringing to his fortunes.

Finally, the boy who could persuade the irresolute Li Yüan to take the hazardous step of open rebellion against Yang Ti, was now, with all the prestige of great victories behind him, unable to influence his father in matters vital to his own safety. During the years following the foundation of the dynasty Shih-Min's influence at court steadily waned. Though the persistent intrigues of his brothers were no doubt mainly responsible for Li Yüan's changed feelings, it seems probable that had we accounts of this crisis derived from the crown prince's party, more stress would be laid upon Shih-Min's autocratic manner and barely disguised contempt for the silken courtiers of the eastern palace.

Bred to the life of the frontier and the camp, passing his days with officers whose fortunes he had made, and who were devoted to his person, Shih-Min had acquired an authority and habit of command which must have been highly offensive to the crown prince and even to the emperor himself. At T'ai Yüan Fu, when his father was still merely a provincial governor, Shih-Min had shown skill and understanding in gaining his father's consent to the rebellion. But when Li Yüan was raised to the lonely eminence of a supreme auto-crat, Shih-Min seems to have been unable to adapt his methods to these changed conditions. For in the field Shih-Min had been too successful. He outshone the emperor himself and his exploits made the crown prince appear ridiculous. Yet it does not appear that he ever realised the danger of inflicting such "loss of face" upon these important personages.

Shih-Min's political ineptitude is as much in evidence in the final crisis as in the years of intrigue that went before. When, enmeshed in the plots of his enemies, he went in daily danger of his life and was about to lose his position in the army, he resorted to a purely military solution of his difficulties. In their failure to foresee this possibility his brothers, who counted on Shih-Min's political incapacity, made their fatal mistake. Imbued with a courtier's civilian point of view, the crown prince discounted the risk of a military *coup d'état* in the capital. Shih-Min, essentially the soldier, and unable to make headway in a political contest, took what the Chinese call a horseback[1] way out of the

---

[1] "Ma shang", 馬上, the idiom for a violent or extra-legal action probably comes from a story related about the emperor Kao Tsu of the Han dynasty. This emperor, a great conqueror, was of peasant origin and illiterate. One day a Confucian scholar threw himself in front of the imperial cortege and offered the emperor the classical Four Books, exclaiming, "Here is what your majesty requires to govern the empire". Kao Tsu, who was mounted, replied, striking his saddle with his palm, "Ma shang tê tien hsia...", 馬上得天下, "On horseback I obtained the empire, what need have I of your books?" To which the scholar made answer, "On horseback you conquered the empire, but can you also govern it from your saddle?"

difficulty. Applying military methods with which he was familiar to that political world which he did not understand, he left an example of successful and unashamed open violence as an evil precedent to later generations.

In later life, when wider experience as reigning emperor had opened his eyes to the political methods in use at his court, Shih-Min had reason to regret that resort to undisguised military violence which gained him the throne. He was to learn that such examples, which destroy the veil of legality and decency that commonly cloaks a political crime, tend to encourage the ambitious and shake the stability of established laws. Shih-Min found, too late, that in politics hypocrisy is not only inevitable but also valuable and praiseworthy.

A man of great foresight and wide mental horizons, Shih-Min never understood the smaller minds of lesser men. He could choose his ministers and generals with skill and employ them with discrimination. But he did not understand the intriguer. In the army and the council chamber he did not encounter these types of character, or if they showed themselves, they were swiftly dismissed.

But in his own family he had to deal, not with such men as he had chosen, but with men such as they were born. He could not alter the characters of his brothers and sons, and he failed to understand either their motives or their methods. In military life, dealing with objective realities, or with men of action—whether allies or enemies—whose motives he shared and whose mental processes were akin to his own, Shih-Min was unsurpassed, his genius and intuition never at fault. But his talents were ill-suited to the stealthy warfare of palace corridors.

CHAPTER VII

THE CONQUEST OF THE TURKS
A.D. 624–30

When Li Shih-Min ascended the throne the most pressing problem confronting the T'ang empire was the defence of the northern frontiers against the inroads of the Turks. For nearly four thousand years (until in the nineteenth century the rapid decline of the nomad races finally removed the danger), the major, almost the sole, problem of Chinese foreign policy was this Mongolian question. What relationship could be established between the civilised, agricultural people of China and the wandering nomad herdsmen who roamed the vast steppes of Mongolia and northern Central Asia? The problem, in a slightly different form, preoccupied the Roman emperors. It is not unlike that which, at the present day on the North-West Frontier, requires the constant attention of the British rulers of India: the terms on which a civilised and peaceful empire can maintain a common frontier with restless and warlike barbarians.

As in Rome and India, so too in China, there have been three policies, which, with varying success, were adopted in different ages. The "forward" policy, to apply the terms current in India, was first put into effect by the great conquering emperors of the Han dynasty (206 B.C.–A.D. 220). It was based on the assumption that the nomad races could never be good neighbours to China, and that therefore the only solution was to conquer and incorporate their territory in the empire, and drive the nomads into the wastes of Siberia, where they could never menace the frontiers of China.

Later dynasties adopted what Indian administrators call the "half-forward" policy. In China this plan sought to break up the great tribes by intrigue or limited campaigns, and set up a fringe of tributary "tame" hordes to act as a breakwater against the wild tribes beyond.

Finally there was the policy of pure defence, which was expressed in that stupendous monument, the 1400-mile-long Great Wall of China. The Wall has often been derided by unthinking critics as a proof of Chinese incompetence in military matters. These critics might reflect that the Romans, surely a military nation, also built walls in Britain and south Germany. Moreover the Wall, though never intended, as many people suppose, to be in itself a complete defence against nomad incursions, was very effective as a check. Built, with superb disregard of difficulties, along the very crest of precipitous mountains, it formed a barrier which was nearly impassable to raiding cavalry. A Tartar force, which had surprised some unguarded section, had either to breach the Wall, no light task, or haul its horses over this formidable obstruction. When returning from their foray laden with booty, and cumbered with herds of captured animals, the raiders could scarcely hope to pass the barrier except at some gate, where a Chinese garrison would be waiting for them.

When the Wall was guarded it proved a perfectly adequate defence. The objection to this purely defensive policy, of which the Wall was the symbol and chief instrument, was the cost. To guard the 1400 miles of Wall with an adequate force involved maintaining a standing army not less numerous than would be required to conquer inner Mongolia, and make the Gobi Desert, a true frontier, the limit of the empire. The cost of defending the Wall was therefore the best argument for the "half-forward" policy. To the full "forward" policy there were strong objections. Outer Mongolia is a boundless country, inaccessible, largely barren desert, far removed from the frontiers of China. The conquest of this wilderness, itself an immense undertaking, might ensure the permanent or at least prolonged disappearance of the nomad danger, but it could only be achieved by a vast expenditure of money and lives, and only maintained by garrisoning the distant wilderness with large Chinese forces. The conquest in itself added no useful province to the

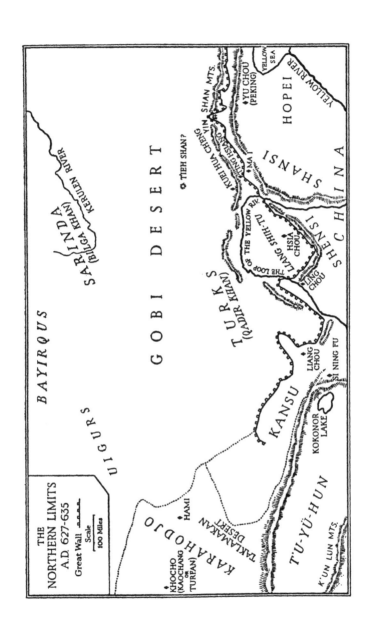

THE
NORTHERN LIMITS
A.D. 627–635
Great Wall ·····
Scale
100 Miles

BAYIRQUS

UIGURS

SARINDA
(BILGA KHAN)
KERULEN RIVER

GOBI DESERT

❖ TIEH SHAN?

KUBI HUA CHENG
YIN SHAN MTS.

TING HSIANG

MA I

YU CHOU
(PEKING)

YELLOW
SEA

HOPEI

SHANSI

SHANSI

CHINA

LIANG SHIH-TU

THE LOOP OF THE YELLOW RIV.

HSIA
CHOU

LING
CHOU

TURKS
(QADIR KHAN)

KANSU

LIANG
CHOU

SI NING FU

KOKONOR
LAKE

TU-YÜ-HUN

KARAHODJO

TAKLAMAKAN
DESERT

HAMI

KHOCHO
(KAOCHANG
OR
TURFAN)

K'UN LUN MTS.

YELLOW RIVER

Chinese empire, and produced no revenue to repay the expense.

Li Shih-Min adopted the "half-forward" policy, which aimed to secure the frontier by conquering all the country south of the Gobi Desert, and so guarantee a lasting peace at a cost which would not beggar the treasury. Even this limited objective seems a gigantic undertaking when the nature of the task is examined. Inner Mongolia was then dominated by the Turks, ancestors of the race which some centuries later invaded the Byzantine empire.[1] These nomads and their predecessors had been undisputed masters of the lands beyond the Wall for nearly four centuries. Not since the fall of the Han dynasty had any Chinese ruler thought of advancing his frontier to the Gobi; indeed the nomad hordes had for many years been free to conquer and invade the northern provinces of China. A Chinese counter-invasion of the Mongolian steppe was regarded as impossible.

The Tartars were formidable foes. Relying entirely on their cavalry and bowmen, they employed exactly the same tactics as, according to Herodotus, their kin the Scythians of the Russian steppe used against Darius of Persia a thousand years before. Rarely could they be induced to stand and fight; instead, riding round their enemies on their fleet horses, they harassed them with showers of arrows, dispersing if charged, only to reform the moment the pursuit slackened. They had no cities which could be captured, no base except a temporary encampment in the boundless grass-lands of the north. They were only vulnerable in one respect. They relied upon their flocks and herds for sustenance and upon the rare streams and wells for water. Experienced Chinese

---

[1] According to the Chinese traditional account the Turks were descended from a tribe of Hsiung-Nu or Huns who fled westward following a defeat by another Tartar horde. They settled under the Altai mountains in an iron-producing district, and there became skilled metal-workers. The name "Turk", which in their language meant a helmet, was taken from a helmet-shaped hill near their settlements. In A.D. 545 under the first great khan, Tumen, they became the dominant power in the steppe, subsequently dividing into eastern and western branches. The Ottoman Turks derived from the western branch.

generals fighting the nomads always sought to capture the flocks rather than defeat the enemy in battle, and to occupy the wells rather than pursue the elusive foe across the steppes.

The regular Chinese army, usually equally composed o cavalry and infantry, was not of great use in this peculiar warfare. The tactics which could be used against other Chinese armies, or against such nations as the Koreans, were useless in the steppe. Shih-Min on these campaigns used heavy armed cavalry combining something of the Turkish mobility with the protective armour of the infantry soldier. But the chief aid to the Chinese arms was the incoherence of the Turkish tribal system, which offered their enemies many opportunities of stirring up dissensions and enmity between the different hordes.

In the early seventh century the Tartar peoples along the Chinese frontier were divided into three main groups. The eastern Turks occupied the country on both sides of the Gobi Desert, from Manchuria to the western extremity of the Chinese frontier. The western Turks were settled in the region of Central Asia north of the T'ien Shan mountains; lastly the T'u-yü-hun had migrated from the east to the mountain region of Koko-Nor or Ch'ing Hai lying north-east of Tibet, beyond the western frontier of the Chinese province of Kansu. The western Turks were remote from the border of the T'ang empire, and their relations with China did not constitute a problem during the reign of Shih-Min. The eastern Turks were the principal enemies of the Chinese empire. They were divided into fifteen hordes, all of which acknowledged the suzerainty of the Great Khan, who maintained a sort of central organisation, and appointed or confirmed the lesser khans.

Ever since Yang Ti's attempt to foment dissension among the tribes, the Turkish rulers had been hostile to China. As has already been related in chap. II, Sibir Khan had assisted the T'ang revolt, until, after the fall of Ch'ang An, he feared that the new dynasty was growing too strong. Then he changed about, conferring his favour upon their enemies. Liu Wu-Chou and Liang Shih-Tu received Turkish assistance; a fugitive Sui prince was acknowledged as emperor by the Turks, who gave him as subjects all those Chinese who, whether for their crimes, or to seek peace, had fled beyond the Wall.

Nor had Turkish hostility to the T'ang dynasty been confined to aiding the rival pretenders. In A.D. 619 Sibir Khan entered Shansi at the head of his entire horde, with the apparent intention of founding a Turkish dynasty in north China. His death on the march dissipated the danger, for his brother and successor, Chur Khan, was not so bold. Chur died in A.D. 620, to be succeeded by yet another brother, Qadir Khan, a far more formidable antagonist.

Qadir owed his elevation to the intrigues of the Sui Princess I Ch'êng. This lady had had a remarkable matrimonial career. Originally wedded to Tutar Khan, she had, on the death of her husband, married his son Sibir, and then successively espoused that khan's brothers, Chur and lastly Qadir. As long as the Sui dynasty reigned in China she used her influence to keep the Turks friendly, as on the occasion when Yang Ti was besieged in Yen Mên, but after the fall of her family she became the inveterate foe of the T'ang dynasty, constantly urging her successive husbands to acts of hostility.

From the moment of his accession Qadir manifested his enmity to the T'ang empire. He raided the frontier, supported the rebellions of Liu Hei-T'a and Kao K'ai-Tao, and at last, in A.D. 622, invaded Shansi at the head of 150,000 horsemen, while another horde crossed the frontier to the west in Kansu. Shih-Min, recently returned from the war against Liu Hei-T'a, was sent to oppose this menace, while another army blocked the passes north-west of modern Peking. The Turks, faced by these preparations, and fearful of an encounter with the famous Shih-Min, fresh from his victory at the Ming river, were not very successful. One division of their army was routed near Fên Chou in Shansi with a loss of 5000 slain, and after this check Qadir was willing to entertain the T'ang peace proposals. His disgust with the war was increased when he learned that his western army in Kansu had been repulsed; and his ally, Liang Shih-Tu, had suffered a great defeat at the hands of the T'ang general, Prince Jên Ch'êng, Shih-Min's cousin (Li Tao-Tsung). Qadir, finding no profit in this invasion, retired to await a better opportunity.

The next year the T'ang generals had to contend with an invasion in another quarter. This time it was the T'u-yü-hun who decided that the troubles of the empire were their opportunity. In A.D. 623 they descended from their mountain strongholds in Koko-Nor to invade Kansu. Chai Shao, husband of the Lady Li, Shih-Min's heroic sister, was the general in command of the army on this frontier. He took the field against the invaders, but by a mischance found himself almost surrounded upon a mountain, where, since there was no water, it would have been difficult to resist for long. Chai Shao, however, was a general of many, if unorthodox, resources. To one side of the mountain on which he was confined was a small, isolated hill, which it was still possible to approach from the T'ang position. The Chinese general sent two singing girls to climb up this hill, where, when they reached the top, they performed curious and obscene dances in full view of the Tartar army. The T'u-yü-hun were completely distracted by this unusual spectacle. While their undisciplined warriors flocked to the little hill to obtain a better view of the proceedings, the cunning Chinese made a sudden descent from the other side of the mountain, and fell upon the inattentive enemy. The unwary Tartars, completely routed, were driven back to their mountains; there to reflect that it is most unwise, in the midst of battle, to let the mind dwell on the delights of peace.

Qadir Khan did not long abide by the truce which he had made with the T'ang empire. In the same year, A.D. 623,

Shih-Min had to take the field, though he did not need to engage battle; his appearance on the frontier was enough to make the Turks withdraw without risking an engagement. But no sooner had the T'ang prince returned to Ch'ang An than the marauders crossed the frontier as frequently as before. In the year A.D. 624 these incursions became so serious that a party of faint-hearts at Ch'ang An advised Li Yüan to abandon the city and fix his capital elsewhere. It was the wealth of Ch'ang An, they declared, that attracted the Turks; if the city was destroyed they would cease raiding.

The proposal, raised in full council, was supported by the crown prince, Chien-Ch'êng, and Yüan-Chi, never conspicuous for courage in the field; also by P'ei Chi, whose disastrous experiences when he commanded against Liu Wu-Chou had given him a mortal fear of the Turks. Hsiao Yü was not in favour, but always rather a timid character, he did not voice his opinion. The emperor, who invariably accepted any strongly urged advice, had already sent Yü-Wên Shih-Chi to choose a new site south of the Nan Shan mountains, when Shih-Min once more raised the question and voiced his opposition in a vehement speech. "Down from the most ancient antiquity we have always had to contend with the northern savages", he said, "but Your Majesty has recently arisen like a dragon to re-establish the throne of the empire. Your army exceeds a million picked troops, none of your enemies have been able to withstand it. If now, merely because the barbarians raid the borders, you burn down your capital and seek safety elsewhere, it will be regarded as a national disgrace which will be the derision of future generations. In the time of the Han dynasty the general Huo Ch'ü-P'ing was prepared to face the power of the Huns (Hsiung-Nu) and even I, although unworthy, having some experience of war, will undertake to reduce Qadir Khan to obedience. Should the enterprise fail, there will still be time to change the capital."

Li Yüan, won over by this speech, thought no more of

abandoning Ch'ang An. Instead he gave Shih-Min command of the army which was sent to oppose the Turks. Yüan-Chi was sent with him to gain experience. The T'ang army met the full strength of the Turks under the two khans, Qadir and Tutar, at Pin Chou, on the border of Shensi and Kansu, only seventy miles north-west of Ch'ang An. Tutar Khan, Sibir's son, had been passed over in the succession in favour of Qadir. For this reason Qadir was somewhat suspicious of his nephew's loyalty, the more so as Tutar had in former years been very friendly with Shih-Min during his boyhood in Shansi.

Shih-Min, who had gained an intimate knowledge of Turkish customs in peace and war during those years, was now afraid that the Turks would avoid battle, and so postpone any decision. The T'ang prince therefore decided to work on Qadir's suspicions and jealousy. He proposed to Yüan-Chi that they should challenge the two khans to single combat, though it is likely that he made this suggestion rather to expose his brother's faint-heartedness than as a serious plan. Yüan-Chi had no stomach for such a risk, and declined. Shih-Min then rode out alone towards the Turkish army, and challenged Qadir to fight it out. The khan smiled, but refused to accept, not knowing Shih-Min's real intentions. The prince then sent a herald to Tutar's horde to ask that khan why he had forgotten his former friendship, and an oath of mutual assistance which they had once exchanged. Tutar, afraid that Qadir would suspect him of disloyalty, did not reply.

Shih-Min then tried a piece of bluff. He rode forward quite alone, and started to cross the small stream which divided his army from Tutar's horde. Qadir, noting this seeming confidence in Tutar's friendship, immediately suspected that there was treachery afoot, especially as from his position he had heard something of the conversation about old friendship and the oath of assistance.[1] He sent a message

---

[1] Though it is nowhere stated it seems probable that Shih-Min could speak the Turkish language. Qadir and Tutar may equally have known some Chinese; it is clear that the khans and Shih-Min had some language in common.

to request Shih-Min not to cross the brook, adding that he was willing to make peace, and in proof of sincerity would withdraw his troops a short distance. His real motive for this movement was the fear that Tutar and Shih-Min had made a secret agreement to attack him by surprise.

Shih-Min, finding that his plan was working well, and the seeds of dissension between the khans were already bearing fruit, withdrew to his own camp. That same night, the weather being very wet, he pointed out to his officers that the rain would have unstrung the Tartar bows, the only weapon with which they were formidable. After sending a warning to Tutar not to fear for his horde, Shih-Min made a sudden night attack upon Qadir's camp. The Turks, surprised, and unable to use their bows, were put to flight. Qadir, now convinced that Tutar was in league with the T'ang court, retreated to Mongolia, as did Tutar, who for his part was quite willing to make a lasting peace with the Chinese empire.

Although this formidable invasion was dissipated by Shih-Min's guileful tactics, the Turks did not give up raiding the border, continuing this war of forays all through the year A.D. 625. Shih-Min passed part of that year in Shansi, but had no opportunity to come to grips with an enemy who carefully avoided battle. In the west, Prince Jên Ch'êng inflicted a serious defeat on one horde, which gave Shensi peace for a season.

The crisis at the T'ang court in the summer of A.D. 626 was interpreted by the Turks as a fresh opportunity for an invasion on the grand scale. As soon as Qadir heard that the crown prince and Yüan-Chi were dead, and Shih-Min had ascended the throne, he swept down into Shensi at the head of 100,000 horsemen. Although part of this army was defeated by Yü-Ch'ih Ching-Tê twenty-three miles north of Ch'ang An, Qadir himself pushed on till he encamped on the north bank of the Wei river, opposite the Imperial Park, only ten miles from the capital. There he sent ambassadors into the city to "observe the strength and emptiness of the land";

expecting that Shih-Min, who had not yet been two months on the throne, would be too uncertain of his position to oppose him.

He was very much mistaken. The new emperor, after listening to the boasts of the Turkish herald, calmly replied, "Your khan has often pretended friendship, and I have sent him presents. But now he has dared to invade the heart of my domains, although he has no cause for a quarrel with me. Although you are only savages, you should have the hearts of men, but yet, forgetting my kindness, you come here boasting of your strength. First of all I shall cut off your head".

This speech made a painful impression on the Turkish herald, whose braggart manner swiftly changed to cringing terror. Shih-Min did not carry out his threat; instead the Turk was confined in a prison as an example to his compatriots.

The next day the young emperor rode out to the bridge over the Wei river, opposite Qadir Khan's camp. Attended by only six officers, among whom were Kao Shih-Lien and Fang Hsüan-Ling, Shih-Min came up to the bank, and called for a parley with Qadir. The Turks, greatly surprised at this bold manner, which they supposed must be due to the presence of powerful Chinese forces in the neighbourhood, were so impressed by the appearance of the famous Chinese conqueror, that all dismounted and made obeisance. The emperor's advisers tried to prevent him going near the Turks, fearing treachery, but Shih-Min paid no attention to them, answering, "I know them of old, you do not. They only dared to come so far because they thought we had internal troubles, and that I, being newly seated on the throne, would be unable to oppose them. If I now show fear, close the gates of the city, and remain inactive, they will plunder the countryside without restraint. But if I ride out alone as if despising them, with the army drawn up behind me ready for battle, they will be afraid to fight so far from their home. You stay here and watch".

As Shih-Min had foreseen, Qadir Khan was not anxious to give battle to so formidable an opponent when far from his native steppes. Before the day was out he sent an ambassador to treat for peace. The next day the emperor rode out again, met Qadir at the Wei bridge, and concluded a treaty of peace, which was sealed in Turkish custom by sacrificing a white horse. The Turks then withdrew from China, and this time the peace was carefully observed. The power of the Turks had only been formidable to a weak and distracted China, divided between warring rivals. When the re-united empire was under the rule of an able emperor such as Shih-Min, the Turkish danger was seen to be comparatively insignificant. From the day of the treaty at the Wei bridge the balance of power between the two races tilted in favour of the Chinese, the initiative passed from the Turks to China, and the nomads, divided by internal feuds, were henceforward on the defensive.

The winter of A.D. 627, the year following the treaty, was extremely severe in Mongolia. The great depth of snow which covered the ground for an unusual length of time made it very difficult to feed the flocks upon which the Turks depended for food. Famine, aided by the excessive cold, swept away thousands of the unfortunate nomads, who had no resources of grain to fall back upon. As might be expected the Turks, suffering from such a catastrophe, blamed their rulers, and in particular Qadir Khan, whose arbitrary rule and preference for Central Asiatic advisers was keenly resented by the nomad chiefs. His conduct was held to be the cause of the national misfortunes, for the Turks, like the Chinese, believed that famine and inclement weather were a sign of heaven's displeasure with the rulers of the earth. Qadir Khan, instead of conciliating the tribes by reducing or suspending the tribute they paid to him, increased his exactions to make up for the general loss of revenue, and so brought the unrest to a head.

The Chinese court was informed of these troubles, but though one party urged the emperor to seize this opportunity to exterminate the Turks, Shih-Min refused to break the treaty. Meanwhile the disaffected tribes had broken into open revolt. These tribes were mostly those north of the Gobi, living along the mountains which now separate Siberia from outer Mongolia. The leagued tribes—Sarinda, Uigurs and Bayirqus[1]—completely defeated the army which Qadir sent against them, indeed the khan was forced to move nearer to the Wall to escape their reprisals. Meanwhile the bad weather still continued and the famine in Mongolia became more acute.

The war party at Ch'ang An made another attempt to persuade Shih-Min to attack the hereditary enemy while he was disabled by so many calamities. Shih-Min was a man of his word, and moreover realised that the high prestige of the Chinese court could only be established by a literal fulfilment of all treaties. He replied to these promptings, "To break an oath is treachery, to profit by the distress of others is unrighteous, to triumph over the weakness of an enemy is unchivalrous.[2] Only after they have done me an injury will I be free to make war on them".

Qadir Khan would have been well advised to observe the same good faith, but the rash Turk could not appreciate the wisdom of honesty. When the western Turks sent an embassy to Ch'ang An to obtain a Chinese princess for their khan, Qadir prevented the ambassadors from crossing his country, and warned them that any gesture of friendship to China would be regarded as an act of hostility to himself.

[1] In transliterating Turkish names I have adopted an orthography suggested by my friend Mr G. L. M. Clauson, C.M.G. The Chinese characters give only a very faint indication of the true sound of Turkish words. As there are no contemporary Turkish inscriptions, Mr Clauson wishes to make it clear that with the exception of "Bilgä" and "Bayirqu" which are established by the later Orkhon inscription, all these names, though conforming to old Turkish forms and what is known of seventh century Chinese pronunciation, are quite conjectural. The Chinese characters for these names, as given in the *Tzŭ chih t'ung chien* will be found in the Index.

[2] "Pu Wu", 不 武. The sense of this passage certainly refers to the code of war current among gentlemen, not to military expediency, which regards the weakness of an opponent as the true opportunity for war.

The next year, A.D. 628, was even more disastrous for Qadir Khan. His nephew Tutar Khan, who had been sent against the rebel hordes, was totally defeated by them, only escaping, almost alone, by the speed of his horse. Qadir, furious at this misfortune, treated Tutar with great severity, having him flogged and imprisoned. Tutar, who had always been friendly to Shih-Min, so much resented this treatment that he sent secret messages to Ch'ang An, begging the emperor to send him assistance, and deliver the Turks from Qadir's rule. Shih-Min might have left these appeals unanswered had not Qadir himself had the folly to provoke the T'ang anger by breaking the treaty of the Wei bridge.

Liang Shih-Tu, the last Chinese pretender, still held out in the country north of the Great Wall, in the "loop" of the Yellow river. This pretender, being Chinese, was not included in the peace sworn at the Wei bridge, although he had been an ally and vassal of the Turkish khan. Shih-Min, considering himself free to attack this rival, sent Chai Shao, his brother-in-law, to reduce the rebel. Qadir Khan, at the appeal of Liang Shih-Tu, sent a Turkish force to oppose the T'ang army. This army was defeated by Chai Shao, who then invested Liang Shih-Tu's capital, where, after a few days of siege, the pretender was murdered by a relative, who surrendered the city to the T'ang general. Qadir Khan had thus brought upon himself the just hostility of the T'ang empire without being able to render any effective assistance to his old ally and vassal.

The consequences of this folly were soon made plain to him. The rebel hordes—Sarinda, Uigurs, and Bayirqus—had elected a new paramount chief, Bilgä Khan, as a rival to Qadir. This pretender was now recognised by the Chinese court as legitimate Great Khan. The emperor sent an embassy by devious routes, which invested Bilgä with the insignia of his new rank, for which the T'ang emperor received in return an acknowledgment of his suzerainty. The "half-forward" policy of creating dissensions among the tribes and setting up a group of friendly vassals was thus inaugurated.

Qadir Khan, though greatly alarmed at the progress of his rival, and the favour which Shih-Min now openly bestowed upon Bilgä, did not for that seek a reconciliation with Ch'ang An. Instead, he resorted to the old plan of raiding the frontiers. These hostile acts only served to involve him in the calamity which his faithless conduct had invited. In A.D. 629 Shih-Min decided that, as Qadir had first broken the Wei bridge treaty and then committed other hostile acts, the oath was no longer binding, and he was free to make war and settle the Turkish problem to his liking.

Li Shih-Chi was appointed to the supreme command of an army of 100,000 picked troops, subordinate commands being held by such well-tried generals as Li Ching, Prince Jên Ch'êng (Li Tao-Tsung) and Chai Shao. The very rumour of these preparations induced a number of minor khans, discontented with Qadir, to send in their submission. Among these was Tutar, who came down to Ch'ang An to swear allegiance. Nevertheless Qadir seems to have been taken by surprise when he heard that one T'ang army under Li Ching, which had passed the Wall at Ma I, had surprised and captured the town of Ting Hsiang,[1] which had apparently been in Turkish hands since the fall of the Sui dynasty.

The news that a Chinese army had passed the Wall, and was, for the first time in centuries, invading the Mongolian steppe, made such an impression on Qadir's followers that one of his officers seized the Empress Hsiao, and the Sui prince whom Sibir had set up to rule the Chinese fugitives, and delivered these important captives to the T'ang army. They were brought to Ch'ang An, where Shih-Min allowed them to live in peaceful obscurity, since a Sui restoration was no longer a possibility. The Empress Hsiao, after a life of amazing vicissitudes, which had included the luxury of Yang Ti's splendid court, the night of horror at Yang Chou, the misery of captivity in Yü-Wên Hua-Chi's mutinous camp,

---

[1] Ting Hsiang is given in the Japanese compiled historical atlas, 支那 歷代 疆域 沿革 圖, as a few miles north-west of the modern So P'ing Fu, north Shansi.

and years of exile in a Turkish encampment, was now at last to spend many quiet years in the city where once she had reigned as empress, till her death in A.D. 648.

Li Shih-Chi entered Mongolia to the east, near Ta T'ung Fu, and came up with a Turkish force at a place near the modern Kuei Hua Ch'êng. The Chinese were victorious, Qadir Khan retreating with only 40,000 horsemen to T'ieh Shan, the Iron Hills, a place north of the main chain of the Yin Shan mountains. From this retreat the wily Turk sent an ambassador to China begging for peace, and offering, as proof of sincerity, to come down to Ch'ang An in person. The emperor sent an ambassador to conduct negotiations, at the same time ordering the army to continue the pursuit. Shih-Min knew the Turk too well to trust his promises.

Qadir Khan, in fact, had no intention of submitting. His object in opening negotiations was to delay the Chinese advance until the spring grass had come up, when the horses, fattened on the new pasture, would be strong enough to cross the Gobi Desert, as it was his plan to take refuge in the northern solitudes, far beyond the reach of Chinese armies.[1] Li Ching and Li Shih-Chi were not deceived by the Turkish bluff: realising that once the khan had got across the Gobi he would be beyond the reach of pursuit, they planned a

---

[1] Parker, in *A Thousand Years of the Tartars*, chap. II, places T'ieh Shan, the Iron Hills, in the Kerulen valley, which is north of the Gobi in outer Mongolia. The text of the *Tzŭ chih t'ung chien* does not confirm this view. The commentator Hu San-Shêng states that T'ieh Shan was 遠在陰山北, "far to the north of Yin Shan", but from the description of the operations of Li Ching and Li Shih-Chi it is plain that it was none the less south of the Gobi. It is expressly stated that Qadir Khan, 欲俟草青馬肥亡入漠北, "would wait till the fresh grass had fattened the horses to flee north of the desert". Farther on the T'ang generals decide to attack him before he can cross the Gobi: 若走度磧北追之難. The ultimate destruction of the Turkish army occurred at Chi K'ou, the "Mouth of the Desert", where it is directly stated that Li Shih-Chi cut off the Turkish retreat so that Qadir Khan, 不得度, "could not cross". Clearly T'ieh Shan was a place on the southern side of the Gobi, as the whole plan of Qadir was to put the desert between himself and the Chinese pursuit, and the T'ang strategy directed to achieving a victory before the Turk could do so. If T'ieh Shan is placed north of the Gobi, the subsequent operations of the T'ang generals are incomprehensible and meaningless.

surprise attack. Li Ching took twenty days' provisions and made a forced march on the Turkish camp.

The ambassador sent by the emperor to treat with Qadir had already reached the khan; who, delighted with the success of his diplomacy, believed himself safe from all pursuit until the spring, when his horses would be strong enough to make the desert crossing. The Chinese attack, aided by a fog, thus came as a complete surprise. Qadir himself had just time to escape on a fleet horse, but his horde was utterly defeated. Ten thousand Turks were slain, 100,000 persons of both sexes taken captive; while a still more terrible loss to the nomads was the capture of countless numbers of cattle, horses, and camels—the herds upon which the Turks depended for subsistence. Among those killed in the rout was Qadir's famous Chinese wife, the Sui princess, I Ch'êng, who had been the most persistent enemy of the T'ang dynasty.

The khan fled with a remnant of 10,000 men in a vain attempt to cross the desert, only to find that Li Shih-Chi, advancing by another route, had forestalled him and was lying in waiting at Chi K'ou, the "Mouth of the Desert". There the Turkish power was finally dispersed. While many surrendered, and others were taken prisoners, the khan once more escaped, with a handful of attendants, flying to the west in the hope of reaching the country of the T'u-yü-hun. But this hope was doomed to fail. Prince Jên Ch'êng (Li Tao-Tsung), detached by Li Shih-Chi in pursuit, relentlessly followed the fleeing khan till he was captured, and brought back to China a prisoner.

By this victorious campaign the whole of inner Mongolia up to the edge of the Gobi Desert was made subject to the emperor, and the Turkish tribes which inhabited it became the vassals of the Chinese throne. The emperor, at the suggestion of the submitted khans, assumed the title of "Heavenly Khan", a sort of Turkish equivalent of the Chinese imperial title. To keep the newly submitted hordes in order, two great garrisons were established, the one at Ling Chou, on the Kansu border, and the other in the east at Kuei Hua Ch'êng. The broken hordes were left under the administration of their own khans, now ruling as Chinese officers. Of these khans Tutar was the most notable, and Ashin Ssǔ-Ma, who had been Qadir's most faithful lieutenant.

Apart from Bilgä Khan, ruler of the Sarinda beyond the Gobi, there now remained no independent tribe along the whole length of the Chinese northern border. Shih-Min's "half-forward" policy had thus been crowned with complete success, though only four years had passed since the Turkish hordes had encamped upon the Wei, within ten miles of the Chinese capital. This achievement, due as much to the wise preparations of the emperor as to the skill of his generals, was hailed with universal joy and wonder in Ch'ang An.

Li Yüan, who now rarely emerged from his retirement, gave a banquet to his son the emperor and the entire court. The aged monarch observing the festivity, remarked with a sigh, "Even Han Kao Tsu (founder of the Han dynasty) could not avenge the insults of the Huns, now here is my son, who in a few months has overthrown the power of the Turks!" Li Yüan himself honoured the feast by playing the lute while Shih-Min danced, and the revelry did not cease till morning.

When Qadir Khan, a prisoner who had lost everything, was brought down to Ch'ang An, the emperor received him, seated on a high throne, surrounded by the full panoply of the imperial court. Shih-Min, having solemnly listed the fallen khan's crimes and follies and obtained a public confession of guilt from Qadir, spared his life, giving him a minor post in the imperial stables. But the wild spirit of the Tartar sickened in this captivity. He died within a few years, pining away in the alien atmosphere of civilisation.

CHAPTER VIII

THE COURT OF CH'ANG AN
A.D. 630–40

To the Chinese the name of Li Shih-Min is even more familiar as a wise and beneficent ruler than as the brilliant victor of the battlefield. In the reorganisation of the civil government the emperor accomplished as difficult and as necessary a task as the reunion of the long divided empire. The tyrannical rule of Yang Ti had left a legacy of brigandage and violence, while the short Sui dynasty had done little to restore the vanished prestige of the imperial court. Men had for too long been accustomed to frequent and violent revolutions to feel any great faith in the durability of the new dynasty. The tradition of unswerving loyalty to an established imperial family had to be recreated.

The government of the provinces was in the hands of military officers, often ex-brigands, who had sent in their submission when they realised that the T'ang dynasty was likely to triumph in the civil war. The laws were disregarded, indeed unknown, for Yang Ti's barbarous code had lapsed, although no new system had been formulated to replace it. Education, neglected by the Sui emperors, who had retrenched the provincial colleges existing under their predecessors, had received scant attention in the years of tumult that followed.

Fortunately for the Chinese empire, Shih-Min had the rare gift, equally valuable in the field and in the cabinet, of choosing men of talents, and using them according to their abilities. The glory of the military galaxy which included such men as Li Shih-Chi, Prince Chao and Prince Jên Ch'êng, Li Ching and Hou Chün-Chi, was matched, if not excelled, by the fame of Shih-Min's illustrious ministers. The four most prominent of these were Chang-Sun Wu-Chi, his brother-in-law, who was for more than thirty years the chief minister of the empire, Wei Chêng, Fang Hsüan-Ling and Hsiao Yü.

Of all Shih-Min's court perhaps the generals, Ch'in Shu-Pao and Yü-Ch'ih Ching-Tê, and the minister, Wei Chêng, have achieved the most enduring popular fame, for these three have been immortalised as the "Gate Gods" whose portraits painted upon the door of a house bar the way to evil spirits. The traditional manner in which these three gained their curious distinction is as follows.

When Shih-Min had succeeded to the throne he fell ill, and his sleep was disturbed by devils who battered upon the door of the imperial bedchamber. The empress, alarmed at these manifestations, summoned a council of the most eminent ministers and generals to devise measures against the demon intruders. Ch'in Shu-Pao and Yü-Ch'ih Ching-Tê offered to guard the doors arrayed in their full war panoply. That night the emperor slept in peace, for the evil spirits did not have the courage to try conclusions with the famous warriors. After several nights, Shih-Min, concerned for the health of the two generals, who had not been able to sleep, suggested that their portraits be painted on two tablets of peach wood and the pictures hung up on the door. This device worked well. The devils, who in China, at least, are notoriously stupid, mistook the portraits for the living men and kept their distance.

But after some days the malignant spirits transferred their attacks to the back door, which had been left unguarded. Upon the advice of the empress the portrait of the minister, Wei Chêng, was placed upon that door, and the demons thereafter did not dare to make any further attempt upon the emperor's peace.

The custom soon spread throughout the nation until to-day no representations of deities are so popular and ubiquitous as the portraits of Shih-Min's two generals and the minister, Wei Chêng.

Wei Chêng, formerly an adviser of Li Mi, and later of the Crown Prince Chien-Ch'eng, was the emperor's most valued counsellor. The relationship between Wei Chêng and Shih-Min was in many ways peculiar. The minister, as one of the most active partisans of the crown prince, had been an avowed and dangerous enemy of Shih-Min before his accession. Pardoned after the morning of the Hsüan Wu gate, Wei Chêng became the most influential member of the new emperor's council. Nevertheless, between Shih-Min and his minister there was a curious hostility woven into their new friendship. Wei Chêng's value as a counsellor, and apparently also his charm for Shih-Min, was his fearless, devastating, frankness. He not only never hesitated to oppose any project of which he did not approve, but he criticised the emperor's conduct in the most outspoken terms.

The annals of the time record many such conversations. One of the most famous occurred at a court banquet in A.D. 637 when Shih-Min had been ten years on the throne. Shih-Min, turning to Wei Chêng, asked him whether in his opinion the government was better conducted than it had been when he first took over the administration. "In matters of magnificence and display, we have progressed, but if popular satisfaction is the test, declined," replied the minister, adding, "In the beginning, although they still suffered from the wars, the people were delighted by the virtue and bravery of Your Majesty. Now, although in the midst of peace, the monotony of events has made them bored and depressed. Your Majesty yourself has changed. In the beginning you feared that we would not dare to tell you of your mistakes, later you received our admonitions with pleasure; now one must say you accept them with difficulty".

The emperor replied, "You must prove all this to us with facts".

"In the first year of your reign", replied Wei Chêng, "you rewarded, with the gift of a country estate, an officer who pointed out to Your Majesty that you were about to punish with death a criminal who had not merited such a penalty. When people said that this recompense was excessive, you replied that it was intended to encourage the ministers to point out your mistakes. Is not that fearing lest we should not admonish you? Later you pardoned, for reasons which a minister advanced, a false accuser who had been condemned to die. Is not that accepting advice with pleasure? Recently, when you wished to rebuild the Lo Yang palace, which Your Majesty yourself burned down twelve years ago, a member of your court thought it his duty to oppose you. Your Majesty became enraged, and although, on my entreaty, you refrained from penalising this man, one must say that his pardon was dragged out of you! It is a proof that you no longer take any pleasure in hearing contrary opinions."

The emperor, greatly struck by these incontestable proofs of Wei Chêng's contention, remarked to the court, "How dangerous it is not to know oneself, I would never have known that my character was changing, unless Wei Chêng had proved it to me by these personal instances".

Shih-Min esteemed Wei Chêng above every member of the court, and relished his uncourtly candour.

Fang Hsüan-Ling and Hsiao Yü were, after Wei Chêng, the most eminent men at the T'ang court. Fang, expert and prudent financier, an indefatigable worker conversant with every detail of the government business, was the perfect administrator, the brain which guided the working of the government machine, the architect of victories. Throughout the reign of Shih-Min, Fang Hsüan-Ling's careful and meticulous attention to government affairs fostered the finances of the empire, making possible victory abroad and reforms at home. Hsiao Yü, younger brother of Yang Ti's empress, had first risen to fame as the counsellor who had devised the stratagem by which the Turkish siege of Yen Mên was raised. Subsequently submitting to the T'ang dynasty after the fall of Ch'ang An, he became an influential counsellor on Shih-Min's staff. When the prince ascended the throne

Hsiao Yü became one of the chief ministers of state. Although always rather timid and favouring the cautious plan, Hsiao Yü was upright, honest and loyal, conspicuous in the T'ang court as the principal champion of the Buddhist faith, in which he was an ardent believer.

Besides the four chief ministers, there were many notable men, some of whom in later years rose to the highest posts. Ma Chou, who originated the plan for the reform of the provincial administration, first came to Ch'ang An as the guest of a relation who was a military officer. This officer, having in the course of his duties to submit a report to the emperor, and being rather unskilful with the pen, sought the assistance of his learned guest. Ma Chou produced such a scholarly and brilliant piece of work that Shih-Min's attention was at once attracted. He enquired who the author was, and when the officer frankly avowed the source of his assistance, Ma Chou was summoned to court and at once given a responsible post.

Kao Shih-Lien, an uncle of the Empress Chang-Sun, and Tu Ju-Hui were old and trusted friends, who had served Shih-Min as prince, and in whom he often confided. Ch'u Sui-Liang, President of the Board of History, was one of the most brilliant men at court during the later years of the reign, playing an increasingly influential part in the state business. Indeed, after the death of Wei Chêng, Ch'u Sui-Liang, who had something of the older statesman's fearless candour, took his place in the inner ring of the emperor's council.

One day, in the year A.D. 642, Shih-Min, curious to know how he would be represented to posterity, said to Ch'u Sui-Liang, "I should like to see what you have recorded concerning me in the history".

"The historians of our department", replied the minister, "record the actions of Your Majesty whether good or bad, your words, whether praiseworthy or reprehensible, and everything meritorious or unworthy which happens in the government. They are exact in these matters, as it is essential to history, which serves as an example to princes and ministers, often preventing them from committing faults. But I have never heard that any emperor hitherto has read what was written concerning him."

"Why!" said Shih-Min, "would you, Ch'u Sui-Liang, write down something discreditable about me?"

"Being entrusted with a position of the importance of President of the Board of History, how could I avoid doing so?" replied the minister. "And even if Ch'u Sui-Liang were unwilling", added one of his subordinates, "we would not hesitate to record the facts."

"There are three things which should be said of me", remarked the emperor. "First, that I have attempted to imitate the wise conduct of the ancient emperors.[1] Secondly, that with the assistance of the able men whom I have chosen, I have restored the laws, which had perished, and revived the power of the government. Thirdly, that rejecting unworthy ministers and incompetent officers, I have never listened to the flattery of those intriguers who are the principal cause of the bad conduct and misgovernment of princes. If I can continue in this way to my death, what evil can be recorded against me?"

"And even the words which Your Majesty has just spoken will infallibly be recorded in the annals of the empire," said Ch'u Sui-Liang.

Two instances among the many anecdotes recording the emperor's justice and moderation will serve to illustrate Shih-Min's attitude to the prevailing vices of an eastern court, flattery and corruption. One of the ministers presented a memorial urging the emperor to remove the flatterers from the ministry, but without naming any person as guilty of this failing. Shih-Min called the author of this petition to his presence, and asked him whom he had intended to accuse.

[1] Yao, Shun, and Yü, the sage emperors of the Chinese Golden Age, about 2300 B.C.

"If Your Majesty wishes to know who are the flatterers in the council," replied the memorialist, "all Your Majesty has to do is to propose in the next council some foolish course of action. Those who support it will be revealed as the flatterers."

"I admit", replied the emperor, "that this plan would succeed; but if a sovereign uses such deceits to his ministers, how can he expect them to be honest and candid with him? The emperor is the spring, and the officers of the state are the waters which flow from it. If the source is pure, the current will be the same. Besides I do not like to use these oblique methods. I prefer to ignore the evil if it exists, rather than discover it by methods which would destroy the frank relationship between sovereign and minister."

Shortly after his accession Shih-Min was shown proof that a member of the empress's family had taken as a bribe several bolts of valuable silk. The crime was considered serious in an officer of this high rank. Shih-Min, instead of applying the law, took a large quantity of silk from the imperial storehouses and sent it to the offending general. When the court, surprised at this action, asked why the general should be rewarded rather than punished, the emperor said, "If he has the feelings of an honest man, the silk which I have sent him will cause him more pain than the penalties established by the law. But if he is not ashamed, I regard him as a brute who would be unaffected by any punishment".

The kindness and tact with which Shih-Min, an absolute monarch, treated his court was instanced in matters less serious. At the New Year festival in A.D. 633 the music and dance called P'o Chên ("Breaking the battle-line") was performed, commemorating the victories which Shih-Min had won over the pretenders before his accession to the throne. Hsiao Yü suggested that another act showing the rival emperors—Tou Chien-Tê, Wang Shih-Ch'ung and others—led captive to execution should be included to complete the series. The P'o Chên dance was first performed in the sixth month of A.D. 632 at a feast at the Ch'ing Shan Kung, the old home of the Li family. The music and dance were composed by a musician named Lü Ts'ai. It was performed by 128 boy dancers dressed in silver armour with lances, who performed evolutions singing the refrain "Ch'in Wang P'o Chên" ("Prince Ch'in breaks the battle line"). Traditionally this refrain was originally a marching song of the T'ang army after the Shansi campaign against Liu Wu-Chou, when the soldiers picked it up from the people of the province who lined the road along which the army marched, singing and dancing to express their joy and gratitude at their deliverance.

Shih-Min rejected Hsiao Yü's suggestion on the ground that many of his ministers and officers, such as Yü-Ch'ih Ching-Tê and Wei Chêng, had at one time served his enemies, and could not be expected to enjoy a drama representing the humiliation of their former masters. It is, in fact, stated that Wei Chêng invariably cast his eyes to the ground when the P'o Chên dance was performed, since it reminded him of the period when he had been the enemy of Shih-Min.

The emperor was very little influenced by the superstitions which were current in his age. Even the time-honoured belief in lucky days met with scant consideration if it conflicted with the interests of the state. When the emperor's son, the Crown Prince Li Ch'êng-Ch'ien, had attained the age of fourteen, in the year A.D. 631, the court suggested that the ritual ceremonies connected with "taking the cap" of virility should be performed in the second month of that year. Shih-Min, however, reflecting that this month, being the planting season, was one in which the people were most occupied on the land, the costly and elaborate ceremonies had better be postponed until midsummer, when there was less pressure of business.

The court astrologers remonstrated, pointing out that the second month was the most lucky in the year, whereas the midsummer season was ill-omened. The emperor refused to listen to these reasons remarking that, "Fortune and calamity are not dependent upon lucky days but upon the good or bad conduct of men themselves".

The ceremonies were in fact postponed until midsummer. It is curious to note that in this matter the astrologers might have considered themselves justified by the event, for the crown prince, whose entry into the status of manhood was thus celebrated in an unlucky month, was destined to an unhappy life, and an early, unhonoured death.

The restatement and reform of the law was the first important administrative task undertaken by the emperor when peace with the Turks left time for internal affairs to be considered. The only code in existence, that of the Sui dynasty, had been draconian in the severity of its penalties, and inapplicable on account of its many unreasonable provisions. Since the general revolt against the Emperor Yang Ti, largely due to the severity of that monarch's legislation, the laws had been disregarded. Magistrates judged cases on their merits, and punished crimes according to their own unguided decisions. In A.D. 631 the emperor gave orders for the old law to be recodified, and reduced to five hundred articles. The penal offences were classified under twenty heads, the Sui death penalty being abolished in ninety-two cases, and the penalty of exile in seventy-one. That it was possible to make these sweeping changes is sufficient indication of the character of Yang Ti's code.

While the T'ang code reduced other criminal penalties proportionately; custom, which in China had always largely replaced civil law, was regularised, and given legal force. The most convincing proof of the justice and tranquillity which the authority of Shih-Min established in China came to light after his death, when his son and successor was informed by the President of the Board of Punishments, on the occasion of a proposed amnesty to inaugurate the new reign, that in all the empire there were only fifty men serving penal sentences, and only two under condemnation of death.

The remodelling of the provincial administration was the most important, and the most enduring of Shih-Min's administrative reforms. During the long period of division the civil service, first adopted by the Han dynasty, had disappeared. Powerful families had usurped feudal authority over wide areas, while elsewhere the government of the country districts was in the hands of military officers or officials appointed direct by the favour of some high personage. Ma Chou, who then held the post of censor, called the emperor's attention to these irregularities, insisting that the foundation of all internal peace and security depended on the conduct of the district officials. In accordance with his recommendations the emperor personally supervised these appointments, making a careful choice of upright and scholarly men, and gradually eliminating the military element.

This reform was the beginning of a civil service exercising the government authority in the provinces, later known to the west as the Mandarin system. Though it has received abuse in the closing years of the last dynasty as antiquated and inflexible, it was for more than a thousand years an instrument of government far in advance of anything found outside China. It served to spread throughout the vast empire and its dependencies the culture and customs of the Chinese court, and so became the mainstay of civilisation in the east of Asia.

The educational policy of the emperor was closely allied to this reformed civil service. Education in the seventh century was regarded principally as a training for state service. For this reason the colleges which Shih-Min founded, or re-established, concentrated on the Chinese classics, particularly the works of Confucius and his school; for the writings of those philosophers are mainly concerned to expound a moral and ethical code for the guidance of kings, ministers and officials. Shih-Min, who had always been noted for his interest in scholarship, paid much personal attention to the progress of these institutions, and left as a monument of his care, the stone tablets, now preserved in the Pei Lin at Ch'ang An, on which the four books of the classics are engraved from his own handwriting.

The T'ang dynasty is usually associated with poetry and a great cultural revival, but this splendid outburst of creative genius really belongs to the generation that followed the reign of Shih-Min. In the early years, when the dynasty had but just restored peace to the exhausted state, literature and art had not yet had time to flower. Shih-Min, opposed to the frivolity and licentiousness of Yang Ti's court, set his face against similar tendencies, and conferred his patronage upon the austere classical scholarship of the Confucian School. Art, however, made progress in his reign, and there are perhaps no finer examples of Chinese sculpture than the famous bas-reliefs of horses which decorated the emperor's tomb. But the great age of T'ang poetry had not yet dawned. Shih-Min's importance in the cultural history of China is therefore indirect. He made possible the political conditions of security and peace which fostered the cultural glories of a later generation.

During these years, which saw the institution of such far-reaching reforms, the court was not exempt from domestic sorrows and bereavements. Li Yüan, the emperor's father, died in A.D. 635 at the age of seventy-one, living long enough to see the flowering of his son's magnificent achievements. During the later years of his abdication, the "Great Superior Emperor", as he was entitled, took no part in the life of the court, spending his time at his own palace and hunting-grounds. Shih-Min carefully avoided any action which might give offence to the retired monarch, although his first act on ascending the throne implied a certain censure of his father's morals. Before attending to other business Shih-Min removed from the palace 3000 women, enrolled among the servants and concubines of Li Yüan, whom he sent back to their families.

In the year A.D. 636 there occurred a death which was far

more distressing to the court and a more serious loss to the empire than that of Li Yüan. In that year died the Empress Chang-Sun, Shih-Min's consort, who by her exceptional virtues has won the enthusiastic praises of later generations, and has been held up as a model, all too rarely copied, to the ladies of similar rank in the dynasties that followed. The empress, although possessed of a shrewd and penetrating judgment, consistently refused to play any part in politics, or interfere with the business of the state. She was wont to declare that the history of earlier dynasties contained too many melancholy examples of ambitious empresses whose activities were not only harmful to the state, but brought ruin upon their own families. Nevertheless she had a great influence over Shih-Min, all the more potent since it was so rarely exercised.

On one occasion the emperor left the council in a state of great irritation with Wei Chêng, who had consistently and vigorously opposed him in the discussion. As he entered the apartments of the empress, she heard him exclaim, "I will never be the master as long as that wretch, whom I have raised from the dust, is alive!"

"Who is the wretch, then?" inquired the empress.

"Wei Chêng, who contradicts me in front of the whole court."

The empress made no further comment, but withdrew to her own room, presently reappearing dressed in her most magnificent robes of ceremony. Shih-Min, surprised, asked the reason for this elaborate toilet. The empress replied, "I have often heard it said that an enlightened emperor will find a faithful minister, upright and sincere. Your Majesty has just admitted that Wei Chêng is such an one. Is this not a proof that you are an enlightened emperor? I have robed myself in honour of the fact, to congratulate you".

The esteem in which the empress held Wei Chêng weighed greatly with Shih-Min, who never subsequently spoke of dismissing the outspoken minister.

Shih-Min was inconsolable at her death, and indeed her loss was a lasting misfortune to the dynasty, for it removed the one influence capable of controlling the eccentric nature of her eldest son, the crown prince. The tragic story of Prince Ch'êng-Ch'ien dates from his mother's untimely death.

Three years later, in A.D. 639, the court was shocked by a conspiracy against the emperor's life. This was the work of a Turk named Qachashar, a half-brother of Tutar Khan. Qachashar planned to slay the emperor to avenge the destruction of the Turkish power, and pave the way for a revolt. Like many of the submitted Turkish khans, he was employed in the imperial stables, and this fact enabled him to enlist some forty confederates of his own race. With this handful of desperate men he made a night attack on the emperor's palace, hoping to overpower the guards and break in.

But his plans were clumsy. The guards were too numerous and reliable to be overcome by so small a band. After a desperate fight Qachashar, seeing that he had failed, made his way to the imperial stables, where, using his authority, he took one of the fastest horses and attempted to escape to Mongolia. Being closely pursued, he was captured, brought back to Ch'ang An, and executed in the market-place. In consequence of this attempt all the submitted Turks were compelled to leave China and settle in inner Mongolia.

While the interior of the empire enjoyed peace and a better government than ever before under the enlightened rule of Shih-Min and his chosen ministers, the distant frontiers were frequently agitated by wars with the less civilised races of Central Asia. The Turkish question had been settled by the defeat of Qadir Khan, but the western frontier still presented problems. The vast region now called Chinese Turkestan or Sin Kiang, was then divided among a number of kingdoms, small in comparison with the boundless size of the whole country, but in fact covering a wide extent of territory. These states had acquired something of the culture of India and Persia, indeed they were all Buddhist in religion, for the

Mohammedan conquerors who later dominated this country had not yet appeared. Under the Han dynasty all Central Asia up to the Caspian and Aral seas had been brought under Chinese rule, but in the subsequent period of partition these conquests had all been lost.

Farther south, in the high mountain land now called Koko-Nor or Ch'ing Hai, was the country of the T'u-yü-hun, nomad Tartars who neither cultivated the soil nor built cities, as did the Central Asiatics. Beyond the T'u-yü-hun were the tribes of Tibet, recently organised and consolidated into a rising kingdom.

The restless conduct of the T'u-yü-hun first provoked the might of the Chinese empire. Unable to learn the lesson of Qadir Khan's defeat, the T'u-yü-hun resorted to the time-honoured Tartar custom of raiding the border districts. Fu-yun Khan, their ruler, was a very old man, who is first mentioned as early as A.D. 597, and was now long past his seventieth year. As his powers diminished, the authority over the horde passed into the hands of an ambitious minister, who adopted a definitely anti-Chinese attitude.

When, not content with raids and forays, he seized a Chinese ambassador who was travelling to Central Asia, the emperor decided that it was time to take firm action against the T'u-yü-hun. Frontier troops and vassal Tartars were first employed, but the T'u-yü-hun, undismayed by these forces, entered China in force and severely ravaged the district of Liang Chou in Kansu province. On hearing this news the emperor ordered a general mobilisation of the T'ang regular army and decided to undertake the permanent conquest of the T'u-yü-hun.

The supreme command of the expedition was confided to Li Ching, with Hou Chün-Chi, Li Ta-Liang and Prince Jên Ch'êng (Li Tao-Tsung) as subordinates. Various tribes of vassal Turks were also employed. The army entered the land of the T'u-yü-hun at K'u Shan near Hsi Ning Fu in Kansu, where Prince Jên Ch'êng inflicted a severe defeat upon the

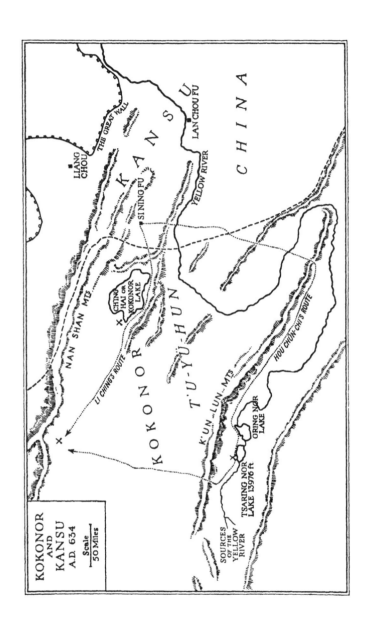

KOKONOR
AND
KANSU
A.D. 634

Scale
50 Miles

THE GREAT WALL

LIANG CHOU

KANSU

LANCHOU FU

SINING FU

YELLOW RIVER

CHINA

CHING HAI OR KOKONOR LAKE

NAN SHAN MTS.

LI CHING'S ROUTE

KOKONOR

T'U-YÜ-HUN

K'UN-LUN MTS.

HOU CHÜN-CHI'S ROUTE

ORING NOR LAKE

TSARING NOR LAKE 13976 ft

SOURCES OF THE YELLOW RIVER

Tartars. Fu-yun Khan then decided to avoid further battles, and in order to hinder the Chinese pursuit, retreated, firing the grass behind him to destroy the pasture.

Li Ching was indeed greatly embarrassed by this device. Many of his generals urged him to abandon the advance. Hou Chün-Chi, however, strongly upheld the opposite view, and his opinion was finally adopted by the commander-in-chief. In order to economise the scanty pasture available, the Chinese army was divided into two corps, Li Ching and Li Ta-Liang moving north, while Hou Chün-Chi and Prince Jên Ch'êng took a southern route through the high mountains. Li Ching followed the Tartars till he defeated them in the heart of the Koko-Nor mountains, capturing huge herds of beasts, a more important gain than the slaughter of men. He then pursued the flying T'u-yü-hun to the north-west, inflicting further defeats upon them.

Meanwhile Hou Chün-Chi with the southern army had struck into the depths of the K'un Lun mountains, one of the highest ranges in the world, advancing by a route which the T'u-yü-hun naturally supposed to be entirely impassable. The Chinese army made one of the most remarkable marches in history, which can be compared without impropriety to Hannibal's crossing of the Alps. For over seven hundred miles they toiled through an uninhabited wilderness, so high that even in the middle of summer the ground was covered with snow, upon which the army depended for water.

"The men sucked ice and the horses fed on snow."

At length they came upon the T'u-yü-hun encamped on the shores of a lake called Wu Hai (either Tsaring Nor or Oring Nor) near the sources of the Yellow river. The Tartars, utterly surprised, for they had never dreamed that an enemy army could pass the mountains to the south, were totally defeated. Hou Chün-Chi, following up this victory, drove the Tartars north-west till they were met by Li Ta-Liang, whom Li Ching had sent in advance to the edge of the

Taklamakan desert. Cut off from further retreat, the remnants
of the T'u-yü-hun were annihilated in the battle that followed.
Fu-yun Khan himself fled almost alone into the desert where
he was shortly after murdered by his attendants.

His death ended the war. Already another khan, repudiat-
ing the rule of Fu-yun, had slain the minister responsible for
the anti-Chinese policy of the late khan, and had sent envoys
begging for peace. This was granted on condition that the
suzerainty of Ch'ang An was acknowledged, and henceforward nothing more is heard of hostility from the T'u-yü-hun.

The fame of this remarkable campaign spread all over
Central Asia. The evidence that the most formidable natural
barriers could not arrest the advance of a T'ang army
produced a deep impression on the peoples of the western
kingdoms. The western Turks sent an embassy bearing
tribute, or rather gifts, which Chinese court etiquette described as tribute. Northern tribes, living far beyond the
confines of outer Mongolia, sent envoys to pay their respects
to the emperor in Ch'ang An. The Tibetans demanded a
princess for their king.

The tone of their embassy was, however, resented at
Ch'ang An, where it was regarded as insolent and even
threatening. The emperor therefore refused to accord them
a princess. The Tibetans, irritated at this rebuff, promptly
invaded the Chinese province bordering their country, now
western Szechuan, and laid siege to the fortress of Sung
P'an. They did not succeed in taking this place before a T'ang
army commanded by the redoubtable Hou Chün-Chi arrived
to its relief. The Tibetans were completely defeated by this
army under the walls of Sung P'an, and forced to fly back to
their mountains.

After thus asserting the superiority of the T'ang arms, Shih-
Min, when the Tibetans sent a more humble and courteous
envoy, permitted them to receive a princess. This lady, it
appears, exercised a civilising influence in the newly formed
kingdom; among other reforms she induced the mountaineers

to give up the custom of painting their faces in various colours, a practice which the Chinese princess found revolting.

The defeat of the T'u-yü-hun and Tibetans did not end the wars in the west. Beyond the extreme north-western border of Kansu province the road to the west, the silk road, by which the ancient caravans carried their precious freight across Asia to Persia and Rome, passes through the cities of Hami and Turfan. Hami had surrendered to the T'ang empire in A.D. 630, and was held as a frontier post. But Turfan was then the capital of the kingdom of Karahodjo,[1] one of the wealthiest and most powerful of the Central Asiatic states. When the Chinese empire reached Hami, the king of Karahodjo decided that it would be safer to offer tribute to the new power in the east, and avert any danger of warfare, for which his people were unprepared. On this basis good relations with China had been maintained for nearly ten years.

In the year A.D. 639 the king of Karahodjo, finding this arrangement inconvenient, decided to discontinue the tribute, and furthermore gave shelter to Chinese criminals and political fugitives who had fled to his kingdom, when the fall of Qadir Khan denied them refuge in Mongolia. When the king was called upon to explain this changed attitude he sent back the reply, "The eagles fly to heaven, the pheasants hide in the brushwood; cats roam through the house, the mice seek safety in holes. If every creature follows its instinct, all can find a way to safeguard their lives".

The emperor, though displeased at what he considered an impertinent answer, still gave the king time to repent. But the Karahodjan, mistaking leniency for weakness, and trusting to the desert which divided his kingdom from China, paid no attention to the envoys from Ch'ang An, and went so far as to menace the Sarinda Turks with war.

---

[1] Parker, *A Thousand Years of the Tartars*, so transliterates the name which the Chinese historians give as Kao Ch'ang. For the question as to who were the Karahodjans and their ethnographic affinities see note on p. 200, chap. x.

The Sarinda, who were ready to hold themselves as vassals of China when that status was convenient, appealed to Ch'ang An for help. Shih-Min, losing patience with Karahodjo, sent Hou Chün-Chi, who had made a great name for himself on the western frontier, to take command of the army and reduce the contumacious king to obedience.

By the middle of summer, A.D. 640, the slow march of the Chinese army reached the frontiers of Karahodjo. At the news that a Chinese army had really crossed the desert where "the winter wind cuts like a knife and the summer heat sears like hot iron" the king of Karahodjo was taken ill with apprehension, and died. His son, after attempting a half-hearted defence, fell back to his capital, which was then besieged by Hou Chün-Chi. The Karahodjans had appealed to the western Turks for assistance, but these hordes, hearing of the advance of the Chinese army, were too much afraid of the name of Hou Chün-Chi to intervene. The besieged city, defrauded of this last hope, surrendered.

The remains of this city of Khocho or Kao Ch'ang (as the Chinese called it) are thus described by A. von Le Coq of the German Turfan archaeological expedition.

The city is an enormous square, of about 256 acres in extent. The massive wall is almost 22 yards high, made of stamped earth. Numerous towers—there are still seventy existing—strengthen the wall, which diminishes in solidity towards the top. The buildings are too much destroyed to allow the course of the streets to be plainly traced, but two wide streets one from north to south and the other from east to west seem to have crossed each other at the centre of the town. The ground plan therefore doubtless follows the pattern of the Roman castra.[1]

[1] A. von Le Coq, *Buried Treasures of Chinese Turkestan*, London: George Allen & Unwin, 1928. Von Le Coq is of the opinion that no Chinese influence is present in the architecture of Khocho. But one must observe that from the facts presented in the above description of the ruins it would seem possible to entertain a contrary opinion. The method of constructing walls "of stamped earth" faced with brick or masonry is precisely the method invariably employed in the city walls of northern China, which are usually far more solid than the walls of cities in Europe. Moreover the rectilinear ground plan with

The whole kingdom of Karahodjo, which the imperial commissioners described as having an area of 133,000 square miles, containing twenty-two cities with a population of 8000 families,[1] was garrisoned by Chinese troops, and annexed as an integral province of the empire. This decision was taken against the advice of Wei Chêng, who favoured setting up a new king as vassal ruler of a subject state. His objection to outright annexation was based on the two counts that China did not get an adequate return for the trouble of administering this distant province, while if it should revolt, the empire might be involved in a difficult and expensive war for the sake of prestige. Shih-Min did not deny the weight of these arguments, but nevertheless decided to retain the country as a province. He was justified by the event, for Karahodjo never gave any trouble to the Chinese empire.

Although the Sarinda Turks had appealed for Chinese help when threatened by Karahodjo, they were quite ready to attack the empire the moment they believed the opportunity had come. The western wars induced them to believe that the defences of inner Mongolia had been depleted. The

two straight streets bisecting each other at the centre of the town is not, as von Le Coq assumes, necessarily following "the pattern of the Roman castra". This ground plan is found in every city, great or small, in the northern provinces of China. It differs from the Roman plan only in one respect, the intersection of the two streets is defended by a massive drum Tower. Nor is there any reason to suppose that this plan was derived from contact with the West. In China the rectilinear ground plan is very ancient, going back to the Feudal Age in the seventh century B.C. The late Professor Haverfield was of the opinion that the Chinese town plan owed nothing to Roman influence, but had originated separately at a date anterior to the rise of the Roman Republic. See F. Haverfield, *Ancient Town Planning*, Oxford: Clarendon Press, 1913. Appendix: "Chinese Town Planning". Seeing that Khocho was conquered by the T'ang army under Hou Chün-Chi in A.D. 640, and remained a Chinese possession for more than a century, it is surely more probable that the city which von Le Coq describes obtained its rectilinear plan and massive walls from the Chinese conquerors rather than from some faint tradition of the Roman castra. For the Romans never constructed a castra within 3000 miles of the Turfan oasis.

[1] Probably tax-paying families. If the usual multiple of five is applied to this total, the tax-paying population would number 40,000 persons; the total population was probably more than double that number.

next year, A.D. 641, profiting by the emperor's absence on a pilgrimage to make sacrifice at the sacred mountain of T'ai Shan in Shantung, the Sarinda crossed the Gobi, and swept down into inner Mongolia, the submitted hordes fleeing before them inside the Great Wall.

The defence of these borders was entrusted to Li Shih-Chi, "my Great Wall", as the emperor used to call him. Collecting the garrison troops, and assisted by another border force under Li Ta-Liang, the T'ang general met the Sarinda north of Kuei Hua Ch'êng, where he defeated them in a battle which cost the nomads the most terrible loss they had yet sustained. No less than 50,000 were made prisoners, while the remainder, flying back across the Gobi, encountered a snow blizzard in which nine-tenths of the horde perished. For many years the Sarinda were crippled by this disaster, which shattered the power of the northern khan.

These wars and conquests spread the fame and fear of the T'ang empire throughout Asia. Embassies from Persia, the states of India, and the most distant tribes of Siberia, flocked to Ch'ang An to pay respects and lay gifts before the Son of Heaven. Never since the Han dynasty had the Chinese empire attained such power and prestige. It was in these years that wandering Syrian missionaries brought Nestorian Christianity to China, where, as the famous tablet now at Ch'ang An records, they were permitted to found a Church which received the protection of the enlightened emperor.

According to Mohammedan tradition it was at this time that Arab traders brought the faith of Islam to Canton. They state that when Mohammed was about to send out his armies to convert the world at the point of the sword, he addressed a letter, urging acceptance of his creed, to the three greatest emperors in the world—Heraclius of Rome, Chosroes of Persia and Shih-Min who reigned in China. Heraclius ignored the fanatic's letter. Chosroes tore it across in a rage, whereupon the Arab envoy exclaimed, "So shall God rend your kingdom from you". Only the sage emperor of China gave careful and tolerant attention to the Prophet's words, permitting the Arabs to build the first mosque in China at Canton.

At this moment, when Li Shih-Min was the acknowledged master of the eastern world, he had to sustain, in the heart of his family, a series of tragedies which cast a shadow over his life and dimmed the glory of the reign.

CHAPTER IX

THE TRAGEDY OF CROWN PRINCE
CH'ÊNG-CH'IEN, A.D. 643

Up to the year A.D. 640 the life and reign of Shih-Min had been unbrokenly glorious and successful. He had never met with failure in any enterprise of importance, and his domestic life, apart from the fatal quarrel with his brothers, had been serene and fortunate. It is true that he had already, four years previously, had to bear the sad loss of the Empress Chang-Sun, a lady of virtues as rare and outstanding as those of the emperor himself. Seldom indeed has a monarch of the genius and wisdom of Shih-Min been blessed with a consort of an equally admirable character.

It might have been hoped that the children which this remarkable lady bore to Shih-Min would inherit some of the virtues and strength of character which so signally distinguished their parents. But it was here that the jealous gods reserved for the great emperor the nemesis which lies in wait for the over-fortunate. Li Ch'êng-Ch'ien, the eldest son of the Empress Chang-Sun, had been appointed crown prince when Shih-Min succeeded to the throne in A.D. 626. Although the boy was then eight years old, and his father only twenty-six, Ch'êng-Ch'ien was not the eldest of Shih-Min's sons. Li T'ai Prince Wei was a year older, but T'ai was the son of a concubine, and therefore had no claim to the throne while any son or grandson of the empress was living.

Shih-Min had several other sons, some by the empress, and others by concubines, but of all these only two played a prominent part in the politics of the time, Li Chih Prince Chin, second son of the Empress Chang-Sun, and Li Yu Prince Chi, son of the concubine Queen Yin.[1]

---

[1] The genealogical table on p. xi should be consulted.

It was in the year A.D. 640, when he was twenty-two years old, that the conduct and character of the Crown Prince Ch'êng-Ch'ien first began to attract the unfavourable notice of the court, presaging a repetition of the terrible quarrel between Shih-Min and his brothers, which had convulsed the capital fourteen years earlier. The character of Prince Ch'êng-Ch'ien, as described by the historians of the time, is especially interesting to an age which has made psychology a science. The old historians, steeped in the traditional Confucian morality, naturally regarded Ch'êng-Ch'ien as the perfect type of what a Confucian prince should not be. They were not interested in psychology, nor did they understand the influence of heredity.

When the actions and words of this seventh-century prince are regarded in the light of modern psychological knowledge, it becomes perfectly plain that Ch'êng-Ch'ien was an unbalanced neurotic with tastes and inclinations derived from his far-off Tartar ancestry. He was also lame in one leg, and as it is nowhere stated that this was due to an accident, it was more probably an inherited defect. Ch'êng-Ch'ien's curiously atavistic tastes took the form of a passionate admiration for everything Turkish: he craved the simplicity of Tartar life, and the crude barbarity of nomad social customs. As was inevitable with these inclinations, he took a violent dislike to the tutors and courtiers who endeavoured to perfect him in the polite civilisation of China.

Already, in A.D. 640, his delight in wild, barbarian music, and his persistent neglect of the ministers of the court brought him rebukes from the emperor and from his tutors. The next year, as these improper habits grew upon him, and he began to keep Turks among his retainers, the chief tutor admonished the prince so strongly that the unbalanced youth attempted to have this zealous official assassinated. The prince sent two desperadoes in secret to his tutor's house, but the ruffians, having found the old man peacefully asleep, were unable to nerve themselves to commit such a crime, and withdrew, leaving him unharmed. This murderous plot was therefore undiscovered at the time.

While the crown prince was becoming the object of unfavourable court gossip on account of his extravagant behaviour, his elder half-brother, T'ai Prince Wei, of an utterly different character, gained the esteem and affection of all by his accomplishments and personal charm. The fatal antithesis of Chien-Ch'êng and Shih-Min seemed to be repeated, as if the gods, with cruel irony, were determined to revenge the morning at the Hsüan Wu gate by enacting a similar tragedy with Shih-Min's own sons as participants.

T'ai was talented and fond of literature, indifferent to the lusts of the flesh, courteous and respectful to the scholars who frequented his palace and eagerly sought his friendship. But the prince had one fault, which in one of his rank could not be considered trivial. He was ambitious. His position as a concubine's son, though the eldest of all the emperor's children, was galling, especially when he observed the improper conduct of his half-brother, the crown prince, who would one day inherit the throne. T'ai knew that he was the more suitable character to be crown prince, nor could he banish the hope that the follies of Ch'êng-Ch'ien would one day lead to his degradation and the elevation of himself, T'ai, to that coveted dignity.

T'ai knew himself to be the emperor's favourite son. Shih-Min was much attracted to this talented youth, whose interests and tastes coincided with his own. He could not help recognising that T'ai had inherited his own character and brains, while Ch'êng-Ch'ien seemed to have more of the evil disposition of the dead Li Yüan-Chi, Shih-Min's younger brother. T'ai knew that his father had these thoughts. The example of the fatal morning at the Hsüan Wu gate was always before the prince to suggest the possibility that crown princes do not always live to wear the crown, while brothers not in the direct succession sometimes find a way to win a position which was not theirs by birth.

Ch'ien Lung, the greatest emperor of the Manchu dynasty, who most nearly of all later emperors approaches the greatness of Shih-Min by his conquests in war and sage administration in time of peace, wrote concerning the domestic tragedies of his T'ang predecessor, "The quarrel between the sons of T'ai Tsung (Shih-Min) was the consequence of the quarrel between T'ai Tsung and his own brothers". A profoundly true comment. The example of violence which Shih-Min had given when he slew his brothers, inevitable though it may have been, dominated the minds of his own sons, and beckoned them on to similar extremities.

The ambitions of T'ai Prince Wei were first brought to the notice of the emperor by Ch'u Sui-Liang, President of the Board of History, who in the year A.D. 642 presented a memorial on the behaviour of this prince. Ch'u Sui-Liang asserted that while many officials were giving expression to the opinion that Prince Wei should be made crown prince and Ch'êng-Ch'ien degraded, T'ai himself did not treat his half-brother with the courtesy properly accorded to the crown prince, behaviour which naturally aggravated the jealousy of Ch'êng-Ch'ien.

The emperor, who fully appreciated the arguments put forward by Ch'u Sui-Liang, decided to take positive action to prevent the jealousy of the brothers leading to a serious quarrel. His own experience at the hands of the vacillating Li Yüan had made him fully aware of the dangers of procrastination in affairs of this kind. Ch'êng-Ch'ien had recently given fresh proof of his unbridled nature by violently assaulting an officer who had ventured to remonstrate with him on his wasteful extravagance. As this incident had led to increased talk of the crown prince's degradation by the partisans of Prince Wei, the emperor decided to silence such intrigues by issuing an edict, in which he announced that in the event of the death of the crown prince (who, as has been mentioned, was partly crippled and had delicate health), Ch'êng-Ch'ien's five-year-old son would inherit the position of crown prince; in no circumstances would any one of the sons of the imperial concubines be preferred over the children or grandchildren of the Empress Chang-Sun.

At the same time, in order to reform the character of Ch'êng-Ch'ien, Wei Chêng, the emperor's most respected and eminent minister, was appointed Grand Tutor to the crown prince. It was hoped that the instructions of this statesman, famous for his forthright nature, and the frankness of his criticisms when he did not approve of the conduct or policy of the emperor himself, would make a lasting impression on the wayward prince.

Perhaps Wei Chêng might have reformed Ch'êng-Ch'ien had he lived; unfortunately, early in A.D. 643 this great minister died, to the abiding sorrow of Shih-Min, who was inconsolable at his loss. On the occasion of Wei Chêng's funeral, which the emperor was with difficulty restrained from following in person, Shih-Min said to the court, "In my life I used three mirrors. One of bronze to adjust my dress; the records of history to correct the mistaken policies of the present; and Wei Chêng who served to reveal the faults of my character. Now I have lost the best of my mirrors".

Whether it was due to the influence of Wei Chêng, or to the fear of his father's displeasure, Prince Ch'êng-Ch'ien had made an apparent change in the manner of his life. He no longer showed fury and hatred to those who endeavoured to correct him. Instead he professed in public the most model virtues, frequently citing the maxims of the sages with enthusiasm. If reproved, he would listen docilely to any admonishments, accept the criticism with every sign of gratitude, and feign a most tractable disposition. But in the privacy of his own palace he maintained a very different style of life.

His atavistic passion for nomad simplicity and Turkish customs led him to perform the most astonishing actions. Dressed in Turkish costume, and speaking the Turkish language, he passed his time with a few attendants whom he had chosen for their resemblance to Turks. These men he dressed in Turkish style with sheepskin coats and their hair done in queues.[1] With these mock Turks he passed hours, and even days, in a Turkish tent which he had erected in the grounds of his palace. There, under the floating pennants of Turkish "wolf's head" banners, the prince would feast with his imitation Turks upon the flesh of a sheep roasted whole at a camp fire, and roughly carved up with swords, in the true nomad style. He obtained the animals which were needed for these barbaric repasts by sending his followers out to steal them from the citizens of Ch'ang An, for in his character of a Turkish freebooter he could not bear to feed upon meat purchased in the ordinary legal way.

Another favourite amusement of the eccentric young man was a play, or pageant, which he called the "Funeral of the Khan". While Ch'êng-Ch'ien himself, stretched out upon the ground, impersonated the dead khan, his imitation Turkish followers rode round him on horseback uttering the yells and howls of nomad lamentation. These amusements, though bizarre, and to the Chinese most unseemly, predicted no great harm. It was in casual conversation with his intimates that the crown prince gave expression to views and plans which raised the gravest doubts as to his fitness for the imperial throne. "When I am emperor", Ch'êng-Ch'ien was wont to remark, "the first thing I shall do is to take an army of several thousands of horsemen and go hunting in the Turkish country. There I shall live and dress in true Turkish style and have a free life."

This aspiration gives striking proof of the nature of Ch'êng-Ch'ien's obsession. To a character which seemed to have harked back to some distant Tartar ancestor,[2] the civilised life of seventh-century China presented no attractions. Ch'êng-Ch'ien found the restraints and ceremonies of

[1] This is an interesting proof that the typical Manchu coiffure, imposed upon the Chinese by those conquerors, was the national style of the Tartar and Turkish tribes 1000 years before the Manchu conquest of China.

[2] The prince's great-grandmother was a member of the Duku family which, though resident in China, was of Tartar origin.

Chinese court life an intolerable and meaningless bore. His soul craved the free life of the Mongolian steppe. The well-meant attempts of his father and tutors to mould him to the pattern of a Chinese prince merely made him more intractable and savage. Had he been granted his wish, and sent to rule the vassal Turkish tribes as khan, he might have passed a useful and happy life; instead, doomed to perform the part of a Chinese prince, his brusque and wilful character became warped to a savage melancholy.

Almost the only friend of the crown prince was his half-uncle, Li Yüan-Ch'ang Prince Han, one of the youngest of Li Yüan's many concubine-born sons. Yüan-Ch'ang, who was about the same age as the crown prince, was a cheerful libertine, who though content with the life of a Chinese prince, and free from Turkish longings, cultivated the friendship of his half-nephew in the hope of gratifying to the full his own passion for wine and women. Yüan-Ch'ang and the crown prince became inseparable companions; and the former, more corrupt by nature than the eccentric Ch'êng-Ch'ien, soon introduced the crown prince to more question-able amusements.

Ch'êng-Ch'ien's liking for drama and pageantry was stimulated by Yüan-Ch'ang's devices. The two princes divided their followers into two corps, between whom they staged sham battles, and although the combatants were only armed with bamboo spears, and were protected by felt armour, the princes urged them on so furiously that serious casualties were not uncommon. Ch'êng-Ch'ien was so taken with this sport that he planned, when emperor, to divided the regular army into two camps and stage a grand gladiatorial combat between them at Ch'ang An.

Any qualms the people of China may have felt at the prospect of such a ruler were not diminished by another of his sayings, "When I am emperor", the prince used to remark, "I must have my way in all matters. If anyone remonstrates with me, I will have him put to death. After

I have done that to a few hundreds the rest will keep silent of their own accord".

It certainly seems probable that Ch'êng-Ch'ien would have found this prediction confirmed in the event.

Although the crown prince kept the expression of such sentiments for the ears of his intimates, there were not lacking spies who reported his extravagant words to his half-brother, T'ai Prince Wei, who was only too anxious to hear anything which was to Ch'êng-Ch'ien's discredit. T'ai began to cultivate the court more assiduously than ever, and foment the belief that Ch'êng-Ch'ien ought to be degraded. These intrigues were in due course reported to the crown prince himself, for in China, then as now, nothing can ever be kept hidden for long. Ch'êng-Ch'ien conceived a furious hatred and jealousy of his brother, and henceforward began to entertain murderous projects.

From the account of Ch'êng-Ch'ien's character so far presented, it will have been made plain that he was a neurotic to whom the exotic and the perverted made a natural appeal. It is therefore in no way surprising that this love of perversion manifested itself in his sexual life.

Mention has already been made of the dramatic dances such as the P'o Chên which were performed at the T'ang court. These dances were performed by boys specially trained to dance and sing. In this year, A.D. 643, Ch'êng-Ch'ien fell madly in love with one of these boys, Ch'êng Hsin by name, who was about thirteen years old, and not only had a beautiful voice but was also exceptionally handsome. Before long this connection, which the prince was at no pains to keep secret, was brought to the knowledge of the emperor.

The luckless Ch'êng Hsin was executed, and judging by the severity of this sentence and the extreme displeasure which Shih-Min showed to his son, homosexuality was held in horror in seventh-century China.[1]

---

[1] If this was the reason for Ch'êng Hsin's execution, it is interesting in view of the easy tolerance of perversion common in India and the Near East, and

If Shih-Min was indignant at the behaviour of his son, Ch'êng-Ch'ien was not only unrepentant, but desolated by the fate of his young friend. His grief was so real that he became ill, kept entirely to his palace, and spent his time lamenting Ch'êng Hsin. He had a statue of the boy set up in the hall of his palace, and offered libations before it as if mourning the death of a near relative. In his gardens he set up a memorial tablet to the dead boy. In spite of the emperor's displeasure at these manifestations, Ch'êng-Ch'ien avoided the court and remained plunged in sorrow.

It was natural that before long his excessive grief should find an outlet in the desire for revenge. Ch'êng-Ch'ien believed, and it is very likely that he was right, that the emperor had been informed of his relationship with Ch'êng Hsin through the agency of his rival and enemy, his half-brother T'ai Prince Wei. Whether right or wrong, the crown prince acted on this belief, finding solace for his grief in plotting the death of his brother.

There has never been a court, be it ruled never so wisely, that has not harboured malcontents. The very justice of Shih-Min's rule and his firm stand against corruption and the iniquities which commonly flourish under a despotic government had alienated those whose conduct was not above reproach. Among these was one man of no mean importance, the general, Hou Chün-Chi. Hou Chün-Chi was one of the most distinguished officers in the T'ang service. The conqueror in recent years of the T'u-yü-hun, the Tibetans and Karahodjo, he had been one of the emperor's intimate followers, a member of the council which planned the ambush at the Hsüan Wu gate.

But now Hou Chün-Chi was in semi-disgrace. He had been found guilty of appropriating part of the royal treasure

the indifference with which it is regarded in China to-day. It may be remarked that in 1924 Fêng Yü-Hsiang, on the occasion of his *coup d'état* in Peking, executed a youth who was well known to be the favourite of the President Tsao Kun. Fêng Yü-Hsiang, however, is a Christian.

of Karahodjo, and making a false return of the riches found in that kingdom, which by law should have been paid into the imperial treasury. The offence was one which normally entailed the penalty of death, for the emperor, accustomed to reward his generals and ministers with great liberality, expected honest service in return. Hou Chün-Chi had been spared on account of his distinguished services. He had escaped with a reprimand, a reduction in rank, and the loss of his office.

Unfortunately the general, instead of acknowledging this leniency with gratitude, could not endure his disgrace. He became convinced that he was the victim of an unjust persecution, and observed very little reticence in airing his grievance. It happened that the general's son-in-law was an officer of the crown prince's household, and this man, knowing that the prince had some scheme afoot, brought the disgruntled Hou Chün-Chi to see Ch'êng-Ch'ien. The crown prince had so far only planned the murder of his brother T'ai Prince Wei, for which purpose he had enlisted one Hô-Kan Ch'êng-Chi,[1] a bravo who had brought with him a hundred bad characters to form a sort of murder gang.

Once Hou Chün-Chi was brought into the circle of conspiracy the affair became far more serious. Ch'êng-Ch'ien was a love-sick young man who madly hated his half-brother. Hou Chün-Chi was a famous general of great enterprise and ability, well known to the army and the empire, but smarting under a fancied grievance. He was not interested in the murder of Prince Wei, which could not further his ambitions. He wanted a revolution which would restore him to his former importance, and perhaps sooth his vanity by proving to Shih-Min that he, Hou Chün-Chi, was not a man to be lightly reprimanded.

At one interview with the crown prince, the general, baring his right arm, exclaimed, "This good arm is at Your

[1] The surname Hô-Kan is not Chinese. He may have been a Tartar, which would have been a recommendation to Ch'êng-Ch'ien.

Highness's disposition". Forthwith he urged the prince to avenge his wrongs on their real author—his father the emperor. Ch'êng-Ch'ien, far from being shocked at this unnatural proposition, was delighted to gain so valuable and influential a supporter. He richly rewarded Hou Chün-Chi, and followed his advice in every particular. The proposed revolution also found an enthusiastic supporter in Li Yüan-Ch'ang Prince Han, who, however, was actuated by other motives. Yüan-Ch'ang, who had often been rebuked by Shih-Min for his licentiousness, had taken a violent dislike to his imperial half-brother. The light-hearted libertine solicited as his reward, when Ch'êng-Ch'ien should be on the throne, that he be given all the girls and boy musicians in the palace, a proposition to which his nephew readily assented.

The conspiracy also included one or two young noblemen of the court, a son of the dead statesman Tu Ju-Hui, and a half-nephew of the emperor, whose mother was the daughter of another of Li Yüan's many concubines. These youths, who resented the fact that their follies had excluded them from the public service, readily fell in with the plot. All took a blood oath to live or die together.

It was first proposed to seize the palace by open force, but Hou Chün-Chi pointed out that the failure of the similar plan adopted by the Tartar rebel Qachashar, proved that the guards were too strong. Instead it was decided that Ch'êng-Ch'ien should feign a serious illness. The emperor would be sure to pay him a visit, and the other conspirators, who would be lying in wait, could take this opportunity to assassinate the emperor and proclaim Ch'êng-Ch'ien. But the consummation of the iniquity plotted by one of Shih-Min's sons was to be prevented by the flagrant crimes of another.

Li Yu Prince Chi was the son of a concubine, the Queen Yin.[1] Created Prince Chi, a title formerly held by Li Yüan-

---

[1] It is not stated whether the mother of Li Yu was also the mother of T'ai Prince Wei, but the inference is that the two princes were the sons of different queens.

Chi, the young man had been sent to govern that region[1] with headquarters at Chi Nan Fu. It had been the emperor's intention to train the youth to play a useful part in public life by this practical experience in the government of a province. As Yu was still very young, several trustworthy officers of experience were attached to his household as advisers, with orders to report on his conduct to the throne.

Yu did not profit by the counsels of these worthy men. A volatile and foolish young man, he fell, instead, under the influence of corrupt and ambitious members of his mother's family. He was particularly swayed by Yin Hung-Chih, his maternal uncle, who hoped to use the young prince as a ladder by which all the clan might mount to power and wealth. To this end Yin Hung-Chih worked on the youth's ambition. "After ten thousand years have passed (i.e. when the emperor is dead)", he said, "there will perhaps be troubles and a contest for the throne. Unless you have a following and troops of your own, how can you protect yourself and us?"

Acting on this advice Yu started to enlist troops of desperadoes through the agency of one of Yin Hung-Chih's relatives.

These proceedings soon attracted the attention of the officers whom the emperor had appointed to watch over and assist the young prince. They remonstrated with him, not only on the matter of his fondness for the company of worthless intriguers such as Yin Hung-Chih, but also on account of his excessive passion for hunting, a pursuit upon which he wasted much money, inflicting hardship on the farming people of the province.[2] His chief adviser even went so far

[1] Chi Chou, the modern Chi Nan Fu or Tsi Nan Fu, capital of Shantung province, was the capital of the ancient state of Chi, which comprised the western and northern part of the modern province.
[2] Hunting in ancient China involved the co-operation of an army of beaters, who surrounded a wide stretch of country and drove the game inwards to the huntsmen, who waited in the centre. This method, if employed in the summer months, naturally caused much damage to crops, and occupied the people who should have been working on the land. Hence the objections of the officials.

as to dismiss many of the bad characters enlisted by Yin Hung-Chih, but the prince immediately cancelled this order.

The emperor, hearing some report of his son's bad behaviour, wrote him a letter of warning and reproof. This evidence of the imperial displeasure made no impression upon Yu, but the chief tutor, realising what was likely to happen, feared that if some serious scandal arose, he himself would be held responsible for failing to guide and control the young prince in a proper manner. He therefore decided to put himself in the right with the emperor. He suggested to Yu that, in view of his father's letter, it would be best to send someone to Ch'ang An to make explanations, and assure the emperor that he had been misinformed about his son's conduct. The prince thoroughly approved this plan, and the chief tutor adroitly offered to be the messenger.

His real motive for seeking an interview with the emperor was not to defend Yu, but, on the contrary, to report his misbehaviour, and so avoid the accusation of having failed to exercise proper care over the prince. Shih-Min, who did not know that the tutor had deceived his son, rewarded the official for his zeal, and wrote a much stronger letter of admonition to Yu. On receipt of this unexpected rebuke, the prince flew into a furious rage, exclaiming, "The Chief Tutor has sold me, accusing me to acquire merit for himself. He deserves to die!"

From this moment Yu began to hate his tutor with a deadly enmity, which was fully shared by all his loose associates and favourites. The chief tutor, on his return from Ch'ang An, could not but notice the hostile attitude of the court of Chi Nan Fu: indeed the enmity of the prince's followers so worked on his nerves that he began to fear for his life. Accordingly he sent a letter to Ch'ang An declaring that he was menaced with death. This act precipitated the fate he feared.

The emperor, realising that affairs at Chi Nan Fu were coming to a dangerous pass, and finding it difficult to discover the real facts at such a distance, ordered both the prince and his tutor to come up to Ch'ang An and explain matters. Yu was greatly alarmed at this order. He feared that once he reached Ch'ang An the emperor would find out all about his illegal army of desperadoes, as well as his misconduct in other matters. The only way out of this difficulty, according to his friends, was to kill the chief tutor on the road. That official, for his part, had wasted no time once he had the imperial permission to leave Chi Nan Fu, where he went in fear of death. But his hurried departure did not save him. The prince sent some of his bravos in pursuit, who having overtaken the luckless chief tutor, murdered him on the public road.

The controller of the household, another of the imperial officials who had the duty of supervising the young prince, was the next victim. Refusing to become an accessory to the conspiracy and the murder of his colleague, he too fled for his life, but was pursued by the prince's followers and killed in the same manner as the chief tutor.

As the murder of two highly placed imperial officials was not a matter which could be passed over without enquiry, the prince now found himself in a more desperate position than before. On the advice of his harebrained court he decided to seek safety by disobeying the emperor's order and declaring an open revolt. Having issued a proclamation assuming full authority in the province, he seized and opened the government arsenals at Chi Nan Fu, ordering the people of the district to assemble in the city to be enrolled in his army.

The citizens of Chi Nan Fu had more common sense than their governor. They realised that this foolish youth stood no chance at all of withstanding the full power and authority of the whole empire, while, if they assisted him in his revolt, their city would pay bitterly for such folly. Instead of flocking to his standards, they profited by the night to escape over the walls and take refuge elsewhere.

On hearing the news of Yu's disobedience, crimes and rebellion, the emperor reluctantly realised that the matter had passed beyond the stage of rebukes and admonitions. Li Shih-Chi was ordered to assume command of the regular army in the eastern provinces and suppress the revolt. At the same time a final warning was sent to the prince, urging him to surrender before he should incur graver penalties by an armed resistance to the imperial authority. The prince, who apparently thought himself a match for all comers, threw away this last chance, and prepared to defend the city.

His foolhardiness did not, however, appeal to the officers of the regular army forming the Chi Nan Fu garrison. They realised that any attempt to oppose a general such as Li Shih-Chi, with the garrison of one city and the few hundred bravos whom Yu had enlisted, was downright imbecility. The inevitable consequence would be defeat, and the extermination of the clans of all found guilty of open rebellion against the imperial throne. The officers were by no means ready to run the risk of such a penalty. The improvident conduct of the prince himself was the surest augur of his impending ruin. So far from devoting his time to the training of troops, and preparations for the defence of the city, he spent his days in feasting, and his nights in drunken debauches with Yin Hung-Chih and his favourites.

The officers of the garrison, loyal to the emperor, had thus no difficulty in surprising the prince in the midst of a feast, and seizing the city. As they were about to force their way into Yu's palace, a cry was raised that Li Shih-Chi's "Flying Horse"[1] were before the walls. This news rousing the revellers to a realisation of their plight, Yu prepared to defend himself, only to find his palace besieged by the mutinous garrison. With the assistance of his private following he defended the palace throughout the night, till his enemies decided to set fire to the building and burn him out.

When Yu realised their intention, he tried to purchase his safety by offering to surrender Yin Hung-Chih and other favourites, but the officers of the garrison replied that the

[1] The "Flying Horse" were a famous corps of light cavalry.

prince was now a declared rebel, with whom it would be a crime to make any composition. Seeing no hope left, the prince then surrendered unconditionally. Yin Hung-Chih and others of the prince's unworthy court were promptly put to death, while Yu himself was sent up to Ch'ang An to answer for his crimes.

This tragi-comic rebellion, of slight importance in itself, served to unveil the really dangerous and deadly conspiracy of Hou Chün-Chi and the Crown Prince Ch'êng-Ch'ien. When those involved in Yu's rebellion were examined, it was found that among the confederates of Yin Hung-Chih was Hô-Kan Ch'êng-Chi, the bravo whom Ch'êng-Ch'ien had enlisted to murder T'ai Prince Wei. This criminal, knowing that his only hope of avoiding a terrible death was to turn king's evidence, immediately confessed the whole plot.

No time was lost in arresting the accused. Ch'êng-Ch'ien, Yüan-Ch'ang Prince Han, Hou Chün-Chi and the rest were brought before a specially constituted tribunal, composed of the highest and most trusted officials in the emperor's service—Chang-Sun Wu-Chi, Fang Hsüan-Ling, Hsiao Yü and Li Shih-Chi. The proofs being clear and undisputed, the court convicted the accused and reported its findings to the emperor. Shih-Min, who could not conceal his distress at this evidence of his son's unnatural crime, and the treachery of his old friend Hou Chün-Chi, turned to the ministers and asked what they advised him to do. In view of the rank of the chief culprit, no one dared to offer an opinion.

Shih-Min pondered the terrible decision for a long space. He could not resolve to put his own son to death. Instead, Ch'êng-Ch'ien was imprisoned, degraded from his rank to the humble status of the common people, and subsequently exiled to a remote town in southern Szechuan province, then on the frontier of the empire. There, little more than a year later, the wretched youth died, his health, always weak, undermined by the loss of all hope and meaning in a further existence.

The emperor wished to spare the life of his half-brother Yüan-Ch'ang also, but the ministers firmly insisted that an example should be made in this case. Yüan-Ch'ang was therefore permitted to commit suicide in his own home, a more honourable death than public execution. His family were freed from all penalties, which was a rare clemency in the criminal practice of that age. Even to Hou Chün-Chi, whose guilt was black and unpardonable, the emperor, for old friendship's sake, extended the utmost possible clemency. He wished to save the life of his former friend, but the ministers represented that such a pardon would be misconstrued, and would encourage the formation of fresh conspiracies. Shih-Min at length yielded to these reasons. Hou Chün-Chi was led before the emperor, and when he had been told of his sentence Shih-Min said, "It is a last farewell". Hou Chün-Chi, overcome by remorse and the realisation of his own insensate folly, threw himself on the ground in tears. He was then led out to execution.

By an unparalleled leniency the lives of Hou Chün-Chi's wife and son were spared, and they escaped with the lighter sentence of permanent exile to Canton. The minor members of the conspiracy were decapitated, but in their case also their families only suffered lesser penalties. The tutors and officers of the former crown prince's household, held guilty of negligence for their failure to correct his wayward disposition and report his evil conduct, were all cashiered.

When the conspirators had been tried and sentenced, the question of Ch'êng-Ch'ien's successor to the post of crown prince arose to agitate the disturbed court. Shih-Min at first thought of yielding to his natural inclination and appointing T'ai Prince Wei, but the ministers, particularly Chang-Sun Wu-Chi, the brother of the late empress, and Ch'u Sui-Liang, were strongly opposed to the elevation of any concubine's son, so long as there still remained sons of the empress worthy of the post.

T'ai sealed his own fate by that ambition which had provoked Ch'êng-Ch'ien to plot his terrible crime. Fearing that Ch'êng-Ch'ien's younger full-brother, the second son of the Empress Chang-Sun, Chih Prince Chin, would be preferred, he attempted to intimidate the boy (Chih was then sixteen) by accusing him of having been a close friend and companion of Yüan-Ch'ang Prince Han and other conspirators. Chih was so alarmed by his half-brother's menaces that he became quite unwell, and his dejected and terrified appearance attracted the attention of the emperor. When questioned, Chih revealed the reason for his fears.

Ch'êng-Ch'ien, when brought before the emperor, had tried to excuse his conduct by blaming the ambition and intrigues of T'ai Prince Wei. Shih-Min, who desired above all to be just, investigated this accusation, and found that T'ai had indeed been guilty of planning to obtain the succession. When these facts were added to his attempt to intimidate the young Chih, the emperor decided that T'ai was an unsuitable candidate for the throne. "Whoever covets a post is unworthy to occupy it", he said. Thereupon Chih Prince Chin was appointed crown prince with the full approval of the court, while T'ai was punished for his intrigues by being degraded to a lower rank of princes, and was exiled to a city in Hupei province. He did not long survive his disgrace, dying at his place of banishment within two years.

Shih-Min, fully determined to guard the new crown prince against the follies and crimes to which his elder brother had been prone, appointed the most eminent ministers of his court to be the boy's guardians and tutors. With Chang-Sun Wu-Chi, Fang Hsüan-Ling, Hsiao Yü and Li Shih-Chi as tutors, he hoped that no corrupt influence could come near his destined heir. Chih, indeed, gave every proof of filial devotion and loyalty, but his character was weak and timid. When he in due course did succeed and reign as emperor, his indolence and weakness opened the road by which his famous concubine Wu Shih, afterwards the Empress Wu, climbed to supreme power and influence in the T'ang empire.

CHAPTER X

THE KOREAN WAR AND THE CLOSING YEARS

A.D. 645–50

The domestic tragedy which had rocked the court of Ch'ang An in the year A.D. 643 cast a lasting shadow over the later years of Shih-Min's life. The emperor never really recovered from the shock and grief caused by his son's unnatural conspiracy. It was to be expected that an energetic and forceful personality such as his should seek relief in some active and absorbing enterprise. This restlessness, which seized upon the emperor in the months following Ch'êng-Ch'ien's fall, was the primary motive which induced Shih-Min to undertake the personal command of the war with Korea, the least successful of all his campaigns.

It was not merely distaste for court life at Ch'ang An that urged the emperor to make war upon this country. China had substantial grievances against the peninsula kingdom. In the year A.D. 642 P'ing Jang, the Korean capital, had been convulsed by a revolution more sanguinary and more successful than that which had menaced the Chinese court. Ch'uan Kai-Su-Wên,[1] a minister at the Korean court, had assassinated his sovereign and massacred all the officials who did not support his own ambitions. He was now master of the kingdom, ruling through a puppet monarch of the old royal house. The dictator, a man of ruthless strength and great energy, improved and increased the Korean army, planning to conquer the two small kingdoms of Silla and Pai Chi, then occupying the southern part of the peninsula. To raise the money required for this policy the new ruler imposed oppressive taxation and confiscated the property of wealthy families who had opposed his usurpation.

---

[1] According to Hu San-Shêng, commentator of the *Tzŭ chih t'ung chien*, Ch'uan was the surname of this man, Kai-Su-Wên a triple personal name.

Although Korea was, in theory at least, a tributary kingdom, the T'ang court did not exercise any control over the government. Yang Ti's attempts to subject the peninsula to his authority had met with complete failure, and the late king of Korea had only paid "tribute", or sent presents, to the T'ang emperors in order to avert any renewal of the destructive Chinese invasions. Shih-Min would never have engaged in a costly and difficult war if the usurping Ch'uan Kai-Su-Wên had maintained this attitude. But in A.D. 643 the ambitious dictator of Korea made war upon his neighbour, the king of Silla, which was also tributary to China.[1] The Korean ruler furthermore closed his roads to the ambassadors of Silla to prevent that kingdom holding communication with China. Nevertheless, Silla, by using the sea route, managed to transmit an appeal for assistance to the suzerain power.

The T'ang court, apprised of the aggressive behaviour of Korea, sent a firm warning to the court of P'ing Jang with orders to cease all attacks upon Silla. Ch'uan Kai-Su-Wên, remembering the failure of Yang Ti's successive invasions, believed that the Chinese empire was no more capable of implementing these threats than it had been thirty years before. He paid no attention to the T'ang ambassador, continuing his aggressions upon Silla. Shih-Min, whose armies had crossed the desert to conquer Karahodjo, and pursued the T'u-yü-hun through the eternal snows of the K'un Lun mountains, was not disposed to overlook the insolence of the Korean regicide.

Early in A.D. 644, the emperor decided to punish the tyrant and prove that a tributary did not appeal in vain to suzerain

[1] Korea, or Kao Li as the Chinese pronounce it, has in modern times been used as the name of the former kingdom occupying the entire peninsula. In the seventh century Korea, or Kao Li, did not control the southern half of the peninsula, which was divided between the kingdoms of Silla and Pai Chi. On the other hand, Korea extended as far north-west as the Liao river in what is now called South Manchuria. The Liao Tung peninsula was at this time part of the Korean kingdom, and was a settled country with many cities of importance.

China. The court of Ch'ang An, however, was not in favour
of war. The older ministers, who had most unfortunate
memories of Yang Ti's Korean campaigns, expressed the fear
that Shih-Min would be no more successful. Ch'u Sui-Liang,
President of the Board of History, memorialised to this
effect, and was particularly insistent that even if it was
necessary to punish Korea, the emperor should delegate the
war to his generals. But Shih-Min had found in the projected
war an interest which served to occupy his energies and
distract his mind from the memory of the unhappy events at
Ch'ang An in the preceding year. He rejected Ch'u Sui-
Liang's advice, confident that his military skill far exceeded
that of Yang Ti and the generals of the Sui dynasty.

No preparation was spared to make this demonstration of
the imperial authority mighty and successful. Szechuan, a
rich province, which almost alone had escaped the devastating rebellions at the end of the Sui dynasty, was put under
contribution to provide a fleet. Four hundred large ships
were built upon the banks of the Yangtze so that the Chinese
should obtain command of the Yellow Sea. It is a singular
proof of Shih-Min's many-sided genius, that though he was
born and resided all his life in inland country, he fully appreciated the paramount importance of sea power. Napoleon,
though an islander, never learnt this lesson in twenty years of
warfare with England.

The invasion of Korea by a Chinese army did not necessarily involve a sea passage, but the geographical position of
the peninsula made the sea route both shorter and easier than
the long march round the head of the gulf of Liao Tung,
through a country which in the seventh century was largely
an uninhabited wilderness. Yang Ti's invasions had failed
primarily because his vast hosts starved in the Manchurian
waste, many hundreds of miles from their base in China. The
sea route therefore served to supplement the land invasion,
which could then be made with a smaller force.

The strategic plan formed by the emperor made provision

for two distinct invasions. While Li Shih-Chi and Prince Jên Ch'êng (Li Tao-Tsung) advanced with 60,000 men through South Manchuria to the Liao river on the Korean frontier, another general crossed the sea from Lai Chou, a port on the north coast of Shantung, landing at the mouth of the Yalu river, which forms the modern frontier between Korea and Manchuria. This force, of 40,000 men conveyed in 500 ships, which was not in itself large enough to conquer the Korean kingdom, was intended to create a diversion. By menacing the Korean capital at P'ing Jang it would prevent the Koreans from concentrating their full strength on the Liao river to bar the passage of the land invasion. The emperor himself intended to join the mainland army after the Liao had been crossed.

The news of these preparations caused uneasiness in Korea. The dictator sent an envoy to Ch'ang An who tried to avert the threatened war by offering a large sum of money as tribute. The emperor had, however, determined to suppress the regicide by force. The envoy was not received, and his tribute was rejected. Late in the year A.D. 644 the emperor proceeded to Lo Yang, in spite of the renewed protests of the ministers, who remained unalterably opposed to the emperor personally conducting the campaign. Shih-Min had made up his mind and would not be dissuaded. Fang Hsüan-Ling was left in charge of the capital with Li Ta-Liang, an experienced and trusted general, as commander-in-chief of the military forces in Ch'ang An.

The emperor, accompanied by the new crown prince (Li Chih), reached Lo Yang at the end of the year, and from that city issued a proclamation making known his reasons for undertaking the war.

Ch'uan Kai-Su-Wên of Korea has murdered his king and oppresses the people. These things cannot be endured. I am now about to proceed to the northern borders to bring justice to the country beyond the Liao. The army will suffer neither loss nor toil. Those who tell how formerly Yang Ti cruelly sacrificed his soldiers without success, should known that then the king of Korea was a righteous ruler who loved his people. Their nation being united and peaceful, a ruthless invading army could not prevail against them. But to-day there are five great reasons why we shall conquer.

Firstly, Strength must defeat Weakness;
Secondly, Righteousness must prevail over Iniquity;
Thirdly, Justice will strike down Oppression;
Fourthly, Order will triumph over Confusion;
and fifthly, Benevolence will conquer Hatred.

After passing the New Year at Lo Yang the emperor started to join the army, leaving Hsiao Yü in charge of the eastern capital. At Ting Chou, 120 miles south of Peking, the main base of the army, the crown prince was left in charge as regent, with his maternal great uncle, Kao Shih-Lien, to advise him. The emperor accompanied by Chang-Sun Wu-Chi then started for Liao Tung.

Meanwhile the preliminary operations of the T'ang forces, both by land and by sea, had been crowned with success. The fleet descended upon the coasts of Korea, landing troops near the Yalu river, where they captured a city probably on the same site as the modern Wiju. This conquest interrupted the direct road from P'ing Jang, the Korean capital, to Liao Yang, the chief city in the northern part of the kingdom. P'ing Jang itself felt menaced by the near presence of an hostile army on the peninsular coast. As the emperor had foreseen, the fleet and landing force immobilised a large Korean army, which was retained in the peninsula to guard P'ing Jang. At the same time all hostilities against Silla had to be suspended.

The Koreans, pre-occupied with these dangers near home, were unable to concentrate their full strength on the Liao. Li Shih-Chi and Prince Jên Ch'êng were therefore able to turn the right flank of the Korean defences and cross the Liao at an unguarded point far to the north, beyond the position of modern Mukden. After crossing the river the Chinese army seized the city of Kai Niu, the most northerly

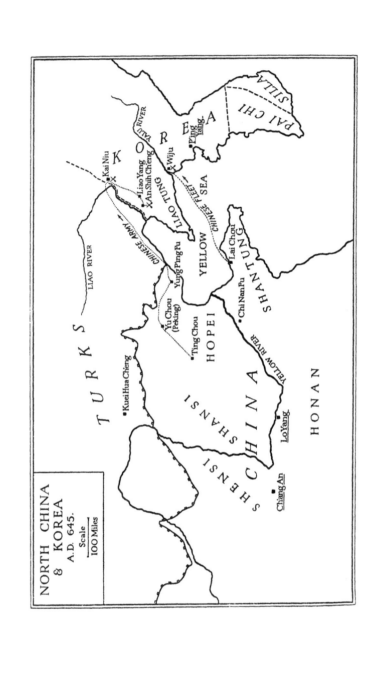

NORTH CHINA & KOREA. A.D. 645.

Scale
100 Miles

fortress of the Korean state.[1] Marching south, Li Shih-Chi then laid siege to Liao Yang, the chief city of Liao Tung, or South Manchuria.

The emperor had already reached the frontier, but before he could join Li Shih-Chi, the Korean army, about 40,000 strong, came hurrying up to the relief of Liao Yang. The Korean approach had been first detected by Prince Jên Ch'êng, who, with an advance guard of 4000 cavalry, was reconnoitring the country. Although so heavily outnumbered, the T'ang prince did not hesitate to engage the enemy. Owing to the flight of one of his lieutenants, less bold than he, Prince Jên Ch'êng was at first repulsed with severe loss, but in spite of the cowardice of his subordinate the prince maintained the action with intrepid courage, repeatedly charging the Koreans, who had no experience of warfare with heavy armed cavalry.

Li Shih-Chi's opportune arrival with the main army restored the fortunes of the day, the Korean army retiring from the field in much disorder after incurring heavy loss. Upon the arrival of Shih-Min, the general who had disgraced the imperial arms by flight was decapitated in view of the assembled army.

The Korean army having thus been beaten off, the siege of Liao Yang was pressed under the direction of the emperor himself. The Koreans in that age were expert and resolute defenders of fortified places. Liao Yang itself had twice resisted the continuous onslaughts of Yang Ti's huge armies. It might have crowned this record by baffling the better directed T'ang invasion had Shih-Min not made skilful use of an opportunity presented by the weather.

During a violent south-west gale the emperor ordered the troops to assault and set fire to the tower upon the south-west angle of the city wall. This building once aflame, the fire spread swiftly to the town itself. Driven back by the flames and smoke the Korean garrison was unable to repel the

[1] Probably Kai Yuan on the Kai Ho, fifty miles north of Mukden.

attackers, who mounted the walls in the wake of the fire, and carried the city by storm. The Korean loss was heavy. Ten thousand were killed, and the same number made prisoners, together with the 40,000 inhabitants of Liao Yang. The city was proclaimed to be annexed to the T'ang empire.

The fall of Liao Yang made a deep impression on the neighbouring towns in Liao Tung, for it was well remembered that three Chinese invasions under Yang Ti had successively failed to take the capital of northern Korea. Several cities opened their gates without waiting to be attacked. This example was not followed by the strongest remaining fortress in Liao Tung, An Shih Ch'êng.[1] The T'ang army accordingly marched upon this place, and in the middle of summer laid siege to An Shih Ch'êng. The Koreans, unable to collect a new army in time to save Liao Yang, were determined to succour An Shih Ch'êng. With a reinforced army, which now amounted to 150,000 men, they advanced confidently to give battle to the far smaller Chinese force. When three miles from the walls of the besieged city the Korean army encamped at the base of a steep hill, to observe the dispositions of the invading army.

In the emperor's council opinions differed on the best course to pursue. Prince Jên Ch'êng (Li Tao-Tsung) considered that as the Korean army represented all the remaining strength of the kingdom, the emperor should occupy this force with desultory operations while another Chinese army, only 10,000 strong, should strike straight at the Korean capital, P'ing Jang. Prince Jên Ch'êng offered to take command of this force himself, for he believed that with the main Korean army occupied before An Shih Ch'êng, he would encounter no real opposition on the march, and after joining with the troops landed on the coast, could take P'ing Jang and end the war.

Shih-Min, who usually favoured the bold course in war, on

---

[1] This city does not now exist. It appears to have been at or near the site of Newchuang City (not Newchuang Port), seventy miles south of Mukden.

this occasion decided upon more prudent measures. He was haunted by the memory of Yang Ti's disastrous invasion of the peninsula, when, after failing to take P'ing Jang, the Sui emperor's army had been cut to pieces on its retreat at the crossing of the Yalu. He rejected Prince Jên Ch'êng's daring plan, preferring to wait till the Korean field army had been defeated and An Shih Ch'êng taken, before invading the heart of the kingdom.

The historians consider that the emperor was mistaken in this decision; and that had he followed Prince Jên Ch'êng's plan the war would have ended in a complete Chinese victory. This wisdom after the event ignores the dangers which Shih-Min was bound to consider. The failure of an invasion of peninsular Korea and an attempt to take P'ing Jang would have been a military disaster of no mean importance, a severe blow to the prestige of the empire; whereas even if operations in South Manchuria proved unfortunate, the army would not be exposed to the perils of a disastrous retreat, and its ill-success would be less conspicuous.

The emperor therefore decided to give battle before An Shih Ch'êng, but not without making careful preparations to ensure a victorious outcome. Li Shih-Chi with 15,000 men formed up in battle line opposite the Korean camp, while the emperor with 4000 picked horsemen remained upon a ridge some miles north of the city, beyond the extreme right flank of the Korean position, as if intent upon maintaining the blockade of An Shih Ch'êng. Other T'ang forces were in fact so engaged, but these were stationed in positions out of sight of the Korean army. Finally Chang-Sun Wu-Chi was detached with 11,000 men to work his way round by a wide detour till he reached an agreed position behind the Korean camp. When he had reached the assigned position he informed the emperor by making smoke signals from the hill tops, and awaited a similar signal from the emperor before he made his presence known to the enemy.

The Korean general, unaware of these elaborate manœuvres,

saw nothing but Li Shih-Chi's 15,000 men, a force vastly
inferior in numbers to his own, and the distant division which
Shih-Min himself commanded. Thinking that these last
troops were not likely to join in the battle, the Korean
engaged Li Shih-Chi, who retreated slowly before the weight
of the enemy attack till the Koreans had advanced far from
the hills into the plain. Their rear being no longer protected
by the mountain, Shih-Min sent up the agreed smoke signal
to Chang-Sun Wu-Chi, at the same time attacking the Korean
right flank with his own force. The Koreans, at first seeing
only Shih-Min's attack, wheeled their right flank round to
receive him, but while this deployment was in progress,
Chang-Sun Wu-Chi unexpectedly appeared behind them.
His attack threw the whole Korean line into confusion.

Their retreat being cut off, the Korean army suffered a
complete defeat. Twenty thousand were left dead on the field,
while 36,000, who succeeded in retiring to the base of a steep
hill, were surrounded and compelled to surrender. With this
force was the commander of the Korean army himself. Those
who escaped capture or the sword dispersed in confusion,
the panic being so great that every town and village for a
hundred miles around was deserted by its inhabitants. The
Korean army had ceased to exist, and nothing, it seemed, but
the city of An Shih Ch'êng, stood between the emperor and
the conquest of Korea.

Shih-Min was justifiably proud of this brilliant victory,
which proved that after twenty years of peace his military
genius was still unimpaired. He sent a triumphant message
to the crown prince giving an account of the battle, adding in
his own hand, "When I am at the head of the army, what else
should we expect?"

This rash boast reveals very clearly the underlying motives
which had induced the emperor to take personal command
of the army in this war. After the sordid tragedy of Prince
Ch'êng-Ch'ien, for which, perhaps, he felt that his own
example years before at the Hsüan Wu gate had been in part

responsible, he felt an overpowering desire to regain, in the free atmosphere of the camp, the undimmed lustre of his youthful fame, when he commanded the ever-victorious army of the rising T'ang dynasty.

But if the battle of An Shih Ch'êng revived the glories of Squirrel pass and Ssŭ Shui, it was to be the last military success of this war. The siege of the city of An Shih Ch'êng, which was now pressed with unexampled vigour, exhausted the strength of the army and consumed the remaining summer months in unprofitable operations. The Koreans, though no match for the T'ang armies in the field, were redoubtable on the walls of their cities. Shih-Min was to find that An Shih Ch'êng resisted every plan of attack which seventh-century military science, directed by a great military genius, could devise.

When the walls were breached by the action of battering rams it was found that the Koreans had raised another and stronger defence behind them. When the Chinese constructed a mound level with the wall and assaulted the city, Prince Jên Ch'êng was wounded in the attack, and the undaunted Koreans, counter-attacking, seized the Chinese mound and incorporated it in their own defences. But though the Koreans were indomitable in defence, Shih-Min's vigilance frustrated their sorties with an equal care.

One day, as he rode round the city on reconnaissance, the emperor, attentive to every indication of enemy activity, heard an unusual squawking of fowls. Shih-Min at once ordered Li Shih-Chi to keep the camp under arms that night in expectation of a sortie. When, in fact, the Koreans made the attack which the emperor expected, they found the Chinese fully prepared, and were driven back into the city with severe loss. The generals, marvelling at the emperor's prescience, asked him how he had divined the enemy's intention. Shih-Min replied, "The squawking of many fowls after so long a siege, when their provisions must be low, proved that the enemy were making a large slaughter of the birds. From that I deduced that their purpose was to give a feast to a body of picked troops, who would be used to make a sortie; as you see, I was correct".

Time and weather, so often Shih-Min's allies in war, now fought on the opposing side. The short Manchurian autumn was drawing to a close, and the severe cold winter of this northern land was now at hand. Already the pasture had withered away, so that fodder for the horses as well as food for the troops was becoming hard to find. The emperor, who knew too well what swift disaster lies in wait for the general who ignores the factors of commissariat and weather, reluctantly decided to abandon the siege before his army, trapped by winter, suffered the fate of Yang Ti's unhappy invasions. After a fruitless siege of sixty-three days the T'ang army marched away from An Shih Ch'êng, while the Korean garrison commander insolently mounted on the walls to wish them farewell.

The decision to retire was taken none too soon. The cold weather comes down in these countries with dangerous suddenness, and although the Chinese retreat was un-molested by the enemy, the troops suffered severely from the rigours of approaching winter. As some compensation for the failure before An Shih Ch'êng, and the continued existence of the contumacious regicide ruler of Korea, Liao Yang and several other cities were annexed; while 70,000 Koreans were led captive to China, where they were settled in the district of modern Peking. These people showed no unwillingness at becoming the subjects of the great emperor, and so escaping the exactions of Ch'uan Kai-Su-Wên's hard rule. At Ting Chou, the emperor, distressed by the spectacle of families divided by his soldiers, who had made slaves of their prisoners, ransomed these unfortunates out of his private revenues, and settled them in China. These new subjects were so delighted at this unheard-of clemency that they lined the road along which his chariot passed, manifesting their joy in shouts and cheers.

The addition of a few cities to the empire could not conceal the fact that the Korean campaign had failed in its avowed object, the punishment of the regicide. Shih-Min returned saddened to Ch'ang An and, which was far more serious, weakened in health. Korea remained rebellious, though chastened; nor was the emperor ever granted the gratification of avenging his check before An Shih Ch'êng.

The partial failure of the Korean war had inevitable repercussions among the Turkish tribes beyond the Gobi. The Sarinda, who believed that the moment had come to avenge their catastrophic defeat in A.D. 641, crossed the desert early in A.D. 646 and endeavoured to invade the territories of the empire. The Turks were entirely mistaken in their estimate of the position. In spite of the absence of a large part of the T'ang army in the north-east, there remained ample troops for the defence of the northern frontier. The Sarinda were met by the frontier troops at Hsia Chou, a city now no longer inhabited, in the loop of the Yellow river beyond the Great Wall. The battle went in favour of the Chinese who scored a complete victory.

This defeat was the beginning of the break-up of the Sarinda confederacy. Troubles broke out among the tribes, which ended in the open rebellion of the most powerful, the Uigurs.[1] The emperor decided to assist this tribe in order to effect a lasting division of the Sarinda power. Li Shih-Chi and Prince Jên Ch'êng were sent at the head of an army to help the Uigurs. With this assistance the independent position of the Uigurs was established, though the tribe was induced to acknowledge the suzerainty of Ch'ang An.

This campaign, which had seen Chinese armies in action beyond the Gobi, not only restored the T'ang prestige, but spread the fame and reputation of the great emperor into

[1] The Uigurs subsequently became very powerful. They were converted in later centuries to Islam, and the Chinese term "Hui Hui", the common word for a Mohammedan, is believed to be a corruption of Hui Kê, the Chinese form of the Turkish Uigur.

distant lands which had never before held communication with China. In the next year the envoys of a people called Kulikan arrived at Ch'ang An. Their land was beyond the Western Sea (either the Caspian or Aral), but so far to the north that the historian remarks that "the days there are very long and the nights very short". Evidently this country lay close to the Arctic Circle, as it was only known to travellers who penetrated in the summer months. It would appear that Kulikan was in the north-west of Siberia, or even west of the Urals.

From some similar part of the world came the ambassadors of Chieh Ku,[1] who arrived in Ch'ang An in A.D. 648. The people of Chieh Ku made a great impression on the Chinese, for they had an appearance hitherto unheard of. These strangers, in fact, "had red hair and blue eyes, they were very tall, and though there were dark-haired people among them, these were not well regarded". Their country, "3000 li (1000 miles) north-west of the Uigurs", must have been somewhere on the eastern slopes of the Ural mountains. After their envoys had been feasted and entertained they were given gifts, and, what was even more to their liking, titles of rank in the T'ang army.

From this account it will be plain that the Chieh Ku, by whatever name they really called themselves, were a people of Nordic race, a white ruling clan with a subject "dark-haired" race, perhaps Mongol, under their authority. The possibility that they were some early settlement of Vikings, who had established a kingdom on one of the great rivers of Siberia, seems not improbable. Byzantium was in a few years to be employing Varangian guards drawn from the same far-wandering stock.[2]

---

[1] Chieh Ku is the modern pronunciation of the characters 結 骨 in the Mandarin dialect. In T'ang times the name may have been pronounced in a very different way.

[2] The impression produced by the Chieh Ku ambassadors is inexplicable if, as von Le Coq and other archeologists believe, the inhabitants of Khocho in Turfan, the Tokharians, were a people of Indo-European origin. The Tok-

The prestige and power of the T'ang empire was as much respected in the tropical lands of the south as in the frozen solitudes of northern Asia. The astonishing exploits of Wang Hsüan-Ts'ê, Chinese ambassador to the states of India, strikingly exemplify the weight which the emperor's name carried in the most distant countries. In the year A.D. 649 the ambassador with an escort of only thirty Chinese officers and attendants was collecting "tribute", i.e. presents, from the kings of northern India, when he was attacked and despoiled of this treasure by Alanashun, king of Tinafuti, which was in central India. This king, who is said to have been a usurper, had refused to hold diplomatic intercourse with China.

Wang Hsüan-Ts'ê, nothing daunted by his misfortune, escaped with his suit to Nepal, where using the name of the emperor, he demanded troops from the king of that country and his neighbour the king of Tibet; both of whom had accepted the alliance and vague suzerainty of the T'ang empire (cf. "friend and ally of the Roman people"). It speaks volumes for the majesty of the T'ang court that this isolated official, hundreds of miles from the nearest Chinese

harian language, as deciphered from manuscripts found in Turfan, is an Indo-European language, and the wall paintings in cave-monasteries at Bäzäklik and Kyzyl show people with blue eyes, red hair and European styles of dress (von Le Coq, *Buried Treasures of Chinese Turkestan*, pp. 88, 124). Von Le Coq dates these paintings as *circa* A.D. 700, that is nearly seventy years after the conquest of Turfan (Karahodjo) by the T'ang army under Hou Chün-Chi. But he regards the Tokharians as a remnant of the Yüeh-Chi, who had been driven westward some centuries earlier. Consequently the people whom Hou Chün-Chi conquered, and who were well known before that event to the Chinese, were a blue-eyed, red-haired, Indo-European race. It is at least curious that no mention of these characteristics of the Karahodjans (Tokharians) is made in the Chinese texts, whereas the red hair, tall stature and blue eyes of the Chieh Ku, who reached Ch'ang An eight years after the conquest of Khocho, excited the keenest interest and astonishment at the Chinese court.

Should further investigation in Turfan prove that the wall paintings of Kyzyl and Bäzäklik, and consequently the arrival of the Indo-European Tokharians, are of a date rather later than has hitherto been suggested, the impression made by the appearance of the Chieh Ku would be explained. For this mysterious embassy may have been the precursor of a later Indo-European intrusion into Central Asia.

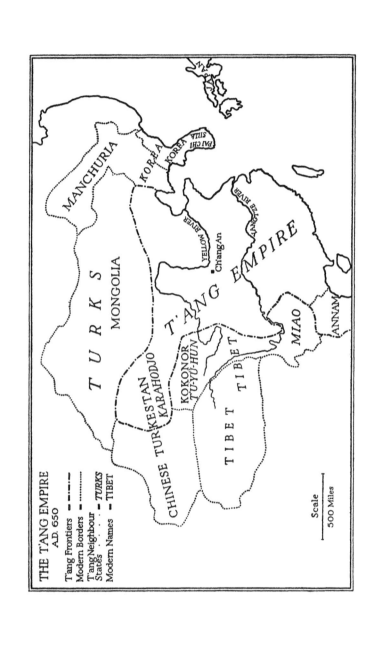

THE T'ANG EMPIRE
A.D. 650

T'ang Frontiers ▬ ▪ ▬ ▪ ▬
Modern Borders ▪▪▪▪▪▪▪▪▪▪
T'ang Neighbour
States ▪ ▪ ▬ ▪ ▪ ▬ *TURKS*
Modern Names ▬ TIBET

Scale
500 Miles

MANCHURIA

T U R K S

MONGOLIA

KOREA

KOREA

PAI CHI

SILLA

YELLOW RIVER

Chang An

T'ANG EMPIRE

YANGTZE RIVER

MIAO

ANNAM

CHINESE TURKESTAN

KARAHODJO

KOKONOR
TU-YÜ-HUN

TIBET TIBET

TIBET

frontier, could obtain from these kings the troops he required. Tibet contributed 1200 men, and Nepal 7000.

At the head of this army Wang Hsüan-Ts'ê entered India, and met King Alanashun at a city which the Chinese call Cha Po Ho La on the River Kan Tu Wei, possibly Chapra on the Ganges. The Indian king gave battle, which was renewed on three successive days, until complete victory rested with the Chinese general. Alanashun fled, but was pursued, defeated again, and taken prisoner, together with his wives and children, attendants and followers, to the number of 12,000 people. The kingdom having been pacified and restored to its rightful prince, Wang Hsüan-Ts'ê returned in triumph to Ch'ang An leading the captive king in his train. All the kings of India sent "tribute" and polite messages to the Chinese emperor.[1]

But while the generals of the empire were enforcing respect, and taking "tribute" from these distant countries, the emperor who had raised China to this commanding position in Asia was nearing the end of his life. Shih-Min never recovered from the hardships of the Korean war. Although he was now only forty-nine years old, his constitution had perhaps been weakened by the ardours of his early life, and not least by the poison draught with which his eldest brother had so nearly achieved his murder. During the years that followed the Korean war the emperor was continuously in bad health. A journey to the north-west, the highlands of Kansu, did not improve his health, and the attacks of his malady became more frequent.

The increasing illness of the emperor was not the only shadow which fell over the glories of Ch'ang An in these years. Death was taking steady toll of the famous ministers and generals who had done so much to second the emperor

[1] This account is drawn from the Chinese history *Tzŭ chih t'ung chien*. The histories of India are silen t on the subject, but that is perhaps because a raid from the Himalayas was too frequent and commonplace an event to deserve mention. It is likely enough that King Alanashun was but a petty rajah whose life and reign has escaped the notice of the historians.

in his life work. Kao Shih-Lien died in A.D. 646. Ma Chou, the censor and author of the reform of the provincial administration, died two years later. In A.D. 649 the court sustained the more serious loss of two of the most eminent statesmen, Fang Hsüan-Ling and Hsiao Yü. The general Li Ta-Liang died at Ch'ang An during the Korean war.

These deaths, and the manifestly failing health of the emperor himself, gave rise to a certain unrest, a stirring of dormant ambitions, which in an eastern court is the first response to the breath of approaching change. The court no less than the emperor were concerned at the prevalence of another of those curious prophecies, such as had heralded the fall of Yang Ti. Everywhere it was being whispered, "After three generations of T'ang emperors, the dynasty of a woman, 'Prince Wu', will rule the empire".

Unlike the prophecy which foretold the imperial greatness of the name of Li, this forecast did not prove entirely accurate,[1] though it greatly influenced the men of the time. The fact that the prophecy was in part fulfilled in after years might lead to the suspicion that it had been concocted in later times, but for the incident concerning an officer whose title, rank and first name all had "Wu" characters, although his surname was not Wu. This officer was so much influenced by the prophecy that he believed himself to be the subject of it. He became involved in a conspiracy, and was executed for high treason. This severity was necessary, for such prophecies in an age and land where they gain easy credence, tend to fulfil themselves by rallying support to a pretender who is popularly believed to be the individual whose future fortune has been pre-destined.

[1] The Lady Wu, who had been taken into the palace late in Shih-Min's reign, was taken as a concubine by his son and successor. In later years she won her way to the rank of empress, and, after her husband's death, actually ruled China in her own name as the Empress Wu. Although she did plan to substitute her own family for the imperial house and found a new dynasty, she failed to accomplish this design, and in extreme old age was forced to resign her power. The legitimate line of T'ang princes was then restored to the throne.

This particular intrigue was the more serious as the emperor was now so ill that those about him realised that his death was near. The youth of the crown prince and the recent death of many of the most responsible ministers made a dangerous situation, which the dying emperor did his best to foresee and provide against. The death of Li Ching in the early months of this year, A.D. 649, left Li Shih-Chi by far the most powerful and influential military officer in the empire. In the civil administration, death had left only Chang-Sun Wu-Chi and Ch'u Sui-Liang among the intimate circle of Shih-Min's cabinet. It was to be feared that with a youthful and inexperienced prince on the throne, Li Shih-Chi, forgetting the loyalty of a lifetime, might be tempted to make some revolutionary change.

Shih-Min, although he believed and trusted in the loyalty of the great general, did not feel justified in taking the risk. He called the crown prince to his bedside and gave him his final counsels on this matter. "I am going to appoint Li Shih-Chi to a post in the provinces", he said, "if he goes without question or delay, you will recall him after my death and confide in him, as I have done, as great general of the empire. But if he hesitates, or refuses the position, when I am dead you must put him to death without delay."

The emperor's reasons for this advice were sound. If Li Shih-Chi, who knew that Shih-Min was dying, accepted his removal from the capital and the army at such a critical time, it could be safely assumed that he entertained no disloyal ambitions. But if he tried to delay or refused the offered post, it would be plain that he cherished secret schemes, and was anxiously awaiting the emperor's death to further his plans. The event proved that Li Shih-Chi was entirely loyal to his sovereign. On receiving his appointment he departed from Ch'ang An without even taking the time to return to his own house. The crown prince, when emperor, followed Shih-Min's advice, and recalled Li Shih-Chi to his former position.

The foresight and prudence with which Shih-Min arranged

the affairs of the government prevented any disturbance, permitting his son to inherit the throne without the slightest difficulty.

In the summer of A.D. 649, Shih-Min, knowing that his end was near, left Ch'ang An for the last time and retired to his favourite summer residence, the Kingfisher Blue Palace (Ts'ui Wei Kung) in the Nan Shan mountains south of the capital. There, attended by his faithful friend, Chang-Sun Wu-Chi, and his son the crown prince, who was overcome with a real grief, he died in the forty-ninth year of his age.

The histories of all nations plentifully record the careers of conquerors who, conceiving that their work was done when the last battle had been gained, devoted the succeeding years of peace to a life of luxury and careless ease. There have been few great commanders, who, on the morrow of victory, not only understood that the hardest task, the organisation of enduring peace, still lay ahead, but also possessed the talents to achieve it. Peace and unity are not in themselves enough. For Li Shih-Min the tragic example of the Sui dynasty proved that an empire conquered and united by successful wars can be as speedily lost by tyrannical misgovernment. To re-establish a unified empire on a lasting foundation the emperor needed as much ability in the council chamber as he had been proved to possess on the battlefield.

Li Shih-Min's true title to greatness is his success in this new sphere. He became far more famous as a wise, far-seeing administrator, than he had been as a conquering hero. To the Chinese the name of the great emperor is more familiar as the model of the Confucian prince, than as the brilliant victor of many battles. In this their judgment is correct. Other young generals have gained a meteoric reputation, but their conquests hardly endured beyond their lifetime. The work of Li Shih-Min was permanent. Before his time unity in China had been the exception, the achievement of a few strong dynasties: feudalism and partition had been the rule.

But from the seventh century onwards China has far more

often, and for far longer, been united than divided. Partitions have been the consequence of partial foreign conquest, or a temporary interlude between strong dynasties. Always the T'ang tradition has re-asserted itself. That tradition, of a unified empire, administered by a civil service taking its orders from one supreme central authority, was the life's work of Li Shih-Min, and it has maintained and spread in the Far East the Chinese culture, one of the great civilising forces in the world's history.

DYNASTIC PERIODS OF UNITY AND DIVISION IN CHINA BEFORE AND AFTER THE T'ANG DYNASTY

BEFORE

Divided			United		
Name	Date B.C.	Duration (years)	Name	Date B.C.	Duration (years)
Hsia	2205–1766	439			
Shang	1766–1122	644			
Chou	1122– 255	867			
(The above were dynasties of the Chinese Feudal Age)			Ch'in	255–206	49
	A.D.		Han	B.C. 206–A.D. 221	427
Three Kingdoms	221–265	44		A.D.	
			Tsin	265–317	52
Partition of North and South	317–589	272	Sui	589–618	29
		2266			557

AFTER

			T'ang	618–907	289
Five dynasties	907–960	53			
			Sung	960–1127	167
Southern Sung and Northern Tartars	1127–1280	153			
			Yüan (Mongol)	1280–1368	88
			Ming	1368–1644	276
			Ch'ing (Manchu)	1644–1911	267
			Republic	1911–	21
		206			1108

A NEW ESTIMATE OF THE CHINESE POPULATION UNDER THE T'ANG DYNASTY IN A.D. 618

Modern historians of China, depending on the census figures given in the dynastic histories, have subscribed to the belief that the population of China doubled under the Ch'ing dynasty, the increase taking place during the sixty years of Ch'ien Lung's reign. Boulger states "the growth of the population during the reign of Ch'ien Lung was quite extraordinary, within fifty years it appears to have almost doubled".[1]

Hawks Pott says that at the death of Ch'ien Lung, that emperor's authority was acknowledged by "upwards of 400,000,000 people".[2]

Li Ung Bing gives the figures of 27,350,000 for the year A.D. 1735, but states that in 1795, sixty years later, the population had risen to 296,978,968. An astounding increase of more than tenfold in two generations![3]

Though there is thus a wide difference of opinion as to the actual figures of the alleged increase of population in the reign of Ch'ien Lung, all agree that there was in fact an increase. All agree, too, that the population of China in the ages prior to Ch'ien Lung's reign was small. Boulger gives the population in 1394 (early Ming period) as 60,545,812.[4]

Hawks Pott gives the figure of 60,000,000 at the death of the Emperor Ming Hung Wu, founder of the Ming dynasty.[5]

Li Ung Bing says the population of China was 56,000,000 in 1391, but had increased to 60,000,000 two years later in 1393.[6]

According to these historians there was an immense difference between the size of the Chinese population in the Ming dynasty

---

[1] D. C. Boulger, *History of China*, 1, p. 728. London: W. Thacker & Co. 1898.

[2] F. L. Hawks Pott, *Sketch of Chinese History*, p. 122. Shanghai: Kelly & Walsh, 1903.

[3] Li Ung Bing, *Outlines of Chinese History*, p. 466. Shanghai: The Commercial Press, 1914.

[4] D. C. Boulger, *History of China*, 1, p. 428.

[5] F. L. Hawks Pott, *Sketch of Chinese History*, p. 92.

[6] Li Ung Bing, *Outlines of Chinese History*, p. 233.

and the population inhabiting the same area (the eighteen provinces) four hundred years later at the death of Ch'ien Lung. The T'ang dynasty (A.D. 618–907) did not exercise authority over large territories now incorporated in the southern provinces, and which formed part of the Ming empire, yet these historians attribute to this smaller China a population almost as great as that of the Ming empire, which flourished six hundred years later.

Boulger states that the population in the reign of T'ang Ming Ti, A.D. 712, was "more than 50,000,000", but adds that by A.D. 764, after the rebellion of An Lu Shan, "the population... did not reach 17,000,000".[1]

Hawks Pott and Li Ung Bing do not commit themselves to figures for the T'ang population, but another authority, Wells Williams, gives the population in A.D. 722 as 52,884,818.[2]

These authorities, therefore, contend that the population had hardly increased at all during the six hundred years between the reign of T'ang Ming Ti and the foundation of the Ming dynasty, although the southern provinces, which did not form part of the T'ang empire, had been colonised and conquered during these six hundred years. No increase is attributed to the Ming period, but in the short sixty years of Ch'ien Lung's reign, the population, stabilised round 60,000,000 for more than a thousand years, suddenly increased beyond all reasonable expectation. One is forced to admire the fecundity of the Chinese people in the Ch'ien Lung period.

The phenomenal increase of the population in eighteenth-century China, if a fact, must be due to a discoverable cause, and it is the purpose of this appendix to test the estimates of population in all three periods, T'ang, Ming and Ch'ing, by approaching the matter from a new angle with the primary object of making an estimate of the population of the T'ang empire in A.D. 618.

Data other than census figures can be used to estimate the population of a past age. The activities of the people, as attested by irrigation systems and other monuments which they constructed, are proof of the existence of a certain minimum population in a specific district. A better, because more universal, indication is to be found in the record of the number of cities built and inhabited by the people of a given age. The city in the economic system of the ancient Chinese world was a by-product of the agrarian economic order, and, as such, its prosperity or

[1] D. C. Boulger, *History of China*, I, p. 205.
[2] S. Wells Williams, *History of China*, p. 37. New York: Charles Scribner, 1897.

decay depended on the size of the farming population. When the rural population increased, the number of cities increased; and when the land was less thickly populated, the surplus cities decayed and were abandoned.

This condition prevailed throughout the ancient world. Professor Haverfield, discussing a similar point in connection with the empire of Alexander, remarks, "For the connection between towns and their local food supply note the story of Alexander the Great and the architect Dinocrates, told by Vitruvius. Dinocrates had planned a new town. Alexander asked if there were lands round it to supply it with corn, and on hearing that there were none, at once ruled out the proposed site".[1]

Up to the beginning of the nineteenth century China was a self-contained agrarian state, having very little contact with foreign countries.[2] Her exports and imports were few and played an insignificant part in her economic system. She consumed her own food and produced her own industrial necessities. In 1793 Ch'ien Lung could still say with perfect truth: "The Celestial Empire possesses all things in prolific abundance and lacks no product within its borders. There is therefore no need to import the manufactures of outside barbarians in exchange for our own products".[3]

The foreign importer, since the fall in silver values, has discovered to his cost that there is still a great deal of truth in Ch'ien Lung's dictum, and China can get along without the "manufactures of outside barbarians", which he has to offer.

This self-sufficiency, which Ch'ien Lung regarded as a virtue, was also a necessity. Before the invention of railways and of steam ships, which were independent of the winds and weather, the importation of large quantities of food stuffs was a matter of great difficulty, and could only be effected by an elaborate and very costly organisation. The grain ships which fed the Roman proletariat and the tribute rice upon which the Peking bannermen lived are rare examples of ancient food imports on the grand scale. The fame of these two organisations, and the importance

F. Haverfield, *Ancient Town Planning*, p. 13 n. Oxford: Clarendon Press, 1913.

[2] An exception must be made for the great trade route from the north-western provinces through Turkestan to Persia. But this trade was entirely in silk and other luxuries, and was not used to import food.

[3] Mandate of the Emperor Ch'ien Lung to King George III, on the occasion of Lord Macartney's Embassy to China. E. Backhouse and J. O. P. Bland, *Annals and Memoirs of the Court of Peking*, pp. 322–34. William Heinemann: London, 1914.

the respective governments attached to their smooth working and maintenance, testify alike to the difficulties and the exceptional character of these enterprises.

In a self-contained agrarian country, such as old China, cities were bound to the country by strict economic ties. They could only exist where the rural population was thick enough to supply the citizens with food from their surplus harvests, and in return the city fulfilled three functions. It supplied the farmers with manufactured goods; it formed a place of residence for the richer landowners and of refuge for all classes in time of war; and it was the centre of government for the district. Where there was no farming population thick enough to support a non-producing town population, or not rich enough to need protection or to attract a tax-hungry government, there was no city. Under these conditions very few cities grew too big to live on the produce of the adjoining country, and these exceptions were only found along the great rivers or on the sea coast. These riparian cities were the only places where industries with a wider market than the neighbouring countryside could flourish. Elsewhere transport was too difficult and too expensive. Even these semi-industrial cities sold their products only in other parts of China and consumed food brought from adjoining provinces. There were no cities of the modern Western type manufacturing for world markets and living on food imported from distant countries.

The walled city was thus the standard Chinese urban type. Unwalled towns were not accounted as cities. But in old China unwalled towns were rarely if ever large or important, a city was *ipso facto* a walled city (a village surrounded with a mud wall was not, of course, accorded this status, the city being girt with a regular well-built wall of brick or stone). Therefore, the list of walled cities occupied at any given time is a list of all the urban centres in the empire.

This would no longer be quite true to-day. Unwalled markets, such as Tongshan in Hopei (Chihli) and Shasi in Hupei, have grown under the influence of modern commerce and industry till they are far larger than their old walled neighbours. But before the era of overseas trade and modern industrial enterprises this did not happen. A city which grew was walled (Tientsin, for instance, was only walled under the early Ch'ing emperors), and most cities did not grow: they fulfilled the functions for which they had been built, and these functions, being to supply the needs of an agrarian community, did not alter with the passage of time.

There was, therefore, a well-defined ratio between the number of cities existing and the size of the population at any given time. If the number of cities and the ratio between them and the population as a whole can be established, it is possible to estimate the number of inhabitants living in the country at the period in question.

But three factors can derange this ratio.

Firstly, a climatic change or the introduction of a new disease, such as malaria, which, by depopulating an agricultural region, leaves its cities half-filled and decaying, stranded, perhaps for some centuries, before they finally disappear. Secondly, a change in the line of a trade route, which may cause the decay of a prosperous chain of cities and bring sudden importance to a region hitherto deserted. Thirdly, the presence of a fluctuating, ill-defined, man-made political frontier, requiring the construction of many economically unnecessary cities as fortresses and places of refuge. There are, or have been, examples of all these disturbing factors in different parts of China. But, if the existence of any one of these factors is noted and allowance made for it, it is still possible to use the city records as a basis for estimating the population.

Moreover, if the number of cities occupied at any one period is found to be approximately the same as the number occupied at another period, it follows that the population in these two periods must have been approximately the same, unless it can be proved that sudden intense industrialisation has occurred, or that new agricultural methods, very greatly increasing the productivity of the soil, have been introduced.

It is common knowledge that up to the end of the nineteenth century no industrialisation of China had taken place, and, therefore, the economic order under the Ch'ing, Ming, and T'ang dynasties was equally agrarian. No proof exists that the agricultural methods in use under the Ch'ing dynasty were in any respect superior to those employed under previous dynasties. Nor have I been able to find any evidence that a new crop, capable of revolutionising the food supply, was introduced at any time between the T'ang dynasty and the reign of Ch'ien Lung.

Using data on the age of cities obtained from the encyclopedia *Ch'in ting ku chin t'u shu chi ch'êng*, and a ratio of population to cities obtained from an average of the census figures for 1885 and 1910 in the province of Kueichou, the least affected by the advent of modern commerce and industry, an estimate for the population of the T'ang empire in 618 has been worked out.[1]

[1] The detailed figures, tables and calculations on which this estimate is based were published in an article called "A New estimate of the Chinese

This gives a total of 129,450,000 for the whole empire, divided as to 102,300,000 for the nine northern and Yangtze provinces, Hopei, Shansi, Shensi, Kansu, Shantung, Honan, Hupei, Anhui, and Kiangsu, which were older and more closely settled in the seventh century than the southern provinces. For these, Chekiang, Kiangsi, Hunan, Szechuan, Fukien, Kuangtung, Kuangsi and Yunnan, the total was 27,150,000. Kueichou, as well as the greater part of Yunnan, did not form part of the T'ang empire.

These results lead to the conclusion that the population of China as a whole has only trebled in the past thousand years, that the increase is mainly to be accounted for by the concurrent expansion of the area of the state, and that the population of the older northern provinces is but slightly greater now than it was in 618, and in the case of Shensi and Shansi is actually less.

These conclusions are not at all in accord with the figures quoted from various modern historians at the beginning of this appendix, if those figures are accepted at their face value. But it must be realised that they represent a count of households multiplied by five, and were taken for the purposes of taxation. Consequently only tax-paying households were assessed. The poor were of no interest to the government and so no attempt to enumerate them was made. Abstract statistics were not esteemed in the ancient world. There must, too, have been a large class who succeeded in avoiding the invidious distinction of being listed as taxpayers.

The figures quoted at the beginning of this appendix, viewed in this light, immediately become intelligible. It may be assumed that the authorities succeeded in their object and drew up a fairly complete list of taxpayers. Then, on the basis of this estimate, the taxpayers in the reign of T'ang Ming Ti, A.D. 712, almost a hundred years after the date to which this estimate applies, were "more than 50,000,000", or about half the population. In view of the fact that the century in question was one of the most prosperous and peaceful ages in all Chinese history, this is not incredible. Nor is the fact that in A.D. 764, after the devastating rebellion of An Lu Shan, the *taxpaying* population had fallen to 17,000,000 in any way surprising. The taxpayers would naturally have suffered from the ravages of the war, the population as a whole would not have been much diminished.

The same considerations explain the extraordinary legend that the population of China was multiplied by five or even ten in the reign of Ch'ien Lung. That, too, was an age of unbroken peace

population under the T'ang dynasty in A.D. 618", in the *China Journal*, January and February 1932, Vol. XVI, Nos. 1 and 2.

(internally) and prosperity. That the taxpaying population rapidly increased under the careful and exact scrutiny of Ch'ien Lung's highly efficient administration will cause little surprise: that the population as a whole increased by more than ten times in sixty years is frankly incredible.

Thus the figures quoted from the ancient census, though not to be taken literally, give a valuable cross bearing which confirms the estimate undertaken in this appendix and the theory upon which it was constructed.

INDEX

.

For EU product safety concerns, contact us at Calle de José Abascal, 56–1°, 28003 Madrid, Spain or eugpsr@cambridge.org.

www.ingramcontent.com/pod-product-compliance
Ingram Content Group UK Ltd.
Pitfield, Milton Keynes, MK11 3LW, UK
UKHW010340140625
459647UK00010B/729